'A sense of wonder permeates every page in this book. It
things happen in classes, and presents stories about the ps
an engaging style based on so many fascinating research
moments.'

Professor John Hattie, *Emeritus Laureate Professor, Melbourne G...*
Education, University of Melbourne

'It is important for teachers to have the opportunity to bring the wide range of disciplinary
knowledge they possess to the task of teaching. Readers will benefit from this example of
how an experienced practitioner is able to combine a wealth of classroom experience with a
depth of understanding from their study of economics. The result is an engaging, entertaining
and well-informed book on pedagogy that merits a place on every educationalist's
bookshelves.'

Vivienne Baumfield, *Professor of Professional Learning,*
University of Exeter

'A perfect balance between insightful behavioural theory and practical strategies for the
classroom, Mallard's accessible style will prove welcome for any open-minded teacher
looking to make their learning environment just that little bit special. A step on the road to
the truly inspirational classroom we always seek!'

Dr Alex Peterken, *Headmaster,*
Charterhouse School

THE BEHAVIOURAL LEARNING CLASSROOM

Teachers are virtually never taught how learners make decisions about studying, concentration and participation, and are not able to find this in educational literature. *The Behavioural Learning Classroom* breaks new ground, allowing teachers to harness their students' traits and quirks to produce a more effective and compassionate classroom.

- Important lessons from behavioural science
- Optimising lesson design
- Effective (home)work
- Marking and feedback
- Rewards and sanctions
- The physical environment of the classroom
- Pupil behaviour
- Designing behavioural experiments and analysing data

Supported by fundamental findings in behavioural science, this book provides practical, accessible, tried and tested techniques to improve the mental wellbeing of pupils and teachers alike. It is an enjoyable and accessible read for any teacher or school leader who wants to enhance their pupils' experience of learning.

Graham Mallard is Assistant Head (Academic) at Clifton College, UK. He has a PhD in economic decision-making from the University of Bath, UK, which he combines with over 16 years of teaching experience. In 2011 he was shortlisted for the University of Bath 'Innovation in Learning and Teaching Award'. This is his sixth published book.

THE BEHAVIOURAL LEARNING CLASSROOM

Making Schools More Effective and Compassionate

Graham Mallard

Routledge
Taylor & Francis Group

LONDON AND NEW YORK

Designed cover image: © Getty Images

First published 2023
by Routledge
4 Park Square, Milton Park, Abingdon, Oxon OX14 4RN

and by Routledge
605 Third Avenue, New York, NY 10158

Routledge is an imprint of the Taylor & Francis Group, an informa business

British Library Cataloguing-in-Publication Data
A catalogue record for this book is available from the British Library

Library of Congress Cataloging-in-Publication Data
Names: Mallard, Graham, 1982- author.
Title: The behavioural learning classroom : making our school more effective and
    compassionate through the findings of behavioural science / Graham Mallard.
Other titles: Behavioral learning classroom
Description: First Edition. | New York : Routledge, 2023. | Includes bibliographical
    references and index.
Identifiers: LCCN 2022041120 (print) | LCCN 2022041121 (ebook) |
    ISBN 9781032056388 (Hardback) | ISBN 9781032056395 (Paperback) |
    ISBN 9781003198505 (eBook)
Subjects: LCSH: Behavioral assessment of children. | Classroom environment. |
    Teacher-student relationships. | Interpersonal communication. | Effective teaching.
Classification: LCC LB1124 .M35 2023 (print) | LCC LB1124 (ebook) |
    DDC 370.15/2–dc23/eng/20230103
LC record available at https://lccn.loc.gov/2022041120
LC ebook record available at https://lccn.loc.gov/2022041121

ISBN: 978-1-032-05638-8 (hbk)
ISBN: 978-1-032-05639-5 (pbk)
ISBN: 978-1-003-19850-5 (ebk)

DOI: 10.4324/9781003198505

Typeset in Interstate
by Apex CoVantage, LLC

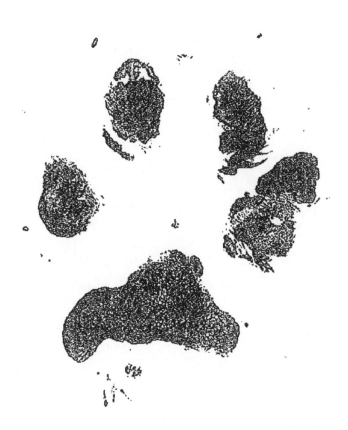

For Bracken

CONTENTS

ACKNOWLEDGEMENTS

I thank Vivienne Baumfield, John Hattie and Alex Peterken for their very generous endorsements; Catherine Bufton-Green, Richard Fairchild, Sarah Johnson, Brian Kenny and Shannon Schrijver for all of their contributions and suggestions; Michael Bond, Chet Khatu, Mo Tanweer and Ruth Tarrant for all of their encouragement and support; Bruce Roberts and Molly Selby for their endless patience and understanding; Lauren Redhead, and Aruna Rajendran and her team for all their work editing and finessing this book; and my family for all they have done and continue to do to help me realise my ambitions: especially Paul for his unfailing interest. Most of all, and as always, I thank Fay for all of her love, encouragement, support and advice, and Oculi, Omni, Monnie and Bracken for all of their love, positivity and energy: what follows would not have been possible without them. Thank you.

LIST ONE: TEN KEY THINGS OUR PUPILS SHOULD KNOW

(1) The mental reserves they use to fuel their thinking and to shape their behaviour are limited. Tip: they should plan how they use them and avoid cutting down on foods that release energy slowly when they particularly need to focus.

(2) They are only able to focus on a very small number of things at any one time. Tip: they should avoid trying to multi-task, and they should cut out distractions when they need to concentrate.

(3) Their behaviour is naturally affected by their feelings of loss and gain. Tip: they should force themselves to be more cautious when they are experiencing loss and to be more ambitious when they are experiencing gain.

(4) They are susceptible to both the planning fallacy and to feeling overconfident. Tip: they should ask others to help them to judge how long tasks will take and how successful they are likely to be at them.

(5) They naturally find it difficult to make a start on tasks, which leads to wasteful procrastination. Tip: they should break tasks down into smaller parts and then quickly make a start on the first of those, and they should avoid asking for deadline extensions.

(6) They naturally fixate on negative feedback and events, which can quickly reduce their mental wellbeing. Tip: they should purposefully savour and celebrate their successes and challenge their negative self-talk.

(7) They can forget to attend to important things in their lives when they fixate on a particular task or feeling, to the overall detriment of their wellbeing. Tip: they can harness the power of precommitment strategies and checklists to overcome this.

(8) There is a trade-off between their ability to shape their lives and their ability to cope with emotions. Tip: they should reduce the demands they place on themselves when dealing with strong emotions, and they should try to release emotions when they need to focus on other things.

(9) They are negatively affected by tasks that are unfinished, which subconsciously drains their mental reserves. Tip: they should plan how, when and where they are going to complete such tasks and then commit to their plans to avoid this effect.

(10) They are susceptible to spending too much time on tasks that are unfruitful, either because they have little to learn from them or because they do not want to crystallise a feeling of loss. Tip: they should try to view stopping work on a task as an opportunity for gain.

LIST TWO: THE BEHAVIOURAL STUDIES

Behavioural Experiment	Section	Cognitive Trait
Culture and ultimatum games	2.6	Inequity aversion
Parole court	3.1	Decision fatigue
Jams	3.1	Decision fatigue
Interruption	3.1	Decision fatigue
Moral dilemma	3.2	Bandwidth tax
Colonoscopes	3.3	Peak-end rule
Mugs – students	3.4	Loss aversion
Mugs – professionals	3.4	Loss aversion
Ellsberg paradox	3.5	Ambiguity aversion
Consecutive letters	4.1	Sisyphus effect
Lego building	4.1	Sisyphus effect
IKEA boxes – identity	4.2	IKEA effect
Craft designs	4.2	IKEA effect
IKEA boxes – completion	4.2	IKEA effect
Origami frogs	4.2	IKEA effect
Pizza choice	5.1	Order effects
Cafè choice	5.1	Order effects
Decoy effect	5.1	Irrelevant alternatives
Marking	5.2	Halo effect
Stanford suicide note – personal	5.2	Confirmation bias
Stanford suicide note – observer	5.2	Confirmation bias
Images	5.3	Negativity bias
Teacher performance	6.2	Endowment effect
Haifa nurseries	6.4	Motivational crowding-out
Environmental protection	6.4	Motivational crowding-out
Radishes and cookies	7.1	Decision fatigue
Trainline distraction	7.1	Bandwidth tax
Word pairing	7.2	Availability heuristic
Wall displays	7.2	Bandwidth tax
Course evaluation	7.2	Availability heuristic
Childhood memory	7.2	Availability heuristic
Electric shock	7.3	Omission predisposition
Electricity tariff	7.3	Omission predisposition
Unpleasant drink	8.1	Decision fatigue
Cold water	8.1	Decision fatigue
Smoking	8.1	Precommitment
Snack choice – original	8.2	Bandwidth tax
Snack choice – personality	8.2	Bandwidth tax
Emotion control impact	8.3	Decision fatigue
Emotion control effectiveness	8.3	Decision fatigue
Saving for retirement	8.4	Procrastination

Behavioural Experiment	Section	Cognitive Trait
French cafè	8.4	Procrastination
Death and salvation	9.1	Framing
Financial investment	9.1	Framing
Shopper scenarios	9.2	Bandwidth tax
Sugarcane harvest	9.2	Bandwidth tax
Angry birds	9.2	Bandwidth tax
Thinking of items	9.3	Zeigarnick effect
Plastic bags	10.0	Default choice
Eyes	10.1	Inequity aversion
Radio fund-raising	10.1	Social comparison
Showering	10.1	Social comparison
Petrified forest	10.1	Social comparison
Fly in the urinal	10.2	Choice architecture effects
Piano staircase	10.2	Choice architecture effects
Ballot bins	10.2	Choice architecture effects
Fine collection	10.3	Personalisation
Charitable donations	10.3	Personalisation
Personal goal-setting	10.3	Personalisation
Organ donation	10.4	Default choice
Parental communication: text messages	10.4	Default choice
Parental communication: phone calls	10.4	Default choice
Plate size	10.4	Relative decision-making
Glucose and mental performance	11.1	Decision fatigue
Glucose and behaviour	11.1	Decision fatigue
Glucose and recall	11.1	Decision fatigue
Scientist in residence	11.3	Representativeness
Representativeness	11.3	Representativeness
Line matching	11.4	Groupthink
Self-esteem	11.5	Negativity bias

1 Introduction

1.1 Birds of prey and pigs

There it was again: the sound of bells jingling somewhere nearby. We had been hearing it from the very start of our hack and our horse, Monnie, became rigidly alert every time we did so. Ears pricked, Monnie was ready to race back to the stables if she needed to. As it turned out, this was for good reason. The latest jingle heralded the appearance of what seemed to be an enormous bird of prey that glided by within a few metres of us, just the other side of the hedge, with its talons and bell hanging underneath and the falconer riding a quad bike in pursuit.

We had covered that particular loop dozens of times, but that was the only time we saw the falconer and his bird. A more regular feature of our hacks were the pigs, either in their pen or being moved about the lanes in a trailer. Monnie hated those pigs and was desperate to turn on the spot and head for home whenever she saw, heard or smelled them. The most we could coax her to do was to tentatively pass by on the other side of the lane, pressed into the hedge and as far from the pigs as possible.

The falconer incident made perfect sense to me. Seeing those talons and the size of the body to which they were attached, it was an understandable response from Monnie as a prey animal to want to remove herself from the situation as quickly as possible. With Monnie being three times the size and weight of an average pig, though, her swine fear was always less clear. It is an instinct seemingly pre-programmed in horses. An evolutionary throwback, possibly arising from horses falling prey to wild boars in the past. Monnie was simply reacting in the way she had evolved to react.

1.2 Understanding evolutionary throwbacks

We too are characterised by evolutionary throwbacks. We regularly behave in ways that on the surface seem irrational, foolish and incomprehensible but are perfectly understandable when we consider them from the perspective of the distant past. And precisely the same is true of the pupils we teach, perhaps even more so for them as they are yet to develop ways of overcoming their initial impulses, which are at best only partially effective for adults. I have sat for hours during inset days listening to talks about new teaching methods, strategies for improving discipline and, increasingly, the use of technology in lessons. But all of that is of

DOI: 10.4324/9781003198505-1

relatively little importance if we fail to consider how our pupils instinctively react in different situations. And I have never heard anything about that, apart from a brief mention of cognitive load theory.

Let me use a final horsey analogy. My wife and I went to see the horse whisperer, Monty Roberts, work his magic one evening in a freezing cold arena south of Bristol, UK. After a short introduction, a solitary horse was led into the ring by his owner; brown, probably about 16 hands tall. His eyes were wide as he scanned the crowd looking down on him, no doubt afraid of whatever was going to happen next. Monty approached the horse from the side and as he reached up to stroke the horse's mane, the horse reared and spun away. Monty tried again, this time head-on, only to elicit the same response. Monty explained that this horse had been beaten around the head by a former owner; that he had been conditioned to expect pain from an approaching human, particularly a male reaching up to him from the ground. The horse's owner had exhausted all her ideas about how to calm him, but her efforts had been in vain, and he remained unhandable. Seeking Monty's help was possibly the final attempt to save her horse.

Monty asked for his own horse to be brought into the ring. Once mounted, he again approached the horse from the side, reaching across to stroke the horse's mane. This time there was no rearing or spinning. It was the first time in years that the horse had been comforted by a human. Monty gradually extended the area he stroked and within what seemed to be only a few minutes, he and the owner were brushing the horse from the ground. It looked to everyone in the crowd as though a physical weight had been lifted from the horse.

Surprisingly, Monty then asked the owner to repeatedly drive her horse away from them, driving him around the circular ring in one direction and then the other. After a few minutes of this, Monty asked the owner to turn and walk away from her horse. Immediately, the horse followed his owner from behind. He almost put his head on her shoulder as she led him around the arena. And when she turned towards him, he allowed her to touch his face.

In what must have been less than half an hour, Monty had transformed the situation. Beforehand there had been a terrified horse, scarred from past mistreatment, and a desperate owner who had never been able to groom him. Afterwards there was a horse that looked completely new and welcomed his owner's affection. Beforehand, the horse had to be caught and led with a lead. Afterwards, the horse followed his owner freely. But there was no magic displayed that evening. What we saw from Monty was what he refers to as natural horsemanship. Having spent years watching wild mustangs in America, Monty understood the herdlike nature of horses and all the quirky, seemingly irrational responses that come from that. He knew that horses like to groom one another as it creates bonds between them, which is why he initially approached the horse that evening whilst mounted on another horse rather than from the ground. By mimicking their natural grooming behaviour, Monty disarmed the horse and slipped through his defences. Monty also knew that horses look for a dominant companion, one that will protect them. In the wild, these bonds are forged by the leader driving away a member of the herd, establishing its dominance before welcoming him back into the group. By asking the owner to mimic this behaviour, Monty established her as the horse's protector: a process he calls join-up.

We have traditionally trained horses to obey us in rather barbaric ways. Even the phrase we use for it – breaking-in – sounds cruel. Monty has spent his life demonstrating that such practices are not only unnecessary, they are often counterproductive: as demonstrated by the horse that evening. By understanding the natural, instinctive, evolutionary behaviours of horses, we can be more humane and more effective. A win-win.

Precisely the same logic applies to how we teach in our schools, classrooms and lecture theatres. A body of work has grown since the 1950s that demonstrates we are characterised by common, and at times seemingly irrational, cognitive traits: evolutionary throwbacks that once served a purpose but are often now seemingly irrational. These traits naturally constrain our abilities to start and complete tasks, to take risks and challenge ourselves, to respond effectively to feedback and to prevent a bad behavioural situation escalating out of control. And that is naming just a few. By recognising these traits in both our pupils and ourselves, and shaping our teaching accordingly, we can remove these constraints from our teaching and from our pupils' learning. We can become better, more compassionate, more efficient and ultimately more successful teachers.

Key term: cognitive traits

The preferences, biases and likely responses in different situations that are naturally common to us all.

1.3 Why not 'nudge education'?

Behavioural scientists have shown how businesses and governments can manipulate our decisions and behaviours by changing the situations in which we find ourselves, often in very subtle and seemingly inconsequential ways. By changing the way advertisements are worded ('Available for a limited time only – do not lose out', for example), the way they are priced (such as £10,000 with £500 cash back rather than £9,500), and the way we make our decisions (changing the default option, for instance), they get us to spend more and to make choices we otherwise would not have done. This approach has become known as nudging. David Cameron established the UK Behavioural Insights Team (known as the Nudge Unit) for precisely this purpose in 2010. Barack Obama followed suit in 2014 by creating the White House's Social and Behavioral Sciences Team and then, a year later, signing an executive order instructing federal agencies to incorporate behavioural scientific findings into their policymaking. It is not much of an exaggeration to say that every situation in which we make decisions nowadays has been deliberately shaped by someone or something for one purpose or another. And the range of applications of this work continues to grow. A cursory glance at the results from searching for 'nudge' on Amazon reveals applications to business management, marketing, self-help, inclusive leadership and healthy workplaces.

The purpose of this book is to examine how we can harness the cognitive traits of both our pupils and ourselves to make our teaching and schools more effective. Part of this focuses on the ways in which we can alter the situations in which we interact with our pupils and in which our pupils learn. This includes managing the distractions that are inevitably present, changing the way we word questions and design activities, and manipulating the order in which we present them. This part of what follows can be thought of as nudge education as it is concerned with how we can deliberately increase the likelihood of our pupils engaging productively with their learning, often without them being aware of us doing so. However, what follows is far wider than nudging alone. By teaching our pupils about the cognitive traits they naturally possess and how they can harness and overcome them, we can empower our pupils to be more effective and more independent learners, both now and throughout their lives. And by understanding how we can harness and overcome these cognitive traits in ourselves, we can be more successful, and at the same time, we can save ourselves considerable amounts of time and stress. Once again, a win-win.

The behavioural science literature is divided in its interpretation of these cognitive traits. On the one hand there are leading academics who view them as evidence of our mental weakness and our tendency to make mistakes. On the other hand, there are equally eminent figures who view them as instruments in our mental toolboxes that help us to make effective decisions in situations in which we could easily become overwhelmed; that they actually make us smart. Irrespective of the view taken, understanding our own minds and helping our pupils to understand theirs will make us better teachers and our pupils better lifelong learners. This is what the chapters that follow are all about.

1.4 Behavioural science and neuroscience

The traditional view of decision-making is illustrated in Figure 1.1. It involves the decision maker receiving information from the environment in which she finds herself, processing that information internally and then, on the basis of that, making her choice. In this view, we are simply computing devices in a linear process, with full autonomy over the options we eventually select.

According to the modern view of decision-making, we are much more active in the process and yet, at the same time, have less control over the resulting choice we make. According to this view, illustrated in Figure 1.2, we interact in a two-way manner with our environment, extracting information from it but also shaping it to help us to make decisions. It is on the basis of this repeated interaction that we make our decision, but in many cases we have relatively little conscious control of the choice we make. Have you ever driven somewhere and yet not remembered passing through some of the junctions on the route? Much of our behaviour is determined by forces outside of our control; forces that have been pre-programmed in us.

Neuroscience is concerned with the physical processes that happen within the 'Decision maker' arrows in Figures 1.1 and 1.2. It looks at which regions of the brain are activated when we make different decisions and the nature of that activation. Behavioural science, on the

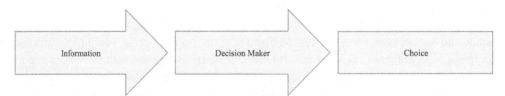

Information   Decision Maker   Choice

Figure 1.1 The traditional view of decision-making

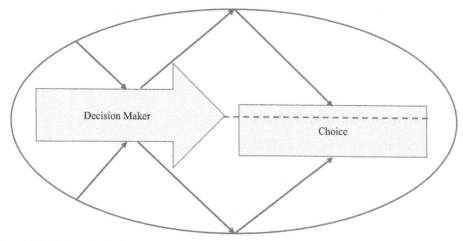

Figure 1.2 The modern view of decision-making

other hand, focuses on the association between the nature of the environment in which we find ourselves and the resulting choices we make. The physical processing part remains a black box.

1.5 The relationship with educational psychology

There is inevitably a considerable overlap between what follows here and the field of educational psychology, with both being concerned about issues such as pupil motivation, pupil responsiveness to instruction and feedback, and pupil behaviour. Educational psychologists have made tremendous strides towards understanding the importance to learning of a whole host of factors, including

- The level of challenge - the 'educational approach' advocated by researchers such as William James and John Dewey;
- Incentives - the 'behavioural approach' advocated by researchers such as Edward Thorndike and Burrhus Skinner;
- Different types of thinking - the 'cognitive approach' advocated by researchers such as Benjamin Bloom;
- Pupil participation - the 'constructivist approach' advocated by researchers such as Jean Piaget; and
- The social and cultural context - the 'social constructivist approach' advocated by researchers such as Lev Vygotsky.

What follows does not challenge any of this work. Instead, it is intended to contribute to the wider field of educational psychology by focusing on the cognitive traits that are common to us all, how we as teachers can alter situations in the light of these traits to enhance pupil learning and how pupils can harness and overcome their own cognitive traits to be more successful learners.

It is important to note here that this book is not concerned with the development of our cognitive traits. It focuses on pupils (and adults) who already possess them. As these pupils are likely to be in the formal operational stage of Piaget's model of cognitive development, in which they can think in abstract terms, what follows perhaps most strongly applies to pupils aged 12 years and upwards.

1.6 The structure of what follows

The chapters that follow are divided into three sections:

- The first and largest section is concerned with pupil learning within the classroom. These five chapters examine the implications of our cognitive traits for lesson design, homework setting, marking and feedback, rewards and sanctions and the physical environment.
- The second section is concerned with pupil behaviour. These three chapters consider the implications of our cognitive traits for pupils controlling their 'naughty selves'; behaviour that can escalate in both positive and negative directions, and how we can purposefully nudge pupils towards better behaviour.
- The third section focuses on a range of wider issues. The first of these chapters explores the implications of our cognitive traits for timetabling, pupils' subject choices, meetings and staff wellbeing. The penultimate chapter of the book takes a step back and explores the general themes that run through everything preceding it, and the final chapter offers a simple toolkit for teachers and schools to use in validating and extending the findings of behavioural science examined in the book in their own teacher-led research.

The intention is for this book to be as useful, interesting and enjoyable as possible. Unnecessary terminology has been purposefully kept to a minimum, and each chapter ends with either a set of 'practical takeaways' that outline the steps we can take as teachers to enhance our pupils' learning or a short summary.

It would be an impossible task to survey and reflect on all the studies in behavioural science that are relevant to teaching, learning and schools. And attempting to do so would no doubt result in a rather tedious and unwieldy tome of a book. Instead, the findings on which the practical takeaways are based are illustrated through 70 behavioural experiments that have been deliberately chosen because of their interestingness, relevance, availability and significance. Every experiment included in the chapters that follow was freely available online at the time of writing and every result presented is statistically significant, meaning the probability of it being spurious is negligible, usually lower than 1%. These experiments are outlined in List Two, along with the cognitive traits on which they shed light. The purpose, nature, strengths and limitations of these experiments are examined in Chapter 2. Recommendations for further reading are offered at the end of the book for those wanting to explore the relevant behavioural science in more detail, each with an explanation for their recommendation.

1.7 Three pupils in my past

James was a member of one of my first Year Seven tutor groups. He was never comfortable in school and went from one disciplinary incident to another. He had a phase during which he would hide under his desk, and on one occasion he even slipped unnoticed through the window of his ground-floor classroom to escape from what was to him a seemingly unbearable situation. He once explained to me that the blame lay squarely with the Head of Year. If only she could control him, he reasoned, he would not get into trouble, and she would not need to punish him. Despite us all trying to help him, at both school and home, the situation went from bad to worse, and he became increasingly disruptive and unmanageable.

Eleanor was perhaps the most talented A-level economics pupil I have taught, who has gone on to secure an impressive job in the financial sector having earned a high-class degree from a leading Russell Group university. The way she thought about the subject was outstanding. She could master models and concepts with apparent ease and then challenge them as though she had already studied the subject at undergraduate level. And this was common across all her subjects. It came as a surprise to everyone, then, when she fell short of achieving the As she expected and needed in her public AS-level exams.

And then there was Jayden, who was a member of another Sixth Form class. He was unfailingly polite in class but would rarely volunteer contributions to our lessons, and he never completed the homework I set. He seemed resistant to any form of encouragement and sanction, politely letting anything his teachers did wash over him and then continuing in his disengaged manner. Through subsequent discussions between the school and Jayden's mother, it transpired that his father had passed away just before he started in the Sixth Form, and he continued to spend large parts of his school holidays standing outside his father's house, waiting for him to step through the front door.

The experiences of James, Eleanor and Jayden are examined and explained in more detail later in the book. For now, when I look back, I cannot help thinking I could have helped all three of them overcome or avoid the difficulties they faced had I known why they were responding as they were to the situations they were in. If only I had known what follows in this book . . .

1.8 Summary

- We are all naturally characterised by common preferences, biases and likely responses in situations. These are our cognitive traits.
- Some researchers view these cognitive traits as mental weaknesses whilst others view them as devices that actually make us smart. Either way, understanding these cognitive traits can help us to make our teaching and schools more effective and more compassionate.
- The modern view of decision-making is one in which we repeatedly interact with our environment in order to make a selection from the available options. Behavioural science is interested in the relationship between our environment and our eventual decision.
- Behavioural science should not be viewed as a challenge to educational psychology but as an extension, opening up a new direction of educational research.

2 The science

Its purpose, strengths and limitations

In May 1747, James Lind found himself on the HMS *Salisbury*, a 50-gun Royal Navy ship patrolling the English Channel during the War of Austrian Succession between Britain and the combined forces of France and Spain. A doctor from Scotland, Lind had been appointed surgeon of the ship two months earlier (Yanes 2016). Eight weeks into the posting, Lind noticed the unmistakable signs of scurvy amongst the 140-strong crew, which probably included 'lethargy, weakness, anemia, discolored and waxen skin and "dropsical effusion" - a buildup of liquid - under the eyes, around the ankles, and in other parts of the body' (Sancton 2021, p. 186). And so, on 20 May, Lind selected 12 of the afflicted sailors on the basis of the similarity of their symptoms and divided them into six pairs. He then administered a different dietary supplement to each pair: cider, diluted sulfuric acid, vinegar, sea water, a purgative mixture and citrus fruit (specifically, two oranges and a lemon). Not only was the pair treated with citrus fruit no doubt grateful from a taste perspective, they were the only pair whose symptoms receded, even though Lind ran out of citrus fruit after only six days.

Lind's work is generally considered to be the first application of the experimental method to people, in which participants are separated into differently treated groups in order for the researcher to identify the effects of the different treatments (although there is no definitive proof that Lind actually conducted the experiment he reported). The first use of this research approach in the social sciences came 136 years later, when Charles Sanders Peirce, an American philosopher and scientist, confirmed his hypothesis that people are usually able to correctly identify different weights even when the differences are very small. Peirce and Joseph Jastrow, one of his students, took it in turns to act as the researcher and the participant in the experiment, with the participant being given a weight from which, unbeknownst to him, weight was then removed or to which weight was added as determined by the colour of the playing card the researcher drew from the pack. The application of the experimental approach to education emerged around the turn of the twentieth century in the form of studies into learning in classrooms. The first book on experimental design in education was published in 1923 (Jamison 2019).

2.1 Behavioural experiments

Throughout this book, the term 'behavioural experiment' refers to a study in which a researcher observes the behaviour or choices of participants in a setting in which one or

DOI: 10.4324/9781003198505-2

more conditions is deliberately altered in some way. The purpose of such a study is to estab-lish the causal link between the aspect of the setting that has been manipulated and the participants' behaviour. The findings of 70 such experiments, outlined in List Two, are drawn upon in the pages that follow. Of these experiments, over 50 involve randomisation in one of two forms. The first, such as that used by Peirce and Jastrow in their weight experiment, involves the participants in the experiment being subjected to all of the different conditions in a random order. The second, and far more prevalent, involves the participants in the exper-iment being randomly assigned to different groups, each of which is subjected to a different condition. Lind's scurvy experiment is an example of this second approach. And of these randomised experiments, over 30 involve a discernible control group: a group of participants for whom the setting is not altered at all, the outcome from which is used as a comparator for the outcomes from the other groups. These final types of experiments are known as randomised control trials. They have become the standard approach to experimentation in medicine and across the social sciences.

Key term: behavioural experiment

A study in which a researcher observes the behaviour of participants in a setting in which one or more conditions is deliberately altered in some way, isolating the link between the changed condition and behaviour.

Three general types of behavioural experiment are included in the pages that follow. They are summarised in Table 2.1. The first type are laboratory experiments. They involve partici-pants, who have no particular relation to the task they are required to complete, undertaking artificial tasks in artificial settings, often in rooms on university campuses. Being the easiest to arrange and tightly manage, allowing researchers to ensure only the desired condition is altered for each group of participants and thereby maximising the clarity of the eventual link between condition and behaviour, these experiments are the most common. They account for 53% of the experiments that follow. A good example of such an experiment is that con-ducted by Dan Ariely and colleagues into the link between how much a person values an item they have created and the difficulty of creating it (see Section 4.2). This experiment involved university students constructing origami frogs and cranes (which surely they hardly ever do in real life) whilst in a teaching room on campus (which is surely not where origami frogs and cranes are usually made).

The second type are field experiments. These involve participants who have some relation to the task they are required to complete, undertaking artificial tasks in real-life settings. This approach strengthens the real-life applicability of the eventual findings whilst also giv-ing researchers the ability to manage the experimental conditions. A good example of this is the jam experiment, in which Sheena Iyengar and Mark Lepper recorded the behaviour of shoppers in relation to specially designed displays of jams whilst doing their shopping in a supermarket (see Section 3.1). Of the 70 behavioural experiments discussed in what follows, 39% are field experiments.

Table 2.1 Types of behavioural experiments

Experiment Type	Task	Setting	Participants	Example
Laboratory	Artificial	Artificial	Unrelated	Origami frogs experiment (Section 4.2)
Field	Artificial	Real life	Related	Jam experiment (Section 3.1)
Natural	Real life	Real life	Related	Train line distraction experiment (Section 7.1)

The final type are natural experiments. These take place in real-life settings in which conditions are altered for different participants going about their daily lives, without any influence or manipulation from researchers. These are inevitably much rarer and pose greater difficulties for researchers when establishing the link between a single change in the setting and the resulting behaviour. Only 9% of the experiments that follow take this form. However, when researchers stumble across such coveted opportunities, they lead to findings that are most applicable to real life. The best example of a natural experiment is the train line distraction experiment (see Section 7.1). In this, a school in Connecticut noticed a concerning disparity between the academic performance of pupils whose lessons were in classrooms on the same side of the building as a busy train line and that of pupils whose lessons were on the opposite side. Researchers were able to investigate the causal link between noise distraction and the academic performance of pupils going about their daily lives in a real-life and unadulterated setting.

2.2 Procedural strengths

Experiments such as these have become something of a gold standard in medical and social science research. There are three main reasons for this:

- They allow researchers to isolate the specific effects caused by changing one of the conditions in a given setting. For James Lind, for example, ensuring the 12 sailors in his study were all treated in exactly the same way during his study apart from the dietary supplements they consumed allowed him to clearly see the impact of each of his different prescriptions.
- With a large enough number of participants, randomly assigning the participants to different condition groups should remove the influence of any other determining factors, which would cloud the effect of the condition of interest. Take the Stanford suicide note experiment as an example (see Section 5.2). Lee Ross and colleagues randomly told each of the 60 pupils participating in the experiment they had achieved one of three different rates of success in a task that had involved them distinguishing between real and fabricated suicide notes. Through such randomisation, they ensured the pupils were evenly distributed across the three experimental groups in terms of factors such as their age, academic attainment and family socioeconomic status, thereby removing the possible effects of these factors from the link between a pupil's performance in the initial note identification task and the pupil's ultimate belief in their ability in such a task.

- With a large enough number of participants, drawn randomly from the population, the findings should be applicable to the population in general. For example, by observing the impact of altering the order of items on a cafè's menu on almost 500 orders placed by customers over a 30-day period, Eran Dayan and Maya Bar-Hillel have revealed that all of us are more likely to purchase items that appear at either the top or bottom of a list than items that appear in between (see Section 5.1). It is difficult to think of a reason why our purchase decisions would be influenced by the menu changes differently to those of such a large number of customers going about their lives in Tel Aviv.

2.3 Procedural limitations

However, there are also technical limitations to such experiments that have led eminent academics to challenge their gold standard status (Deaton and Cartwright 2018). Three criticisms particularly stand out:

- It is often difficult to randomly assign participants to different experimental groups. For example, in his study of the impact of a scientist-in-residence programme on the perceptions of scientists amongst Year Six pupils (ages 10-11 years) at a school in Eugene, Oregon, Larry Flick compared the perceptions of pupils in two classes at the school having experienced the programme with those of two Year Seven classes (ages 11-12 years) at a different school (see Section 11.3). Any common differences between the pupils across the two schools and across the two year groups, such as socioeconomic status or parental attitudes, could have contributed to the different perceptions revealed after the programme had been completed. Oftentimes, observed effects of changing a condition in a given setting should be interpreted as the combined effects of changing the condition and the other uncontrolled factors.
- It is difficult for researchers to ensure an experiment is not undermined by those involved knowing about its structure and purpose. Researchers commonly assign participants to experimental groups in ways that ensure the participants are blind to how the conditions they face are altered. This safeguards against possible placebo effects, which subconsciously cause the participants to behave in the way expected. It is less common, though, for those conducting the experiment, recording the outcomes and analysing the final data to be blind to the structure and purpose of the experiment. And it is likely that this knowledge can lead them to subconsciously act in ways that skew the results in the direction the researchers hope they will go. In their study of the effects of parental communication during the 2010 summer programme at a school in Boston, Massachusetts, Matthew Kraft and Shaun Dougherty deliberately removed such unwanted influence by training other people to observe the pupils involved in the study and by ensuring these observers did not know whether or not they were observing pupils whose parents were receiving communications from the school (see Section 10.4). However, in the cafè choice experiment conducted by Eran Dayan and Maya Bar-Hillel, the cafè staff are likely to have known the nature and purpose of the experiment, and this could have, without any intention, led them to talk customers through the options in a way that inadvertently induced them to more regularly select options at the top and bottom of the menus.

- Controlled experiments lead to ethical dilemmas as one or more of their experimental groups are purposefully kept in conditions that deprive them of known benefits. Angus Deaton and Nancy Cartwright give an extreme example from the 1970s, when the efficacy of a new treatment for newborns with persistent pulmonary hypertension was assessed. All of the babies who received the treatment survived, but four of those in the control group lost their lives. Situations such as these have led to the development of adaptive experiments. In these, outcomes are analysed throughout the experiment's duration and experimental groups whose conditions are leading to suboptimal outcomes are collapsed before the end of the experiment and the participants within them reassigned to more beneficial groups requiring further assessment. But even these inevitably lead to ethical dilemmas, albeit likely reduced compared to the standard format. The researchers conducting the 1970s study started with such an approach that resulted in the death of one of the newborns involved. This limitation is inevitably particularly acute in medicine and education.

2.4 The replication crisis

One of the problems pervading the findings throughout this book is that of seeming irreplicability. Many of the findings discussed in the chapters that follow are astonishing, in terms of how surprising they are and in terms of their magnitude. However, when other researchers have tried to repeat them in similar situations, they have often failed to find any sign of the reported effects. An example of this problem, relating to a specifically education-focused study, relates to the work of Dominique Morisano and colleagues explored in Section 10.3. These researchers found that personalised goal and strategy setting considerably improved the academic performance of students at McGill University: a remarkable effect for an almost costless intervention that took students only two and a half hours to complete. Renè Kizilcec and colleagues attempted to replicate this impact, along with that from a similar intervention in one of their own previous studies, in an experiment involving over a quarter of a million students from 247 countries enrolled in online courses offered by Harvard, MIT and Stanford Universities (Kizilcec *et al.* 2020). The experiment required students to describe in detail how and when they were going to complete necessary coursework and to write about how taking their course aligned with the values most important to them. The researchers found that the plan-making activity improved student engagement but only for the first few weeks of the course. The positive impact was small and very short-lived. And the values-based activity had a small positive effect on the average completion rate of students in less-developed countries on courses they tended to complete less frequently than their developed country counterparts, whereas it had the opposite effect for courses in which there was no such initial difference in completion rates.

Key term: replication crisis

The growing and worrying realisation in 2011 that many of the key findings in the social sciences could not be replicated in confirmatory experiments.

Such findings caused something of a crisis in the social sciences in 2011 and triggered a number of projects to assess the extent of the problem. In psychology, for example, the Centre for Open Science launched the Reproducibility Project in November of that year, in which researchers identified and tested key findings in the literature (Open Science Collaboration 2015). The findings of 100 influential studies were subjected to such tests, 97% of which had been statistically significant in the original papers. Concerningly, only 36% of the replication experiments resulted in equally significant findings. This replication rate fits into the range of those from similar studies in different fields within the social sciences. The highest replication rate has been in economics, with 61% of the findings of 18 studies in two of the leading academic journals published in the years 2011–2014 being successfully replicated (Camerer *et al.* 2016).

The cause of this crisis predominantly lies with the publication bias that exists within academia. Researchers wanting to build their careers tend to focus on one thing: publishing research findings in the highest-ranked academic journals they can. It is on such publication records that appointments, promotions and grants are based. As the top, most widely read and most highly valued journals tend only to publish the strongest and most interesting and surprising findings, researchers find themselves in an increasingly fierce race to find such results. Anything less striking than those are not worth their time, which increasingly includes findings that simply replicate those previously published. This pressure in turn leads to two outcomes. The first is that researchers tend only to submit results that are likely to be accepted, which then misrepresents their research. A team may run ten experiments, for example, and will only write up the one trial that led to a significant result, ignoring the nine others that led to ambiguous or even negative findings, as submitting those would erode the power of the one success. The second is that researchers are incentivised to engage in what are known as questionable research practices in order to make their findings stronger, more surprising and, ultimately, more publishable. These practices, to which Leslie John, George Lowenstein and Drazen Prelec refer as the 'steroids of scientific competition' (John *et al.* 2012, p. 524), include removing 'unhelpful' data points in a spreadsheet of findings; stopping the collection of data earlier than planned in order to retain a nice finding, and failing to report unsuccessful trials. Such practices reduce the reliability and replicability of findings. To ascertain the prevalence of such practices, John, Lowenstein and Prelec sent a survey to 5,964 academic psychologists working at leading American universities asking them to anonymously report whether or not they had engaged in each of ten of these practices, the percentage of academic psychologists they thought had engaged in them, and the percentage of academic psychologists they thought would admit to engaging in them. From their responses, the researchers were able to infer the prevalence of these practices, knowing respondents were likely to under-report them. Their findings were stark. There was only a 36% response rate to their survey, a further 33.4% of those who started the survey failed to complete it, and the inferred estimates for the prevalence of some of the questionable research practices approached 100%. The use of these techniques sadly seems to be the norm.

2.5 Academic fraud

Whilst the practices in the previous section fall short of academic fraud, in which data are fabricated, there are also instances of that occurring within the social sciences. Perhaps the most famous example, which contributed to the start of the replication crisis, is that of Diederik Stapel, who reached the pinnacle of a career as a social psychologist, publishing articles in the very best academic journals and rising to be the Dean of the School of Social and Behavioral Sciences at Tilburg University in the Netherlands. Stapel made a strong start to his career, completing his doctorate at the University of Amsterdam, publishing a number of papers that earned him a prize from the European Association of Experimental Social Psychology and being appointed to a professorial role at Groningen University. He increasingly found editors of academic journals asking him if he could make the results of his work sharper before they were published, which in 2004 led to him having an article published in a leading journal despite it being entirely based on data he had made up. Seeing just how enthusiastically this work was received, Stapel increasingly fabricated data, for both himself and his unknowing co-authors and students. By the time his deception was uncovered and an inquiry into his work was released in November 2011, Stapel had published at least 55 articles, and had supervised ten doctoral theses, that involved fraudulent data (Bhattacharjee 2013).

Sadly, the Stapel story is not an isolated case within the social sciences. Similar accusations of academic malpractice have also been levelled at Dan Ariely, for example: a Professor of Psychology and Behavioral Economics at Duke University in the USA who has done more than perhaps anyone else to popularise behavioural economics. The main allegation related to a study that Ariely and co-authors published in 2012, which demonstrated that asking people to confirm the honesty of their responses at the start of a form rather than at the end leads them to lie less. This result has led insurance companies to change their practices and has been incorporated into business management courses around the world. It has since been established that the data on which this conclusion was based were fabricated, at least in part, which has led the journal in which the original article was published to retract it. The five authors have all claimed they were unaware of the fabrication and have asserted they would not have published their findings had they known about it, with Ariely suggesting the deception occurred within the insurance company that was collecting the data for the study. The authors have since published a follow-up article refuting their original findings (Miller 2021). And then there is the 2004 study by Marcial Losada and Emily Heaphy, discussed in Section 5.3, which showed the greatest determinant of a team's effectiveness is the ratio of positive to negative interactions between its team members, with the ratio for the highest performing teams being remarkably close to the famous five-to-one ratio for healthy relationships. The editors of the publishing journal have since raised concerns about the 'data collection, analyses, [and] interpretation of the analyses' in the paper, advising caution when using the findings within it (Editors of American Behavioral Scientist 2014).

2.6 The WEIRD criticism

Thought experiment: the ultimatum game

This simple game involves only two players. One of the players is the Proposer and the other is the Responder. The Proposer starts the game with £100, whilst the Responder starts without anything. In the first stage of the game, the Proposer chooses how to distribute the £100 between himself and the Responder. In the second stage, the Responder then either accepts that distribution, causing the money to be divided in the manner agreed and the game to end, or rejects it, causing the game to end and both players to walk away with nothing at all.

How would you distribute the £100 if you played the part of the Proposer?

The final limitation of the evidence on which this book is based arises from the homogeneity and unrepresentativeness of those on which behavioural experiments are conducted. In a paper published in 2008, Jeffrey Arnett reported his analysis of the articles published in the top psychology journals in the five years between 2003 and 2007. The headlines: 68% of the participants in these studies came from the USA and 96% came from Western, indus- trialised countries (North America, Europe, Australia and Israel). Furthermore, 67% of the American participants and 80% of those from other countries were university undergradu- ates. Not only are behavioural findings drawn almost entirely from countries that account for only 12% of the global population, they are drawn from a remarkably small subset of those populations (Arnett 2008). It cannot be assumed that the findings from behavioural experiments are representative of, or indeed applicable to, the vast majority of the world's population because they are drawn from such a WEIRD (westernised, educated, industri- alised, rich and democratic) sample (Henrich *et al.* 2010). And it is evident from a recent article that revisits this issue that relatively little progress has been made in addressing this limitation. Slightly more than 60% of the participants in studies published in the same six journals that Arnett analysed in his original article but in the five years between 2014 and 2018 were from the USA. However, this reduction seems to have been driven by an increase in the number of studies conducted in other English-speaking and Western European coun- tries (Thalmayer *et al.* 2021).

Sadly, this limitation applies to the behavioural experiments on which the chapters that follow are based, as shown in Figures 2.1 and 2.2. Of the 70 behavioural experiments dis- cussed in this book, 89% of them were conducted in either North America or Europe, with a further 7% being conducted in either Australia, New Zealand or Israel. And of these, over 51% were conducted on university undergraduates and almost 36% on adults, meaning fewer than 13% were conducted on those about whom this book is primarily concerned: schoolchildren.

The reason this composition of participants in behavioural experiments is concerning can be seen in the study of the behaviours of people when playing the ultimatum game. This very short and rather dull game, outlined in the thought experiment at the start of this section, is a key component in the studies of our concerns for one another. Logically, a Responder should accept any distribution of the £100, however unfair it may be. Receiving any amount is better for the Responder than walking away at the end of the game without anything at all. Knowing this and following cold-hearted reasoning, a Proposer should give the Responder only a single penny, keeping £99.99 for themselves. However, the findings from laboratory behavioural experiments consistently show that when Proposers choose to keep 80% of the initial endowment, Responders tend to reject the distribution 40% to 60% of the time,

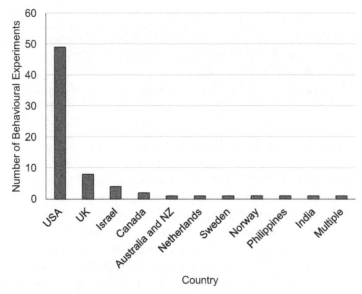

Figure 2.1 The location of the behavioural experiments in this book

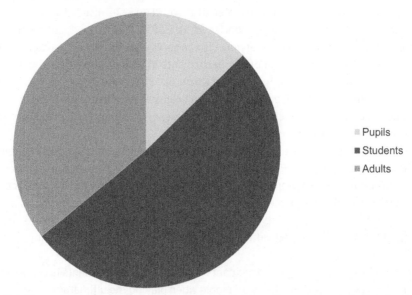

Figure 2.2 The nature of the participants in the behavioural experiments in this book

with the probability of rejection increasing as the Proposer's distribution becomes increasingly unfair. Perhaps subconsciously anticipating this, Proposers in these experiments tend to keep only 50% to 60% of the initial endowment, giving their counterparts the remainder (Mallard 2017).

Unsurprisingly, these outcomes were not replicated when this game was conducted in field experiments with players from 15 different indigenous, small-scale populations around the world (Henrich *et al.* 2001). Two populations that particularly stand out from this study are the Machiguenga and the Lamalera. The Machiguenga are a people from Southeast Peru who are predominantly hunter-gatherers. They live in small and widely dispersed family groups and refer to one another with kinship-based names, such as mother and brother. They do not possess personal names. The Lamalera, on the other hand, live in a village on the slopes of an Indonesian volcanic island. The structure of Lamalera society is based around whale-hunting, its traditional source of protein, with lead harpooners being held in particularly high esteem and with an individual's share of a catch being determined by their role in the hunt. Far from the outcomes of ultimatum games played in lecture rooms on Western university campuses being common across all human societies, Joseph Henrich and his colleagues found that behaviour in this game is closely related to the everyday relationships within society. The more players depend on one another in their daily lives, the fairer Proposers' distributions are likely to be. Proposers from the Machiguenga, a society in which there is very little cooperation outside of close-knit family groups, were seen giving on average 26% of the initial endowment to Responders, whilst those from the Lamalera, in which cooperation is essential for a successful hunt, gave an average of 58%. The findings of behavioural experiments cannot simply be assumed to represent the behaviour of people different to those who participated in generating them.

2.7 Overall assessment

There are undoubtedly limitations to behavioural experiments and their findings. However, through using them, behavioural scientists have uncovered a wealth of insights into how our minds work, why we behave the way we do and the factors that most acutely influence our mental health and wellbeing. That governments around the world are making their policies more effective by shaping them according to behavioural science is testament to the potential power of the experimental approach. The 70 behavioural experiments examined in the chapters that follow have been selected because the statistical likelihood of their findings having arisen randomly is tiny, usually less than 1%; because they were freely available online at the time of writing for you to read for yourself; but, most importantly of all, because the insights to which they lead could have profound implications for both the way we teach and how we manage our schools. That they have been mostly conducted on university students and adults from the USA and UK, and the articles in which their results have been published have undoubtedly been influenced by publication bias, means we cannot take their findings at face value, though. They may not all apply to the pupils we teach or to our individual schools. And so I encourage you to read the next nine chapters with open minds but also with a sense of scepticism, mentally testing what follows against your own experiences of teaching and your understanding of the pupils you teach. And then, if you can, to use the toolkit outlined in Chapter 13 to run your own behavioural experiments to more concretely test the value of the suggestions that follow in your own classrooms and schools and to push our understanding forward.

By cautiously harnessing the lessons from behavioural science, we can make our teaching and schools more effective and more compassionate. That is the purpose of the pages that follow.

2.8 Summary

- The primary sources of evidence in behavioural science are behavioural experiments. These involve researchers observing the behaviour of participants in settings in which one or more conditions is deliberately altered in some way, isolating the link between the changed condition and behaviour.
- There are three general types of behavioural experiment: laboratory, field and natural experiments. The first of these is by far the most prevalent in behavioural science.
- Behavioural experiments allow researchers to isolate the impact of specific interventions, to remove the effects of other influences, and to draw conclusions about the behaviour of people in general. These are the strengths of such experiments.
- Behavioural experiments suffer from difficulties in assigning participants to groups randomly, susceptibility to subconscious distortion by those who know their design, and ethical dilemmas that arise from depriving some participants from potential beneficial treatments.
- Behavioural science suffers from the replication crisis, in which researchers have found it difficult to replicate key findings in the literature; academic fraud, in which researchers have fabricated their data and findings; and the WEIRD criticism, which arises from the unrepresentative nature of those who tend to participate in behavioural experiments.
- Behavioural scientists have uncovered a wealth of insights into how our minds work that can help us to improve the experiences of our pupils. However, these insights should be tested against our own experiences and in our individual school settings.

Bibliography

Arnett, J.J., 2008. The neglected 95%: Why American psychology needs to become less American. *American Psychologist*, 63 (7), 602-614.

Bhattacharjee, Y., 2013. The mind of a con man. *New York Times Magazine*, 26 April. Available from: www.nytimes.com/2013/04/28/magazine/diederik-stapels-audacious-academic-fraud.html.

Camerer, C.F., *et al.*, 2016. Evaluating replicability of laboratory experiments in economics. *Science*, 351 (6280), 1433-1436.

Deaton, A., and Cartwright, N., 2018. Understanding and misunderstanding randomized controlled trials. *Social Science and Medicine*, 210, 2-21.

Editors of American Behavioral Scientist, 2014. Expression of concern. *American Behavioral Scientist*, 58 (8), 1100-1101. Available from: https://journals.sagepub.com/doi/full/10.1177/0002764214537204.

Henrich, J., *et al.*, 2001. In search of homo economicus: Behavioral experiments in 15 small-scale societies. *American Economic Review Papers and Proceedings*, 91, 73-78.

Henrich, J., Heine, S., and Norenzayan, A., 2010. The weirdest people in the world? *Behavioral and Brain Sciences*, 33 (2-3), 61-83.

Jamison, J.C., 2019. The entry of randomized assignment into the social sciences. *Journal of Causal Inference*, 1-16.

John, L.K., Loewenstein, G., and Prelec, D., 2012. Measuring the prevalence of questionable research practices with incentives for truth telling. *Psychological Science*, 23 (5), 524-532.

Kizilcec, R.F., *et al.*, 2020. Scaling up behavioral science interventions in online education. *Proceedings of the National Academy of Sciences*, 117 (26), 14900-14905.

Mallard, G., 2017. *Behavioural Economics (The Economy Key Ideas)*. Newcastle upon Tyne: Agenda Publishing, pp. 59–60.

Miller, C.B., 2021. An influential study of dishonesty was dishonest. *Forbes*, 30 August. Available from: www.forbes.com/sites/christianmiller/2021/08/30/an-influential-study-of-dishonesty-was-dishonest/?sh=48f9df702c72.

Open Science Collaboration, 2015. Estimating the reproducibility of psychological science. *Science*, 349 (6251), 1–10.

Sancton, J., 2021. *Madhouse at the End of the Earth: The Belgica's Journey into the Dark Antarctic Night*. London, UK: Penguin Publishing.

Thalmayer, A.G., Toscanelli, C., and Arnett, J.J., 2021. The neglected 95% revisited: Is American psychology becoming less American? *American Psychologist*, 76 (1), 116–129.

Yanes, J., 2016. James Lind and Scurvy: The first clinical trial in history? *OpenMind: BBVA*. Available from: www.bbvaopenmind.com/en/science/leading-figures/james-lind-and-scurvy-the-first-clinical-trial-in-history/.

SECTION ONE: LEARNING

3 Lesson design

3.1 Mental tasks are tiring

We power all our conscious behaviour using our mental energy reserves: deciding whether the answer to a multiple-choice question is A or C, working through the solution to a mathematical problem on the whiteboard, resisting the temptation to check emails whilst our pupils are busy reading the exemplar answer we wrote the night before and trying to cut out the noise of the coach idling outside our classroom. All of these tasks, along with all the others we do on a daily basis, require us to draw on those mental energy reserves. And as we deplete them, we become less and less able to do these tasks, and we increasingly rely on shortcuts or choose to avoid them altogether. You are suffering the effects of having depleted your mental reserve whenever you have got to the point whilst marking when you cannot bear to look at one more book; or you decide to leave planning a lesson until the next day because you just cannot decide which tasks would be most effective; or you react to a pupil who has started talking with a rather harsh sanction, even though you know you were more lenient with another pupil earlier in the day. In each of these cases, you are suffering from decision fatigue.

From their study of over 1,100 of the parole decisions made by judges in an Israeli court over the course of a year, Shai Danziger, Jonathan Levav and Liora Avnaim-Pesso showed that, when all other factors had been taken into account, the probability of a prisoner being released early fell as the day went on (Danziger *et al.* 2011). They found that the average probability that a prisoner would be released early was approximately 33% across the whole year, but the average probability of early release for a prisoner whose hearing was early in the morning was about 70%, whereas that of a prisoner appearing late in the day was less than 10%. The risk for judges in making these decisions lies in releasing a prisoner early and the prisoner then going on to reoffend. A judge faces no risk in refusing to release a prisoner early, beyond having a bad conscience in hindsight from acting unfairly. And so as a day goes on, with judges making one decision after another and depleting their mental reserves, judges increasingly opt for the safe option: not granting parole. Decision fatigue even impacts highly qualified and highly experienced professionals.

DOI: 10.4324/9781003198505-4

Key term: decision fatigue

We find any conscious behaviour mentally tiring, be it making decisions, resisting temptations or making ourselves focus on a task. And as we mentally tire, we become increasingly less able to do these things effectively.

In another study, Sheena Iyengar and Mark Lepper, working at Columbia and Stanford Universities, respectively, set up a display of jams in a supermarket on two separate occasions (Iyengar and Lepper 2000). On the first, the display consisted of 24 different types of jam. It was a visually appealing array of flavours and colours. On the second, the display consisted of only six different jams. The researchers then sat back and recorded how shoppers responded. They saw that 60% of shoppers perused the display when there was a larger number of jams, compared to 40% when the range was more limited. However, only 3% of shoppers actually made a purchase from the more varied display, whereas 30% bought a jar from the more limited display.

We are attracted to the more colourful, more interesting display and so are more likely to stop to look at it. But we find it more tiring to make a choice from a larger range of options, which makes us more likely to walk away without having made one. This is the excessive choice effect. The shopping example can seem rather trivial, but this effect has also been documented in elections, during which we are less likely to cast a vote when there are a large number of candidates on the ballot slip than when there are only a few.

Key term: excessive choice effect

Increasing the number of options from which we can choose quickly overwhelms us mentally and makes it more likely that we walk away without making a decision.

I have always been told that an effective lesson starts with an easy-to-access starter exercise, ideally one that links to the previous lesson or to pupils' prior learning. After that, there should be a number of different tasks, all directly focused on helping pupils achieve the desired learning outcomes and varied in order to maintain their interest and engagement. The first of these is likely to be an activity designed to transfer knowledge to pupils, which is followed by a separate activity in which pupils practise using what they have learned, such as them answering exam-style questions, having a debate or applying their new knowledge in different situations. This model lesson then ends with a plenary exercise, during which pupils review what they have learned, helping them to consolidate and organise the new information in their minds. This pattern of a lesson seems logical until the effect of decision fatigue is taken into account. Every task we ask our pupils to complete is mentally tiring for them: concentrating on us speaking, taking notes, answering questions, making contributions to a class discussion and everything else we ask them to do. As the lesson progresses, our pupils become increasingly tired. And as they become tired, they become less able to do the things we ask of them, and just as in the case of the judges, they take fewer deliberate risks, which in this case probably means they contribute less. As Figure 3.1 illustrates, our lessons typically demand an increasing amount of mental effort and active participation from our pupils at precisely the time they are becoming less able to do those things. This is why our pupils seemingly lose the ability to concentrate as a lesson goes on, why they struggle to engage with the more active tasks in the second half of lessons, and why our carefully designed plenary exercises are not as effective as we had expected. These can all be explained through the effects of decision fatigue: through something that is not the wilful behaviour of our pupils, but something they cannot control.

The inevitable implications of what is shown in Figure 3.1 are compounded by the finding that what mentally tires us most is having to switch from one task to another. Studies have shown that it takes us considerably longer than we realise to refocus on a task after having been interrupted or distracted from it. Indeed, the average time to do so is 23 minutes and 15 seconds. This is lower when the source of the interruption is external (such as a phone call) rather than internal (such as checking our emails), but only very slightly so. And not only that, these studies have shown we also suffer from knowing that an interruption is coming.

In an experiment for the *New York Times*, 136 people were asked to read a short piece of writing and then answer questions about it (Sullivan and Thompson 2013). The participants were randomly split into three groups. Those assigned to the first group took a single test without interruption or expectation of interruption. This was the control group. Those in the second and third groups took the test twice and were told they might be interrupted during each. Those in the second group were interrupted twice during the first test and then again during the re-run. Those in the third group were also interrupted twice during the first test but not at all during the re-run. The researchers found that those in the interrupted groups answered 20% fewer questions correctly on average than those in the control group. Not only does it take us a surprisingly long time to resume interrupted tasks, interruptions also make us less effective in completing those tasks. However, in the second part of the experiment, those in the second group answered 14% fewer questions correctly on average, whilst

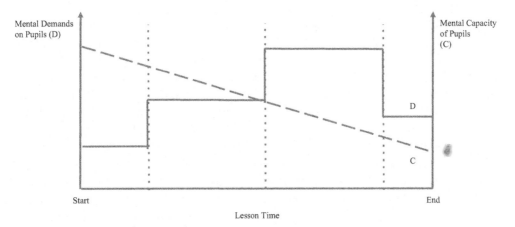

Figure 3.1 Pupil mental load during a typical lesson

those in the third group, who were expecting an interruption that never came, improved their performance by 43%, even outperforming those in the control group. This somewhat counterintuitive finding fits with the other findings in this area that suggest we alter our way of completing tasks, becoming more efficient, when we expect interruptions. However, this comes at a cost to our mental wellbeing, stress levels and feelings of being both under time pressure and frustrated.

If we want to maximise our productivity, we should set aside a prolonged period of uninterrupted time in which we can focus on the task at hand. And we should focus on only one task during that time. We certainly should not attempt to multi-task. Yet in a typical 50-minute lesson, we ask our pupils to switch tasks perhaps three or four times, and we constantly interrupt them as we try to monitor their learning and to help them as much as we can. (I am even susceptible to interrupting my pupils as they work because I feel I need to be doing something and even because I am bored.) Paradoxically, though, by doing this we are inadvertently either reducing the productivity of our pupils or, if they are able to respond in a way that makes them more efficient, worsening their mental wellbeing. We can help our pupils by planning lessons that allow them to focus on a single task for a prolonged period of time, by resisting the urge to interrupt them unnecessarily and by monitoring their progress through observation rather than questioning whenever they are task focused.

3.2 We can only process so much at one time

Not only do we find conscious behaviour tiring, we can also only retain and process a certain amount of information at any one time. To use the proper terminology, our mental bandwidth is constrained. Psychologist George Miller famously reported that our mental bandwidth allows us to process five pieces of information plus or minus two. This figure has more recently been reduced to four. That equates to a processing capacity of approximately 120 bits per second. As processing what a single person is saying requires around 60 bits per second, it is no wonder we struggle to keep up when in noisy settings (Levitin 2015). Trying to attend to two or more conversations at the same time quickly overwhelms our mental bandwidths and makes us lose track of what everyone is saying. This has become known as the cocktail effect.

Our processing speed also slows down as more of our mental bandwidth is used. A group of over 80 undergraduates from Princeton University were asked by Joshua Greene and some of his colleagues to answer a number of questions, in which they had to make moral judgements about whether or not to allow harm to one person in order to save the lives of others (Greene *et al.* 2008). One such question was the Crying Baby Dilemma, in which the students had to consider how they would behave if they were hiding with some of their neighbours from invading soldiers and their baby began to cry. They could either allow their baby's crying to attract the attention of the soldiers, which would result in the death of everyone hiding, or they could smother their baby to death. Some of the students simply had to read aloud the dilemmas from their computer screens and then make their decisions. Others, who were completing the same task, also had to watch a stream of numbers run across the bottom of their screens and press a button every time the number five appeared.

The nature of the responses was not affected by the additional, bandwidth-consuming task. Both groups of students responded with the utilitarian response, allowing harm to one person for the greater benefit of the group as a whole, in around 60% of cases. The average time it took the participants to make these decisions was noticeably longer for those having to complete the additional task, though: 6.5 seconds per question compared to the 5.8 seconds taken by their less burdened counterparts.

> **Key term: mental bandwidth**
>
> The limit to how much information our brains can process at any one time.

We can help our pupils by deliberately considering in our lesson plans how much information they have to process at any one time and how long they need to do so. There are times when we need to explain something to a class, perhaps the meaning of a particular concept, the logic underpinning a certain argument or the technique for answering a type of exam question. Cognitive psychology tells us that we need to make these times interactive, as pupils commit information to their memories most effectively when they use it in some way. And the work of Robert Bjork's lab at the University of California has shown we should not make those tasks too easy; that there is a desirable level of difficulty that makes pupils mentally engage with the tasks set. And so we ask our pupils questions and set them exercises to complete as we go through our explanations. But it is easy to forget that pupils need to process the information before they can use it, that the content is new to them and so needs organising in their minds, and that we should not expect a response or outcome before they have had the required time to do that properly. Periods of silence in a lesson, as we wait for a response, can be uncomfortable, but they are an essential part of effective assessment for learning.

3.3 Teaching enjoyable lessons

We all want pupils to enjoy the lessons we teach and to look forward to their next lesson with us, so they are receptive to what we have planned as they step through our classroom door. The findings of two behavioural experiments conducted by Donald Redelmeier and Daniel Kahneman on colonoscopy patients at Toronto Hospital shed light on how we can ensure they do so (see Kahneman *et al.* 1997). In the first experiment, patients were asked to rate the level of discomfort they were feeling every 60 seconds during their procedures and then, once they were over, to make judgements about the overall levels of discomfort they had felt. Their ratings showed a strong correlation between the levels of discomfort they felt at their worst and also at the end of their procedures, on one hand, and their hindsight judgements about the overall levels of discomfort they had felt, on the other. As those two reported levels of discomfort worsened, so did the overall judgement. Perhaps curiously, there was very little correlation between the duration of the procedures and the hindsight judgements. In the follow-up experiment, the patients involved were separated into two groups. The patients in both groups were asked to judge the overall levels of discomfort they had felt during their procedures after they had finished. The difference between the two groups was that the colonoscopes were left in place for a short period of time after the procedures had been completed for those in the first group, whilst for those in the second group they were removed immediately (as is usually the case). Prolonging the procedures in this way no doubt increased the total amounts of discomfort felt by the patients in the first group. The surgeon may not have been manipulating the colonoscopes during the additional time, but they were still in place. However, the overall levels of discomfort reported by the affected patients were significantly lower than those reported by the patients in the second group.

In response to our constrained mental bandwidth and our susceptibility to decision fatigue, we employ shortcuts to help us to make decisions more easily and more quickly. These are our decision-making heuristics. An example is the Peak-End Rule. Rather than trying to process the information about the level of discomfort they felt at every minute during their procedures, a task that would quickly become mentally overwhelming, patients unconsciously based their overall judgements on two pieces of information: the levels of discomfort when they were at their worst (the peaks) and those at the end. By leaving the colonoscopes in place and without manipulation for the additional time before the end of the procedures of some patients, the levels of discomfort felt by the patients at the end were reduced and so their hindsight judgements were that they had experienced less discomfort overall.

This is a rather unpleasant example of the Peak-End Rule in action, but we use the very same heuristic in situations of pleasure as well. When we go to a concert, a festival or a show, we tend to remember the very best song, band or moment, as well as the enjoyment we felt at its end. That is the Peak-End Rule. We as teachers can take advantage of this in our lessons. The peak levels of enjoyment felt by our pupils in a lesson are perhaps difficult to control, but the end of the lesson is entirely in our hands. Our training tells us that plenary activities are important in helping pupils to consolidate their learning from the lesson, but they are also important in ensuring our pupils leave our classrooms in positive states of mind and are eager to return the next time we appear on their timetables. Allowing our lessons to over-run, meaning pupils start packing up before we are finished, or using the time at the end to quickly set their homework tasks, is a missed opportunity to use that time to our advantage.

Key term: heuristic

A mental shortcut we use, usually without thinking about it, to make our decision-making easier, quicker and less mentally demanding.

3.4 Losses and gains

One of the most influential diagrams in behavioural science is shown in Figure 3.2: a diagram we return to numerous times in the chapters to come. It illustrates three important facets of how we value something if we either gain or lose it. Only one is important for now, which is the finding that we are loss averse: that we value losing something more (approximately twice as much) than we value gaining that very same thing. This can be seen by assuming we are at zero in the diagram. If we are then given an item, perhaps a bottle of wine from a fellow

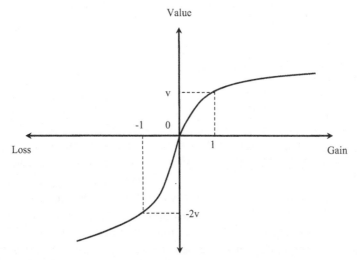

Figure 3.2 Loss aversion
Source: Adapted from Tversky and Kahneman 1981

teacher, we move one step to the right and feel better off to the magnitude of *v*, whatever that might be. If we are in a situation in which we are at zero and another teacher takes the same bottle of wine away from us, though, we move one step to the left and feel like we have lost out to double the magnitude of *v*.

Former world number one tennis player, Jimmy Connors, who won eight major titles during a career that saw him become the first male player to hold the number one spot for over 200 weeks, expressed this nicely when he claimed that he hated to lose more than he liked to win. That we have a greater preference not to lose something than to gain it may seem rather innocuous and, from an evolutionary perspective, perfectly logical, but it has serious implications for how we make judgements and decisions. This was shown in an experiment conducted by Daniel Kahneman, Jack Knetsch and Richard Thaler at Cornell and Simon Fraser Universities (Kahneman *et al*. 1990). Undergraduate students sitting randomly on alternating seats in their lecture halls were given university-branded mugs, which they were invited to sell to the other students in a variety of situations. Having been told that mutually acceptable trades would possibly be enforced, the students were asked to record the prices at which they were willing to sell the mugs, the prices at which their peers were willing to buy them and so the prices at which trade was viable. As shown in Figure 3.2, the average price at which the students were willing to sell (or lose) the mugs was approximately twice as high as that at which the other students were willing to buy (or gain) them. To ensure this result was not simply the product of running the experiment on students, Dan Ariely has since tested it on car salespeople and estate agents (Ariely 2012). That experiment generated an even greater difference in valuation, with the average recorded selling price being almost three times greater than the average recorded buying price. There is no reason why the students and professionals who were fortunate enough to be given mugs would like them more than their less fortunate counterparts: in both cases the mugs were distributed randomly. That there is such a difference in their valuations arises from loss aversion.

Key term: loss aversion

We feel the impact of losing something approximately twice as much as we feel the impact of gaining the very same thing.

Loss aversion has implications for our teaching, as it affects how our pupils engage in our lessons. Let us assume pupils enter our classes in a neutral state. They feel neither as though they have yet gained anything nor that they have lost anything. They are at zero in Figure 3.2. We then start teaching, and we want them to answer questions, to volunteer suggestions and to ask questions, and to do so out loud so the whole class can benefit from it. Any contribution they make comes with a risk, though. They may make a brilliant point, from which they then feel a gain as they receive our praise; but their contribution may be incorrect, in which case they may feel as though they have lost something, as they are shown-up in front of their peers. Figure 3.2 shows that if we simply declare a contribution to be correct or incorrect, the possible loss faced by our pupils outweighs the possible gain. In this case, the best thing for our pupils to do is to keep quiet, avoiding the risk entirely. Instead, we can overcome our pupils' natural resistance to contribute by

- Focusing on the action of contributing rather than on its outcome. By praising pupils for making contributions, whether or not they turn out to be correct, we can reduce the negative impact they feel from making a mistake. This links to the work on growth mindset by Carol Dweck (2017). We should also counter any negative comments made by other pupils in response to an incorrect contribution, reaffirming the value of the contribution that has been made.
- Finding something positive to highlight in every contribution. This could perhaps be the way of thinking that has been demonstrated or the way the pupil has linked their response to other content. Whatever it is, the important thing is that it is genuine and worthy of praise.
- Being discerning about which errors in our pupils' responses we correct and which we leave. It is important for our pupils to know when they have made mistakes or have misunderstood, but picking up on those that are unnecessary can deter pupils from contributing. There is a balance to be struck between our corrections and our pupils' willingness to speak out.

Of course pupils are unlikely to start lessons in a neutral state. Some enter our classrooms feeling as though they have already gained that day, having had successes in previous lessons, at home or during break times. It is likely that these pupils will be more willing to engage thoughtfully in the tasks we set, feeling confident in their abilities to complete the tasks successfully, and to interact with us in a positive manner. But they are also likely to be less willing to take risks in the contributions they make as they are happy with what they have already achieved that day and do not want to jeopardise those feelings. We can help pupils in such a positive mindset by giving them a greater push than usual to challenge themselves in their learning. Others enter our classrooms already in deficit, having experienced one form of loss or another previously. It is likely that these pupils will feel a need to take risks in the way they engage in tasks in order to offset the feeling of loss they already have. They are likely to engage less effectively with the tasks we set and to interact with us in a defensive manner. We can help pupils in such a negative mindset by reducing the likelihood of them failing again and the pressure we put on them. It is helpful to deliberately spend time establishing strong teacher-pupil relationships with each of our pupils as that enables us, over time, to recognise the loss/gain states they are in when they enter our classrooms.

The timing of the lesson is also influential in how willing pupils are to actively engage. As illustrated by the parole judges in Section 3.1, decision fatigue makes us less willing to take risks. In their case, as they tired mentally from making one judgement after another, they became less willing to release prisoners early. In the case of our pupils, as they complete one activity after another, and go from one lesson to another, they naturally become less willing to speak out. Planning lessons so the activities that occur earlier are those in which we particularly want our pupils to actively engage and take risks, and planning sequences of lessons so we use periods early in the day for lessons in which we want pupils to be particularly active and risk-taking, enables us to avoid the difficulties that can arise due to how they value losses and gains.

Unless we create an environment in which our pupils feel safe, encouraged and rewarded, and we deliberately plan lessons in a way that maximises the chances of them being able to take risks, we cannot expect them to be as active in our lessons as we would like them to be. How often do we write comments in pupils' reports along the lines of them being very able in our subjects but not fulfilling their potential because of their reluctance to fully engage? The implication of loss aversion is that when pupils are not contributing as much as we would like them to, the fault probably lies with us, the environment we have created and the way we have planned our lessons, rather than with the pupils.

3.5 Unknown unknowns

Thought experiment: the Ellsberg Paradox

Consider two large containers, in each of which there are red and black balls. There is an equal number of red and black balls in Container One, whilst in Container Two there is the same number of red and black balls in total but in unknown proportions. Now imagine you have to choose one of the containers, and once you have done so, you will face one of the two related lotteries shown in Table 3.1, which will be selected at random. Which container would you choose?

Table 3.1 The two-container Ellsberg Paradox

Container One (Known Proportions)	Container Two (Unknown Proportions)
Lottery 1A: You win £100 if, without looking, you pull out a red ball.	**Lottery 2A**: You win £100 if, without looking, you pull out a red ball.
Lottery 1B: You win £100 if, without looking, you pull out a black ball.	**Lottery 2B**: You win £100 if, without looking, you pull out a black ball.

Known as the Ellsberg Paradox (named after its creator, American economist and former military advisor Daniel Ellsberg, who is perhaps most well known for leaking the Pentagon Papers, a confidential study of American decision-making during the Vietnam War, to newspapers in the early 1970s), this thought experiment demonstrates that the decisions we make are not just skewed by our perceptions of loss and gain. Most people faced with this decision choose Container One because they prefer to know the probabilities of winning in each of the lotteries: in this case, 50% in each (Ellsberg 1961). Whilst that makes sense when comparing Lottery 1A with Lottery 2A, with the probability of winning in the latter possibly being considerably lower than 50%, it does not stack up when comparing the two sets of lotteries. With only red and black balls in each container, combining the two lotteries in each case means the probability of winning £100 is the same in both. If there is a 20% chance of winning in Lottery 2A, there is then an 80% chance of winning in Lottery 2B. The probability of winning is the same across the two containers and so we should be indifferent between the two. That we have a predilection for wanting to know the probabilities in uncertain situations has become known as our ambiguity aversion.

Key term: ambiguity aversion

We tend to be repelled from situations in which the likelihoods of possible outcomes are unknown.

Since the work of Daniel Ellsberg on this in the 1960s, our natural tendencies have been shown to be a little more complex than that of simply disliking unknown risks. Linking to the evidence of our loss aversion in Section 3.4, it has been established that we actually prefer ambiguous situations when they involve losses. (As a thought experiment, would your choice of container change if each of the lotteries in Table 3.1 were worded along the lines of 'You will lose £100 if, without looking, you pull out a X ball'?) When faced with a choice between uncertain outcomes with known probabilities and uncertain outcomes with unknown probabilities, we naturally lean towards the former if the possible outcomes are positive as we do not want to take the risk of losing out on something positive by inadvertently choosing a situation in which the probability is lower. When it comes to making the same choice but with the possible outcomes being negative, we lean towards the unknown situation because it is worth taking the possible additional risk to avoid the negative outcome.

What is the uncertainty like in our classrooms? Do pupils know the likelihood of being praised if they make a good contribution and that of somehow being shown up if their contribution is incorrect? And what about the likelihood of receiving a sanction in response to misbehaviour? Ideally there should be no uncertainty at all as it helps if pupils know and feel confident about the outcomes of the choices they make within our lessons. Failing that, it helps our pupils if they have a feel for the probabilities of the different possible outcomes. We can ensure this by being consistent in our reactions to what they do. In classrooms in which pupils do not know the probabilities of their choices leading to one outcome or another, their behaviour will be driven by ambiguity aversion and ambiguity seeking. They will do fewer things that could possibly lead to positive outcomes, such as helping their peers, tidying the classroom and contributing to class discussions. And they will do more things that could possibly lead to negative outcomes, such as disturbing their friends, trying to sidetrack our teaching and resisting work. And as with all cognitive traits, this is likely to worsen when our pupils are mentally tired.

3.6 Overconfidence

> ### Thought experiment: driving
>
> How do you score yourself on a ten-point scale in terms of both the quality and safety of your driving in comparison with your colleagues (one = worst/least safe and ten = best/most safe)?

Before we end this chapter, it is time to consider the experience of Eleanor from Section 1.7 and that of probably an uncountable number of other pupils. Ola Svenson effectively asked exactly the questions in the previous thought experiment to 161 undergraduate students drawn almost evenly from the Universities of Stockholm and Oregon (Svenson 1981). On average, the students in the USA scored their relative driving quality seven out of ten, whilst those in Sweden gave their driving quality a score of six. For their relative driving safety, the students in the USA and those in Sweden gave scores of nine and eight, respectively. True values of driving quality and safety are likely to be normally distributed and so the average of the judgements reported should be five out of ten. What Ola Svenson found was that we naturally tend to be overconfident, rating ourselves higher on average than we should. That we are characterised by such an overconfidence bias has been found time and time again, and in a range of different settings. In a more recent study, for example, Chris Chabris and Daniel Simons asked individual players at a chess tournament what their current chess rating was and what they thought it should be (Chabris and Simons 2011). These were experienced players whose ratings were based on their performances in large numbers of matches and yet only 21% of them thought their current rating was reflective of their true ability. The remaining 79% were split, with 4% thinking their rating exceeded their true ability and 75% thinking their rating was lower than their true ability.

> ### Key term: overconfidence bias
>
> We are naturally inclined to rate our knowledge and abilities higher than they actually deserve.

Sadly, Eleanor also suffered from the overconfidence bias. She was good at economics. Very good in fact. She exuded confidence whenever she answered the questions I asked her class, and the thoughtfulness she demonstrated when she asked questions back was impressive. I had only recently graduated with a degree in economics, this being my first teaching position since I completed my teacher training, and so the subject was still fresh in my mind, and yet she asked questions that I had never considered. And she was equally good across all her A-level subjects. All her teachers expected her to achieve straight As in her AS-level exams, which would open up the doors of the top universities for her. However, that was not what transpired. She took the exams, achieved results much lower than we had expected and ultimately missed out on the university offers for which she had been hoping. I distinctly remember my conversation with her afterwards, and her explaining that she had deliberately opted not to revise as thoroughly as she should have done because she thought it was unnecessary. She thought the A-grades were already secured.

It is likely that all our pupils suffer from the overconfidence bias to at least some extent, and they need help to overcome the risks this creates. This is especially so for those who are relatively able compared to the others in their classes and so inevitably get a wrong impression of their ability when compared against their year group on a national scale. Practically, we can do this by gently ensuring our pupils are aware of the areas on which they need to work. In cases in which we regularly give the top score in a class to the same pupil, the danger of the overconfidence bias makes the need for formative feedback even more acute. By just writing a summative comment, such as 'excellent work – well done', we are reinforcing the pupil's perception that they are doing so well that they can relax. Pupils such as this need to know what they can do to secure the remaining marks and to know that doing so is vital if they are to compete with the best from other schools. We can also focus our praise on attitudes rather than achievements, rewarding pupils for displaying attributes such as determination, perseverance, resilience and thoughtfulness, rather than for their ability. Following the work of Carol Dweck, this should encourage our pupils to have growth mindsets, meaning they will focus on improving themselves rather than simply focusing on the things at which they are already proficient.

Related to the overconfidence bias is what Daniel Kahneman and Amos Tversky called the planning fallacy. (This is the cognitive trait that I am feeling more acutely than any other as the deadline for submitting this manuscript looms.) It can be seen clearly in the findings from an experiment conducted by Roger Buehler, Dale Griffin and Michael Ross in the mid-1990s (Buehler *et al.* 1994). In their study, 101 undergraduate psychology students responded to two questionnaires either individually or in small groups. In the first questionnaire, the students were asked to describe two tasks, one academic and the other not, that they intended to complete in the following week, to offer predictions about how long the tasks would take and, on a scale from zero (not at all certain) to 100 (completely certain), to give a judgement about how certain they were of completing each of the tasks on time. A week later, the same students responded to the second questionnaire, which required them to declare whether or not they had finished the two tasks, along with the date and time they did so, and the lengths of any external deadlines that had been set for the tasks. The results, based on 91 academic and 62 nonacademic tasks, are shown in Figure 3.3.

On average, the amount of time the students predicted they would need to complete their chosen tasks, both academic and nonacademic, amounted to only 54% of the time they actually took to complete them. And they only completed 39% of the tasks on time. This is the planning fallacy. Perhaps unsurprisingly, those who gave low predictions about the time they needed did tend to finish their tasks relatively quickly, but participant optimism about how quickly they would complete the tasks was systemic. Just over 60 of the participants declared having been set external deadlines for their academic tasks, 80.6% of which were met. The average number of days they had before those deadlines was 12.9, the average number of days it took them to complete those tasks was 11.9, and the average number of days they predicted they would need was 5.9. The external deadlines exerted more of an impact on completion time than predictions.

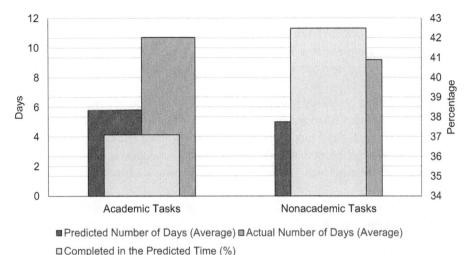

■ Predicted Number of Days (Average) ▣ Actual Number of Days (Average)
□ Completed in the Predicted Time (%)

Figure 3.3 Results from the planning fallacy experiment

Key term: planning fallacy

We naturally tend to underestimate the amount of time it will take us to complete tasks, thinking they will take less time than is actually needed.

Our pupils will inevitably struggle to plan their time effectively, leaving themselves too little time to complete their work. Not only is this likely to lead to their work being of a lower standard than it could otherwise have been and to them stunting their own learning, ineffectual planning during revision periods is likely to lead to under-performance in their public assessments that can have much longer-lasting implications. Thankfully, the researchers demonstrate in two follow-up studies that we can help our pupils to overcome this cognitive trait by making them think carefully, perhaps through answering questions, about similar tasks they completed in the past and how long they took to complete them. Even more effective, though, is to teach them about the benefit of asking others to predict how long their tasks will take. Observers tend to offer more accurate predictions, whilst trying to recall similar events in the past can lead us to become too pessimistic, which according to Parkinson's Law can cause us to waste time on tasks. There are also lessons here for us as we try to manage the demands that compete for our time.

3.7 Practical takeaways

We can help our pupils by

- Planning more challenging and active tasks to be earlier in lessons and more challenging and active lessons to be earlier in the day.
- Resisting the urge to interrupt our pupils whilst they are focusing.

- Giving our pupils enough time to process the information they receive in lessons and reducing distractions so they can do so.
- Ensuring our lessons end in a positive and enjoyable manner.
- Focusing our praise on positive actions and attributes rather than on pupil achievements.
- Finding something genuinely praise-worthy in every contribution our pupils make.
- Being judicious about when and how much we correct mistakes in our pupils' work.
- Developing strong teacher-pupil relationships with all of our pupils.
- Ensuring we are consistent in the way we respond to our pupils' actions.
- Ensuring even the most highly performing pupils know how to improve their knowledge and skills.
- Making pupils consider how long it took them to complete similar tasks in the past when they are planning their time.

Bibliography

Ariely, D., 2012. Real-world endowment. *The Blog*. Available from: www.danariely.com/2012/09/20/real-world-endowment/.

Buehler, R., Griffin, D., and Ross, M., 1994. Exploring the planning fallacy. *Journal of Personality and Social Psychology*, 67 (3), 366-281.

Chabris, C., and Simons, D., 2011. *The Invisible Gorilla: And Other Ways Our Intuition Deceives Us*. London, UK: Harper Collins.

Danziger, S., Levav, J., and Avnaim-Pesso, L., 2011. Extraneous factors in judicial decisions. *Proceedings of the National Academy of Sciences*, 108 (17), 6889-6892.

Dweck, C., 2017. *Mindset - Updated Edition: Changing the Way You Think to Fulfil Your Potential*. London, UK: Robinson.

Ellsberg, D., 1961. Risk, ambiguity and the Savage axioms. *The Quarterly Journal of Economics*, 75, 643-669.

Greene, J.D., *et al.*, 2008. Cognitive load selectively interferes with utilitarian moral judgement. *Cognition*, 107 (3), 1144-54.

Iyengar, S.S., and Lepper, M.R., 2000. When choice is demotivating: Can one desire too much of a good thing? *Journal of Personality and Social Psychology*, 79, 995-1006.

Kahneman, D., Knetsch, J.L., and Thaler, R.H., 1990. Experimental tests of the endowment effect and the Coase Theorem. *Journal of Political Economy*, 98, 1325-1348.

Kahneman, D., Wakker, P.P., and Sarin, R., 1997. Back to Bentham? Explorations of experienced utility. *The Quarterly Journal of Economics*, 112, 375-406.

Levitin, D., 2015. *The Organized Mind: Thinking Straight in the Age of Information Overload*. New York, USA: Penguin Books, p. 7.

Sullivan, B., and Thompson, H., 2013. Brain, interrupted. *The New York Times*.

Svenson, O., 1981. Are we all less risky and more skillful than our fellow drivers? *Acta Psychologica*, 47 (2), 143-148.

Tversky, A., and Kahneman, D., 1981. The framing of decisions and the psychology of choice. *Science*, 211, 454.

4 Effective (home)work

There is a growing debate about the need for, and even the wisdom of, setting pupils work to complete outside of the six or seven hours they spend at school each day. With growing concerns over the mental health of young people, and the average age at which depression is first diagnosed falling from age 29 years in the 1960s to age 15.5 years in the early 2000s, leading figures in education are calling for homework policies to be reviewed, such as Eve Jardin-Young, Principal at the 162-year-old Cheltenham Ladies College (The Guardian 2015). They argue young people should instead be spending greater quality time with their families, which would help them to strengthen their communication skills, or cultivating their own interests and trying new hobbies, which would help them to become more resilient by giving them new outlets for, and distractions from, their emotions and anxieties. Research studies in a number of countries even cast doubt on the benefits of homework for learning. In one such study at the University of Virginia in 2012, for example, researchers examined data from 18,000 pupils and found that homework had no discernable impact on their academic performance. In another study at the Institute of Education in London, homework was found to account for less than 4% of grades achieved (Doug 2019). And yet homework undoubtedly causes our pupils stress, anxiety and frustration.

The inefficacy of homework may, at least in part, be attributed to the approach we as teachers take when we set it. We know we are expected to spend time planning our lessons, ensuring they are well structured, there is differentiation for pupils with differing learning needs and, ultimately, they allow our pupils to make good progress against the specific learning outcomes we have for the lessons. That such lesson planning and delivery are happening throughout a school is monitored by more senior members of staff regularly observing lessons, often without any notice. Schools are increasingly trying to create environments in which classroom doors are left open so that teaching and learning are not only visible but of improving quality. However, when it comes to homework, we are largely left to ourselves. Schools publish their homework policies, which tend to outline the weekly number of hours of homework pupils are expected to complete in each of their subjects and, for younger year groups, the days on which tasks are to be set and those on which they are to be returned. School policies may include clauses about the need for homework to be meaningful and the need for us to promptly and thoroughly mark the work pupils submit; but when it comes to monitoring, senior staff tend to monitor only the frequency, magnitude and marking of homework. I have never once, in my 16 years of teaching, been asked to explain my reasoning

DOI: 10.4324/9781003198505-5

for setting particular tasks for homework. It is unsurprising that we often set homework as an afterthought, with little consideration given to what we actually want our pupils to learn from it and without it being suitably differentiated for pupils with different learning needs. It is often set as a 'tick box exercise', to ensure we comply with the expectations of our schools' policies; with greatest thought often being given to how easy it will be to mark the tasks we set. The behavioural science is silent about whether or not homework should be set, but its findings are clear about how we should set such work (in fact, any work) if it is to be effective.

4.1 The power of purpose

In two experiments conducted on undergraduate students, Dan Ariely, Emir Kamenica and Drazen Prelec examined the impact of acknowledgement and meaningfulness on our productivity when completing simple tasks (Ariely *et al.* 2008). Over 100 students at the Massachusetts Institute of Technology responded to advertisements in their students' union to participate in the first experiment, in which they were given one seemingly random sequence of letters at a time and in exchange for payment were asked to find ten instances of two consecutive letters being the same. Once participants had submitted one completed sheet, they were given another. They were informed of the payments in advance: $0.55 for the first sheet completed, $0.50 for the second, $0.45 for the third and so on, with the payment decreasing by $0.05 for each additional sheet until participants decided to stop working. At that point, they received their total accumulated payments and the experiment ended. The participants worked independently, without any contact with one another. They just had to decide when to stop.

The researchers randomly separated the participants into three roughly even-sized groups. Those in Group One were asked to write their names on the sheets they completed and were told that a researcher would examine and file what they completed at the end of the experiment. Those in Group Two were not asked to write their names on their work and were told that a researcher would simply place it on a high stack of papers without examining it first. Finally, those in Group Three were told that a researcher would shred what they completed as soon as they handed it in and without even looking at it.

The participants in Group One completed an average of 9.03 sheets before deciding to stop. They received an average total payment of $3.01. Those in Groups Two and Three completed an average of 6.77 and 6.34 sheets before deciding to stop and earned average payments of $2.60 and $2.42, respectively. The researchers did not attempt to prevent cheating. Indeed, in the case of Group Three there was no possible way of doing so. And yet the participants who were acknowledged for their work completed a greater amount than their counterparts whose work was not acknowledged or, even worse, simply destroyed.

A further 40 undergraduate students at Harvard University were recruited for the second experiment having responded to posters that had been displayed around their campus. In this experiment, the participants were asked to construct Bionicle LEGO models, each of which consisted of 40 separate pieces that could only be assembled according to the written instructions provided. The participants were told at the outset the amount they would be paid for each model they constructed: $2 for the first and then $0.11 less for each subsequent model, until the 19th, after which they would be paid $0.02 for each model. The participants were all able to follow the instructions without any difficulty and worked alone, without any contact with one another. The only decision they had to make was how many models they constructed. Once they had decided to construct no more, they were paid and the experiment ended.

The researchers randomly assigned the participants to two groups. When a participant in Group One made a model, the participant placed it on a researcher's desk where it stayed for the remainder of the experiment. The researcher then gave the participant a box containing the pieces needed to construct the next model. And so as the experiment progressed, the number of assembled models on the researcher's desk grew. When a participant in Group Two made a model, the participant took it to the researcher who made a note that it had been made and then disassembled it, giving the pieces back to the participant to assemble again.

Perhaps unsurprisingly, the participants in Group One assembled more models on average than their counterparts in Group Two. Those in Group One assembled an average of 10.6 models and received an average payment of $14.40, compared to the average of 7.2 models made, and average payment of $11.52 received, by those in Group Two. We are more productive in our work when we feel as though it has a purpose. This has become known as the Sisyphus effect, after the founder and king of Ephyra in Greek mythology. Sisyphus attracted the displeasure of Zeus, the Father of the Gods, by killing visitors to Ephyra in order to demonstrate his ruthlessness as a king rather than offering them hospitality, by informing the River God Asopus that Zeus had kidnapped his daughter, and by evading capture in the underworld. Zeus eventually punished Sisyphus by condemning him to the eternal fate of having to push a boulder uphill only for it to slip from his grasp and roll back down whenever he got it to the top (Greekmythology.com).

Key term: Sisyphus effect

We find tasks demotivating when we are not acknowledged for completing them.

If our pupils are to complete the work we set them and to push themselves that step further in doing so, they must find purpose in the tasks we set. As the previous experiments show, we can ensure this is the case in two ways. Firstly, by making the tasks we set meaningful for our pupils. Pupils want to know that what they are spending their time on is going to benefit them in some way, which is why they frustratingly often ask if what we are teaching them will be in their final assessments. The reasons we give certainly do not need to be directly related to assessments, but they need to be meaningful. Secondly, by recognising the work our pupils complete for us. Whenever we fail to provide feedback to pupils about their work or fail to make it clear to them that we have looked at what they have accomplished and recognise the effort that has gone into it, we are essentially disassembling the models they have created and allowing the boulder we have asked them to push uphill to roll back down again. Pupils will only be truly motivated if we recognise all of their efforts. Sharing a pupil's work with the others in the class, or putting it up on the wall for all to see (taking into account the findings in Section 7.2), or scanning a copy of it to share with parents and senior members of staff, will all increase the meaningfulness of their work.

4.2 The importance of feeling proud

Michael Norton, Daniel Mochon and Dan Ariely randomly assigned 52 students from a university in southeast America to one of two groups, having paid each of them $5 to participate in a study examining the value of taking pride in their work (Norton *et al.* 2011). Those assigned to Group One were asked to construct a plain black storage box from IKEA, following the instructions provided with the kit. Those assigned to Group Two were each simply given a storage box that had already been constructed and were asked to inspect it. After this initial construct/inspect stage, the students were asked for the maximum amounts they would be willing to pay for the boxes they had either constructed or inspected. To ensure the students offered amounts as honestly as possible, they were told that they would have to honour their offers if they had offered amounts greater than a price that would be randomly chosen and announced by a researcher. In addition to offering amounts to buy the boxes, the students also had to rate how much they liked their boxes on a scale of one (not at all) to seven (very much).

Those in Group One, the box constructors, were willing to pay an average price of $0.78 for their boxes, whilst those in Group Two, the box inspectors, were only willing to pay an average of $0.48. Those who had constructed their own boxes were willing to pay a 63% premium compared to those who had been given boxes that were already constructed. Similarly, the box constructors reported an average score of 3.81 for the extent to which they liked their boxes, whilst the box inspectors reported an average score of only 2.51. We value items more when we have worked to create them. We take pride in our own work. In fact, these researchers have shown that we value our own work almost as highly as that of experts whilst others have shown that children actually value their work more than that of people they might consider to be experts. In a series of experiments by Vivian Li, Alex Shaw and Kristina Olson, for example, four-year-olds were given two identical sets of craft materials, consisting of five paper shapes, two cotton wool balls and glue (Li *et al.* 2013). In the first stage of these experiments, the researchers asked each of the children to think of a design using the materials, which they then constructed for the child. In the second stage of the experiments, the researchers and the children swapped roles. The researchers now thought up their own designs, which the children then constructed. At the end of the experiments, the children were able to pick which of the two pieces of artwork they liked most, which they could take home. A majority of the children took the artwork which they had designed, preferring that to the designs of the adults. The value of having created something is really rather high, and that extends to the creation of ideas and designs.

Norton, Mochon and Ariely also conducted a modified version of their IKEA experiment to test the importance of being able to complete a task. Thirty-nine students were each paid $5 to participate in this modified experiment and were again randomly assigned to one of two groups. Those assigned to Group One were given the parts required to build an IKEA storage box and were asked to follow the instructions to construct it, just as before. These were the constructors. Those assigned to Group Two were given the same parts and written instructions but were asked to stop before completing the final two steps. These were the incomplete constructors. After this construction stage, the students were asked for the maximum amounts that they would be willing to pay for their boxes, in the same way as previously mentioned to ensure their honesty. The amounts stated by the incomplete constructors were those they were willing to pay for their incomplete boxes along with the remaining pieces and instructions, allowing them to complete their boxes with relative ease after the experiment. The students were also asked to rate on a seven-point scale the extent to which they considered themselves to be do-it-yourself people, from one (not at all) to seven (very much).

Constructors were willing to pay more than twice as much for their complete boxes than the incomplete constructors were for their unfinished boxes, offering averages of $1.46 and $0.59, respectively. And this effect was common across all of the students, irrespective of how much they thought of themselves as do-it-yourself people (although it was stronger for those who rated their practical skills more highly). We value work that we have done ourselves and are willing to pay more for it because of the sense of pride it gives us, but that value is eroded if we do not finish the work involved. Completion is key.

We should certainly consider what it is we want each of our pupils to learn when we design tasks for them to complete, and we should design those tasks to maximise that desired and differentiated learning. We can also help our pupils by considering the sense of achievement that they will feel from working on those tasks, ensuring they leave with a feeling of accomplishment. The debate is ongoing about whether or not enquiry-based learning is an effective approach to take. Some authors, such as Deborah Ayres, stress the importance of pupils discovering answers for themselves as it reinforces their retention of that learning (Ayres 2016). Others, such as Adam Boxer, question the evidence for this approach and instead advocate the more traditional teacher and pupil roles in learning, with the teacher communicating the content to the pupil and then using examples and tasks to embed the learning (Boxer 2020). Whatever the answer is in this debate, behavioural science suggests that there is a value to seeing pupils as co-creators of their own learning, providing them with opportunities to construct their own learning and to feel proud of having done so. This is a crucial part of helping our pupils to feel as though what they are doing for us is of value, fostering feelings of fulfilment and enjoyment.

We can also help our pupils by considering the level of difficulty of the tasks we ask them to complete. On the one hand, setting work that is too difficult will mean pupils are unable to complete the task, eliminating the feeling of value they derive from working on it. On the other hand, Dan Ariely and colleagues have shown that the feeling of value increases with the level of difficulty of the task. In a study similar to those outlined earlier, but in which student participants had to make origami frogs and cranes rather than IKEA storage boxes, participants were willing to pay more for their own work when they were not provided with the full set of instructions, making the task much more difficult to complete and requiring them to spend a longer amount of time on it. The amounts others were willing to pay for the resulting models were reduced compared to those made by participants with the full set of instructions, but the additional time and effort spent on making them made the constructors value them more highly. The most effective tasks are those that challenge our pupils as much as possible whilst still allowing our pupils to complete them.

Finally, we can help our pupils by ensuring they have the time they need to complete the work we set. Looking through their books and folders, how many pieces of work are left unfinished? And how many of these are unfinished because we set our pupils tasks that required more time than was available or because we moved on to the next activity or topic unnecessarily soon? In each of these cases, we have inadvertently eliminated the feelings of value and pride our pupils could have felt from the work they did for us.

Returning to the homework debate, Roshan Doug in his article in the *Times Educational Supplement* suggests that we should frame homework as a reward rather than as a punishment, that pupils should earn the right to homework. Practically, he suggests that we should only allow pupils to complete and improve their work outside of lessons when they have worked sufficiently hard on it during them, and that we should inspire our pupils to take advantage of that opportunity (Doug 2019). The findings of behavioural science suggest that our pupils may not need that much external inspiration to do this, being naturally driven to complete the work they have started.

4.3 Making a start

Through the influence of what is now known as the First Triumvirate, consisting of the general Gneaus Pompeius Magnus (Pompey), the wealthy politician Marcus Licinius Crassus and himself, Gaius Julius Caesar in 58 BCE secured a five-year command of 20,000 troops in the Alps. But having not been authorised by the Senate, this posting broke the laws of the Roman Republic. Caesar was setting out on an unsanctioned, personal conquest of Gaul, which today roughly consists of France, parts of Belgium, Western Germany and Northern Italy. Caesar took full advantage of the opportunity, conquering Gaul in nine years so comprehensively that it remained passive under Roman rule throughout the Roman civil wars between 49 and 31 BCE. For Caesar, this conquest was the means by which he could accumulate plunder, and both power and status in Rome. Through the regular, detailed and favourable letters about his exploits that he sent back to Rome, and the use of his plunder from the conquest to hire political support in the capital, he achieved just that.

This growing status caused Pompey to become wary of Caesar's successes. The alliance was renewed at a meeting of the three in 56 BCE, when it was agreed that Pompey and Crassus would continue as consuls and would use their influence to extend Caesar's posting in Gaul. The Senate may not have authorised Caesar's conquest initially, but it extended the posting for a further five years. But this restrengthening of the triumvirate was only temporary. The marriage link between Pompey (then Governor of Spain) and Caesar was broken in 54 BCE with the death of Julia, Caesar's daughter and Pompey's wife. And then in the following year, Crassus, then Governor of Roman Syria, was defeated and killed in the Battle of Carrhae by the Parthians from modern-day Iran. After these events, Pompey increasingly aligned himself with the Roman nobility. Caesar and Pompey were now rivals for power.

The issue on which Caesar's future hung was whether or not there would be an interval between him giving up his provincial governorship of Gaul, and thereby the command of his army, and him taking up his second consulship. He would be a private citizen during such an interval, opening him up to prosecution from his rivals in Rome for his unsanctioned conquest of Gaul and making him vulnerable to losing everything. The question was raised numerous times in the Senate from 51 BCE onwards, but Caesar was able to have his allies veto proposals that would lead to such an interval. In 50 BCE, the Senate declared that Caesar should disband his army, to which Caesar responded with an offer: he would relinquish his command in Gaul if Pompey did the same in Spain. Caesar did not want to be in the situation in which Pompey had command of an army and he did not. The Senate rejected this offer and instead secretly invited Pompey to take command of all Rome's armies in Italy (Editors of Encyclopaedia Britannica 2009).

All of this is just the backdrop to what happened next. In response to the Senate's declaration, Caesar marched the 13th legion south to the Rubicon River in Northern Italy. Now just a stream, the river then represented the boundary of the Republic. Fearing a military coup, the Senate had ruled that an army should never be brought into the Republic and so Caesar had to decide whether to cross the boundary alone, risking death at the hands of his enemies in the capital, or to cross over with his army, instantly sentencing himself and all his soldiers to death. The Roman historian Suetonius tells us how, on the eve of 10 January 49 BCE, no doubt trying to keep warm in front of a fire and sheltered from the rain or snow, Caesar wrestled with the decision until he saw an apparition from the gods. At that, Caesar declared 'Eatur,' inquit, 'quo deorum ostenta et inimicorum inquitas vocat. Iacta alea est.': 'Take we the course which the signs of the gods and the false dealing of our foes point out. The die is cast' (Suetonius, translated by Rolfe 1914). He had made the decision to cross.

This story has become an analogy in cognitive and behavioural science, known as the Rubicon effect. Caesar found it difficult to make the decision about whether or not to take his army across the Rubicon. Suetonius makes that very clear in his biography of Caesar. Once he had made the decision, though, there was no hesitation: he simply had to focus on pressing on into Rome. The die had been cast. There was no going back. And within a few years of civil war, Caesar was able to declare himself sole ruler of Rome, a position he held until his assassination in 44 BCE. The Rubicon effect simply refers to us finding an initial decision the most difficult and mentally tiring to make. Once the initial decision has been made and the chain of events initiated, the decisions that follow are much easier for us.

Key term: Rubicon effect

We find making an initial decision most difficult and mentally tiring. Once behaviour has been initiated, it becomes easier to see it through to its conclusion.

Whenever we have a set of reports to write, or a set of exercise books to mark, or a number of lessons to plan for the next day, and we cannot bring ourselves to actually sit down and do them, we are suffering from the Rubicon effect. We are mentally grappling with the choice of either making a start on the work or leaving it until another time and instead doing something more enjoyable and less taxing. And this struggle only becomes more difficult when we are already mentally tired: a situation in which we are even more likely to procrastinate.

Our pupils experience this struggle just the same. It is the reason why they waste so much time making themselves start the work we set. Our pupils need our help to be efficient with their work, to complete it with as little stress as possible and to have time to spend on beneficial and rewarding activities that are not related to school. We can help them to make a start by setting the first part of the homework as a task to be completed in class. For example, helping them to write the opening paragraph of an essay, in which they set out the structure of the rest of their answer; or having them sketch out the plan of a project so that we can help them to make relevant formatting and aesthetic decisions; or getting them to answer the first few mathematical questions in a problem set before they leave the classroom. All of these will make it easier for them to return to the task at a later time. The Rubicon effect will still be there, as our pupils will still need to decide to recommence the work, but having overcome the initial barrier to making a start on it will make it easier for them to do so.

4.4 Allocating time

In seeking to explain how we make decisions about how we spend our limited finances, about which items we buy and which we disregard, Richard Thaler proposed the model of Mental Accounting (Thaler 1985). There are three, sequential stages to this model:

- In the first stage, we create mental accounts for each type of expenditure that we are going to make, allocating a certain amount of our available money to each. This is the mental equivalent of having a number of tins in which we physically place bank notes, with one tin being for groceries, another for petrol, a third for entertainment and so on. We use this as a device to help us to make sure we do not inadvertently exhaust our budget on one particular type of expenditure.
- In the second stage, we decide how to spend the money within each mental account. Following the logic of loss aversion illustrated in Figure 3.2, we spend the money we have earmarked for a particular type of expenditure in the way that maximises our overall feeling of gain, combining losses and segregating gains. (There is more on this in Section 6.1.)
- In the third and final stage, we make decisions about when we close existing mental accounts and when we open new ones. Also following the logic of loss aversion, we are resistant to closing mental accounts when they are in an overall position of loss. Instead, we keep them open, and we keep spending money on them in the hope of turning them into gains and so avoiding having to crystallise losses when we eventually choose to close them.

Key term: mental accounting

A theory about the way we allocate a scarce resource across competing demands, for example, how we allocate our time across the different tasks we need to complete.

This model has been used effectively in explaining our spending patterns, including those patterns that appear rather irrational. My experiences suggest that the same logic applies to how we use the time we have available. When faced with a 'to-do list' consisting of an array of different jobs, we often assign a certain amount of time to each. When we help our older pupils to prepare for upcoming assessments, we often sketch out revision plans for them, assigning certain amounts of time to different subjects during their revision period. As with the case of spending money, such planning can be effective in ensuring we avoid spending too much time on tasks that bring us relatively little benefit. However, by being naturally loss averse, we are prone to making two types of poor time allocation decisions.

Firstly, we tend to devote too much time to activities we enjoy. We find it difficult to sacrifice instant gratification for longer-term gains, even if the latter by far outweighs the former. When it comes to deciding how we distribute the time we have available across tasks, we naturally focus on those we enjoy most or those at which we are strongest, rather than focusing on those that require greatest effort. The path of improving any skill or knowledge is never perfectly smooth. There will be days when we improve a lot and others when we see hardly any payback from our efforts. However, it is usually characterised by diminishing marginal returns. We see improvement as we invest greater time and effort into mastering a skill or learning information, but the rate of improvement slows as the time and effort we put into doing so increases. We see greater improvement from the first hour we spend on practising a skill or learning information than from the tenth, and we see greater improvement from the tenth than from the hundredth. Being naturally inclined to devote a greater proportion of our time to the tasks at which we are already proficient, we develop our skills and knowledge much less overall than we would by focusing our time on the things we find hardest.

Secondly, we tend to keep going with a task even when it is proving unfruitful. How often do we pick up a book, setting aside an amount of time to relax whilst we read it, to discover that the endorsements on the back cover have been far too generous and it is in fact rather tedious and hard going, and yet we feel reluctant to discard it and choose to press on with it for remarkably little benefit? I have known many pupils, particularly those completing the Extended Project Qualification, tell me about how they read some obscure tome through to the end in the hope of finding something useful in it when in fact the evidence from the first few pages suggested that would be a fruitless endeavour. Just as with our financial decisions, we are reluctant to crystallise time losses by closing mental time accounts when they are in deficit, and so we pour good time after bad. This is the sunk cost effect.

Key term: sunk cost effect

Our natural inclination to continue to invest a resource into an activity beyond the point of realising it is unfruitful: to continue to 'pour good money/time/effort after bad'.

When it comes to setting work, our pupils need us to help them to allocate their time effectively. We can do this as classroom teachers in three ways:

- Differentiating the tasks we set our pupils according to their individual strengths and weaknesses, setting them tasks that are specifically tailored to help them to work on the skills and knowledge acquisition from which they will benefit most. Rather than setting all pupils in a class the same essay question or the same design problem, for example, we should adjust the titles and briefs in the way that forces them to address their individual weaknesses.
- Being more prescriptive about the amount of time our pupils should spend on each part of a task, tailoring the allocation according to their individual needs. When setting a

one-hour piece of work in History that involves both the skills of source analysis and evaluation, for example, some pupils may benefit from being instructed to spend 20 minutes on one and 40 minutes on the other, whilst others may benefit from the opposite instructions.

- Helping our pupils to stop working on tasks that are proving unfruitful. This is particularly relevant to situations in which pupils are working on extended independent projects and coursework, when they have greater freedom over how they use their time to complete the overall task. We can help our pupils by challenging them to consider the payoffs they are seeing from their efforts and encouraging them to change tack when they are at risk of falling, or have already fallen, into a rut. Helping our pupils to see giving up on such things as gains rather than losses is crucial to this.

There is also an important role for a personal tutor in this, especially for younger pupils. We tend to assume that our tutees are using their time effectively when completing the work they have been set, and we often give little further thought to how they are approaching their studies outside of lessons unless we receive reports from colleagues about them not handing in work on time or not finishing it to a satisfactory standard. But effective and efficient time management is a skill that needs to be learned, just as the skills of algebra in Mathematics, grammar in French and evaluation in Religious Studies need to be learned. Indeed, the skill of time management is more important than all of these other skills as it affects the productivity of our pupils in whatever they study, for the rest of their lives. And just as learning these other skills requires guidance from teachers, so does that of time management. As personal tutors, we can help our tutees by discussing with them the work their teachers have set and how it relates to what they find most difficult and the areas in which they would most benefit from improvement, in order to help them plan their time most effectively.

4.5 Practical takeaways

We can help our pupils by

- Ensuring the tasks we set our pupils are meaningful.
- Acknowledging the efforts our pupils make on their work, however great or small they may be.
- Ensuring the tasks we set can be completed in the time we are giving our pupils for them.
- Setting tasks from which our pupils can feel a sense of pride and accomplishment.
- Helping our pupils to get started on tasks.
- Differentiating the tasks we set according to the improvements from which our pupils will most benefit.
- Being prescriptive about the time pupils should spend on different parts of a task.
- Guiding pupils to allocate their time effectively and to stop tasks that are proving unfruitful.

Bibliography

Ariely, D., Kamenica, E., and Prelec, D., 2008. Man's search for meaning: The case of Legos. *Journal of Economic Behavior and Organization*, 67 (3–4), 671–677.

Ayres, D., 2016. *High Performance Learning: How to Become a World Class School*. Abingdon, UK: Routledge.

Boxer, A., 2020. Introducing evidence-informed change. *In*: C. Brown, J. Flood and G. Handscomb, eds. *The Research-Informed Teaching Revolution: A Handbook for the 21st Century Teacher*. Woodbridge, UK: John Catt Educational Ltd, pp. 29–38.

Doug, R., 2019. Don't set homework – get students to find a new hobby. *TES Magazine*. Available from: www.tes.com/news/dont-set-homework-get-students-find-new-hobby.

Editors of Encyclopaedia Britannica, 2009. The first triumvirate and the conquest of Gaul. *Encyclopaedia Britannica*. Available from: www.britannica.com/biography/Julius-Caesar-Roman-ruler/The-first-triumvirate-and-the-conquest-of-Gaul.

GreekMythology.com, 2021. Sisyphus. 7 April. Available from: www.greekmythology.com/Myths/Mortals/Sisyphus/sisyphus.html.

Li, V., Shaw, A., and Olson, K., 2013. Ideas versus labor: What do children value in artistic creation? *Cognition*, 127 (1), 38–45.

Norton, M.I., Mochon, D., and Ariely, D., 2011. The IKEA effect: When labor leads to love. *Journal of Consumer Psychology*, 22 (3), 453–460.

Suetonius, *Lives of the Caesars, Volume I: Julius. Augustus. Tiberius. Gaius. Caligula*. Translated by J.C. Rolfe (1914). Cambridge, MA: Harvard University Press.

Thaler, R.H., 1985. Mental accounting and consumer choice. *Marketing Science*, 27, 15–25.

The Guardian, 2015. Cheltenham Ladies' College considers homework ban over student welfare. Available from: www.theguardian.com/education/2015/jun/06/cheltenham-ladies-college-considers-homework-ban-over-student-welfare.

5 Marking and feedback

The question about how we should provide feedback to our pupils, about the strengths of their work and about how they can improve their performance in future tasks, has been at the forefront of inset days and continuing professional development in recent years. Much has also been written about it, most of which has been summarised by John Hattie and Shirley Clarke (2018). The use of whole-class feedback, peer feedback, written feedback, verbal feedback, continuous feedback and immediate feedback has all been examined. However, the act of marking has largely been overlooked, even though behavioural science shows that rather mundane things, such as the order in which we mark work, the benchmark against which we compare work and our ability to identify the pupil who has completed a piece of work, all play important parts in the scores and, ultimately, the feedback we give. These, along with how our pupils' minds affect how they receive the feedback we provide, potentially driving a wedge between the impact we intend our feedback to have and the impact it actually has, are the focus of this chapter.

Before looking at these, though, it is important to consider again the Rubicon effect as it has implications for our own productivity. How often do we take a whole class set of exercise books home to mark in an evening, only to find the following morning that we have not looked at a single one of them? Starting to mark involves a change in mental operation as we need to switch from the task we are currently working on to do so. It necessitates a deliberate decision to initiate, which we find mentally difficult to make. This is especially the case at the end of a day when it is more than likely that we are also suffering from decision fatigue, having exhausted our mental reserves during the course of the day; when we have unwound by travelling home, relaxing our focus on work, and when there are so many more appealing distractions. By taking our pupils' work home to mark, we are inadvertently creating a situation for ourselves in which the odds of success are stacked against us and from which feelings of stress, anxiety and regret are likely. We cannot avoid the Rubicon effect but, following the logic of Section 4.3, there are three things we can do to tilt the odds back in our favour, at least in part:

- Make a start on the marking whilst at school: just one exercise book or essay. With fewer more appealing distractions around us and with us already focused on work, it is easier for us to focus on this new work-based task. And once we have made that initial decision, we find it easier to continue the marking at a later time. In the supposed words of Caesar, at that point 'the die is cast'.

DOI: 10.4324/9781003198505-6

- Make a start on the marking as early in the day as possible. The Rubicon effect and decision fatigue together create a formidable barrier to us starting the work. We may not be able to avoid the former, but we can certainly alleviate the effect of the latter for ourselves. Marking that first book is easier when we are mentally fresh and means we are more likely to be able to do the rest at a later time, even if by then we are mentally running on fumes.

- Take a smaller number of books home to mark. When we are back at home, surrounded by other things we would prefer to do and in a more relaxed mindset, the prospect of marking thirty books can easily become overwhelming, whereas that of marking ten seems more achievable. Following the logic of mental accounting in Section 4.4, we are more likely to open a mental account for marking the smaller number of books because the chances are greater that we will complete the task and experience a gain from it. By taking a smaller number of books home to mark, we are maximising the chance of us doing any marking at all.

5.1 The order matters

Over 200 students at the Hebrew University in Jerusalem participated in an experiment conducted by Eran Dayan and Maya Bar-Hillel (2011). The students were shown part of a menu from an Israeli pizza chain, which was divided into sections for appetisers, starters, soft drinks and desserts, and was devoid of prices. The students were randomly separated into four groups, with those in all groups being shown the same menu options but in one of four different orders according to the group they were in. Motivated by the prospect of winning their chosen meal from the pizza chain, the students simply had to choose their preferred option from each section of their menu. Without any price information, the logical outcome was for the students to reveal which items they most preferred. In actuality, an item was chosen more frequently when it was placed either top or bottom in its section of the menu than when it was placed in the middle of it. The order in which the menu was written was more important to the choices made than any underlying preferences about taste or perceived nutritional value.

To test this rather surprising finding in a real-life setting, the researchers arranged for a cafè in Tel Aviv to provide its customers with one of two different menus, each for 15 days spread in the same manner across the days of the week. As with the study on the university campus, the cafè's menu consisted of different sections. The only difference between the two menus used during the 30-day experiment was that the orders of the items in three of the sections (coffee with alcohol, soft drinks and desserts) were different. Customers placed 492 orders from these three sections of the menu during the experiment, and just as in the previous study, they more frequently chose items that appeared either top or bottom of a section than those in the middle. In fact, the top and bottom items in a section were chosen 20% more frequently.

We find it difficult to place a list of menu options into the order in which we truly like them, independent of the order in which they appear on the menu. Likewise, we find it difficult to take a set of work and place the pieces within it into their 'true' ranking with 'true' scores assigned to each. The way we rank them is at least in part dependent on the order in which we tackle them. If we are given the same set of work in different orders on different occasions, we will probably rank them differently on each occasion. Even if there is a 'true' rank order for them, the probability that we are able to identify it is low. And the probability that we are able to assign 'true' scores to the individual pieces of work is even lower. This is because we make judgements in a relative rather than absolute manner. When we plunge a hand into a bucket of water, for example, we cannot tell its temperature. All we can tell is whether it is hotter or colder than something else. If we first run the hand under colder water, we will probably overestimate the temperature of the water in the bucket. If we first run the hand under hotter water, we will probably underestimate the temperature of the water in the bucket. We find it difficult to make absolute judgements and so we make them relative to what are called reference points.

Thought experiment: the Gullfoss task

Consider the situation in which you have set your class a Geography task in which you asked the pupils to draw and then annotate with detailed descriptions the Gullfoss waterfall in Iceland, and in which you have told the pupils their work will be scored out of twenty, with ten marks being awarded for the quality of the drawing and ten for the detail of the annotated description.

The first piece of work you mark has a remarkable picture that shows the different levels and directions of the waterfall, is beautifully coloured and even shows the sun glinting off the Langjökull glacier behind. However, there are hardly any annotations, and those the pupil has included are at best perfunctory.

What score do you give to it?

You then turn to the second piece of work. The drawing in this one is very much two-dimensional, drawn in pencil without any colour being added to it and showing no consideration of the wider setting of the waterfall. The annotations are exceptional, though. They cover the illustration, and each describes the relevant feature in a level of detail that required significant additional research.

What score do you give to this one?

And, more importantly, for which of these pieces of work do you give a class reward, knowing you can only give it to one?

You then turn to the third piece of work. This pupil has also drawn a beautiful picture, but it is not quite as impressive as that of the first pupil. It too shows the different levels and directions of the waterfall, and the glacier from which the waters originate in the background, but the colouring is less sophisticated and less accurate, being almost messy in places. And there are even fewer, equally perfunctory, annotations.

What score do you give to this one?

And what rank order do you give to the three pieces of work?

Experiments such as that in the Gullfoss task thought experiment have been conducted on a range of different types of participants and have focused on widely differing items, from paper shredders to popcorn at the cinema. (For the original work on this, see Huber *et al.* 1982.) Together, they have generated a substantial body of evidence for what is known as the decoy effect. We struggle to make a choice between two items that are character-ised by the same two desirable attributes, X and Y (such as speed and cost in the shredder example and 'bucket' size and price in the popcorn example), when one item scores highly for Y but poorly for X, and the second scores highly for X but poorly for Y. The addition of a third item can change this, though, if it is slightly worse than one of the initial items in terms of both attributes. This is the decoy, which we should never choose because it is worse in all respects than one of the others. It should be an irrelevance when it comes to our choice. But that is not what the evidence shows. By being slightly worse than Item 1 in all respects, it makes Item 1 appear to us as being relatively better, and not just to the decoy but to Item 2 as well. The inclusion of Item 3 tends to draw us towards choosing Item 1 over Item 2.

When faced with the situation outlined in the Gullfoss task thought experiment, it is likely that we are initially indifferent between the work of the first two pupils but that the addition of the third then causes us to favour the first piece of work more than the other two. Not only are we likely to rank pieces of work differently if the order in which we look at them changes, the scores we give pieces of work are also likely to be affected by the work of other pupils. This inevitably alters the elements of a pupil's work we focus on and so changes the nature of the feedback we give. This is why, when marking, we often look at a piece of work and then feel the need to go back and change the score and feedback we gave for a previ-ous piece, after which we feel at least somewhat uncomfortable about all the other scores we have awarded. We naturally find it easier to make judgements in a relative rather than an absolute manner.

Key term: decoy effect

The addition of an option that is worse in all respects to an existing option, and so should be irrelevant in how we make judgements, makes us more likely to favour that existing option above the available alternatives.

There are two steps that we can take to reduce these effects in our marking. The first is altering the order in which we mark the work produced by pupils in a class each time we have work of theirs to mark. Over the course of a term or a year, we should then be able to see something that resembles the 'true' ranking of abilities within the class emerge in our mark books. However, implementing this makes the second step even more important, which is making sure we are clear in our own minds about what we are looking for from the work before we start to mark it. For questions taken from past exam papers, it helps us to first understand the published mark schemes. For tasks we devise ourselves, it helps us to write our own mark schemes and model answers in advance. This will enable us to mark in a more absolute manner, establishing the score and feedback for each piece of work in isolation from all the others, comparing it to our mark scheme and model answer rather than to the work of other pupils. The first step makes this one more important because it removes our ability to mark the piece of work that is likely to be strongest first and to then use that as the benchmark against which all the others can be compared.

5.2 Impressions also matter

More than 150 academics and graduate students at universities in Australia and New Zealand were recruited by John Malouff and colleagues to participate in an online study of marking, each for a payment of $15 (Malouff *et al*. 2014). To ensure the participants were all suitably experienced, they each had to have previously marked and scored at least 20 pieces of work produced by university students. The participants were randomly assigned to one of three experimental groups. In the first stage of the experiment, those in Groups One and Three watched and scored a recording of a short oral presentation given by the same student. The difference was that those in Group One watched the student give a poor presentation whilst looking scruffy, whereas those in Group Three watched the student give a strong presentation whilst looking well groomed. Those in Group Two did not watch or score an oral presentation. In the second stage of the experiment, all of the participants read a short piece of written work supposedly produced by the student who had delivered the oral presentations and scored it for its written quality alone. Following the convention common across Australian universities, the participants were asked to use the following grade bands whilst scoring both the oral presentation and the written work: 49 or less being a fail, 51-64 being a pass, 65-74 being a credit, 75-84 being a distinction and 85-94 being a high distinction.

Unsurprisingly, the average score for the oral presentation was 60.5 from those in Group One and 71.5 from those in Group Three. The participants observed the difference in quality of the two presentations. Concerningly, the average score for the written work was 62.2 from those in Group One, 64.5 from those in Group Two and 65.6 from those in Group Three. The scores awarded for the student's written work by these experienced markers were influenced by the quality of the student's oral presentation, with those who had watched the student deliver a poor presentation giving a lower average score for the written work than those who had watched the student deliver a strong presentation. Those who had not watched a presentation gave scores that were, on average, between those of the other two.

We find it difficult not to let our impressions of our pupils' previous work affect the scores we award to their current work. As Daniel Kahneman, arguably the preeminent behavioural psychologist, has observed about the way he marks his own students' work, if a student first submits a strong piece of work and then a weaker piece, the student is likely to receive higher scores for both than if the student submitted them the opposite way round, even though they are the same pieces of work in each case. This is an example of the halo effect and another example of how the order in which we mark work is important, albeit in this case across numerous submissions by the same pupil rather than the same submission by different pupils.

Key term: halo effect

We tend to rate people more highly when we have previously seen that they possess unrelated positive attributes.

Perhaps more surprising is that the influence of the halo effect when we are marking our pupils' work is triggered by much more than the quality of their previous pieces of work. A common finding is that perceptions of our physical attractiveness affect our success, especially for females. Experienced teachers have been observed assigning higher ratings for academic ability to pupils they perceive to be more attractive (Kenealy *et al*. 1987). And undergraduate students have been recorded awarding higher scores for essays supposedly written by attractive authors than for those written by less attractive authors, even though the essays were in fact identical (Kaplan 1978). And this works both ways, with students being seen to rate teachers they deem to be likeable higher for teaching performance than teachers they deem to be less likeable, even in situations in which likeability and actual performance are purposefully kept separate (Cardy and Dobbins 1986). This is why we often find ourselves writing unduly positive reports about the academic performance of pupils we like.

The impact of such halos when we are marking is compounded by another of our cognitive traits, that of confirmation bias. In one rather macabre and intricate study, Lee Ross, Mark Lepper and Michael Hubbard recruited 60 female pupils aged between 14 and 18 years to participate in a study at Stanford University, for which they were each paid $2 (Ross *et al*. 1975). The participants were told it was a study of their physiological responses during decision-making. The experiment was conducted on one individual participant at a time. As participants entered the study room, they were asked to attach electrodes to their left wrists to supposedly measure changes in their sweating during the experiment. They were then given 25 cards, on each of which were two suicide notes, one real and the other fictious. All they had to do in Stage One of the experiment was to work through the cards, one at a time, identifying which was the real suicide note on each. The researcher informed the participants after each card whether or not they had identified the correct note. Without their knowing, the participants had been randomly assigned to one of three groups. Those in Group One, the success group, were told that they had correctly identified 24 of the notes. Those in Group Two, the average group, were told that they had correctly identified 17. And those in Group Three, the failure group, were told that they had identified only 10 correctly. After a short break, the researcher explained to the participants that they had been deceived in order to measure their physiological responses to success or failure (a second deception), that the researcher's responses to their selections had been predetermined. The researcher asked the participants to explain the nature of the deception to ensure they had understood and assimilated it properly, apologised for it, and then asked them to complete a short questionnaire whilst the researcher went to get their payments. The questionnaire, representing Stage Two of the experiment, asked the participants to estimate the actual number of real notes they had correctly identified, the average number of real notes identified by all participants, and the number of real notes they would correctly identify if they were to do a similar test again. The results of these questions are shown in Table 5.1.

As the results in Table 5.1 show, the experimental group to which the participants were assigned had no real impact on their ultimate estimate of the average number of real notes correctly identified by all of the participants. It did affect the levels of personal success participants thought they had in the experiment and thought they would have in the future, though. Those who had been informed of having been successful continued to believe in their success even after they had been told that their success had just been an illusion. Those who had been informed of having been unsuccessful continued to believe in their failure even after they too had been informed of the deception. We tend to stick to our beliefs and impressions even after we are disabused of them.

Even more important for us as teachers are the findings of the second experiment in the Stanford suicide note paper. In order to further investigate these results, the researchers re-ran the experiment, this time on 144 female undergraduates at the university. The main difference between the two experiments was that two participants were involved in each of the repeat trials: a responder (as in the initial experiment) and a randomly chosen observer, both of whom then had to complete the questionnaire from the initial experiment but focusing on only the responder's levels of success. As shown by the results in Table 5.2, observers exhibited an even stronger confirmation bias when estimating the responder's actual and future levels of success than that shown by the participants in the initial experiment about their own actual and future levels of success. Once we have made a judgement about the ability (or indeed character) of a pupil, that goes on to influence the way we treat the pupil even if we are shown the information on which we based our initial judgement was incorrect.

That we tend to stick to our existing beliefs and impressions, even selecting and interpreting new evidence in a way that means we avoid the unpleasant experience of having to acknowledge to ourselves that we were wrong, has been spoken about for thousands of

Table 5.1 Results from experiment one in the Stanford suicide note experiment

Question	Group One Average	Group Three Average
Estimate of the number they had correctly identified	17.1	12.8
Estimate of the average number correctly identified by all participants	15.5	14.2
Prediction of the number they would correctly identify in a repeat of the test	16.7	13.5

Table 5.2 Results from experiment two in the Stanford suicide note experiment

Question	Group One Observer Average	Group Three Observer Average
Estimate of the number correctly identified by the responder	19.0	12.4
Estimate of the average number correctly identified by all responders	18.3	13.8
Prediction of the number the responder would correctly identify in a repeat of the task	19.1	14.5

years. The Ancient Greek historian Thucydides has been translated as saying in his History of the Peloponnesian War that 'it is a habit of mankind to entrust to careless hope what they long for, and to use sovereign reason to thrust aside what they do not fancy' (Book 4, page 276). He wrote that around 400 BCE. It has also been blamed for playing a central role in 50 wrongful conviction cases and other criminal investigative failures in a paper written by Kim Rossmo and Jocelyn Pollock at Texas State University (Rossmo and Pollock 2019). It is likely that many of the scores we give to our pupils, and many of the reports we write for them, are influenced by our pre-existing impressions of them rather than being true reflections of their academic performance.

Key term: confirmation bias

We are inclined to retain beliefs and impressions even when they have been proved to be incorrect, and to interpret and purposefully seek information to support them.

We will always be susceptible to the effect of halos and the confirmation bias. They are two important examples of our cognitive traits. However, we can reduce their impact on us and our marking by

- Heeding our initial, 'gut' feelings. We are often aware of giving into confirmation bias, not out of any ill will towards our pupils but because we try to avoid the feeling of having been wrong. In the case of a pupil whom we rate highly having handed in a disappointing piece of work, we might look further for positives within it or we might give that pupil the benefit of the doubt for something the pupil has written that could, perhaps at a push, be interpreted as being ambiguous. Usually we know deep down that we are doing this. And so the first step is to listen to those gut feelings and to resist the temptation to find a way of overruling them.
- Instructing our pupils to anonymise the work they submit. Of course, this is most effective when the pupils have used word processors for their work and so we cannot recognise their handwriting. It can also work in the case of handwritten work, though, if we simply spread out marked work on a table for the pupils to collect and then ask them to tell us their scores and feedback, weakening our mental link between our feedback and the style of handwriting.
- Regularly asking a colleague who does not know our class to randomly mark a small sample of the work we have already marked. This acts as a test of our objectivity and, as we know a colleague is essentially going to look at our marking, it motivates us to resist these two biases. It also has the added benefit for a department of helping the different teachers within it keep their marking in alignment with one another, of ensuring a stronger and more consistent degree of standardisation across classes.

The debate about what constitutes effective assessment is never-ending. There are arguments that it should be more continuous, with pupils being assessed on a regular basis throughout their programmes of study rather than in terminal assessments that could fall on days when things simply do not go their way. There are also arguments that it should be more situational, reflecting the real-life environments in which the skills being assessed will ultimately be exercised. As an instructor of agricultural skills was quoted in the AQA report on this issue, 'isn't it strange how the tractor's wheel always seems to come loose in a dark and muddy ditch and never in the controlled conditions of the college workshop?' (Ahmed *et al.* 2015, p. 32). And there are arguments that it should focus more on aptitudes than on knowledge, as exemplified in the 2012 PISA tests that assessed pupils' interactive problem-solving skills (OECD 2014). These arguments have all been brought to the fore in the UK as a result of the Covid-19 pandemic, with teachers and schools having to determine the grades for those in year groups that would normally have sat public exams. Whilst these arguments all have merit in an ideal world, the effects of our cognitive traits make us unready to bear the responsibility of being assessors of our own pupils and, perhaps sadly, mean the fairest approach to assessment remains that of public exams in which assessors mark the work of anonymised candidates.

5.3 Negative feedback hurts

In a study at Ohio State University, Tiffany Ito and three of her colleagues recruited 25 under-graduates to take part in a study into the level of electrical activity in their brains as they viewed different types of images (Ito *et al.* 1998). Sitting in a neutral environment, in a comfortable reclining chair in a sound- and electrical-proofed room, and having had the necessary electrodes attached to various parts of their scalps, the participants were shown 40 different images on a computer screen. The vast majority of these images were neutral, purposefully chosen to not cause arousal in the viewers, such as a dinner plate and a hair dryer. Two of the images were chosen to cause positive arousal: a Ferrari and a group of people enjoying a roller-coaster. The final two images were chosen to cause negative arousal: a mutilated face and a gun pointing at the camera. The participants were shown these images in 120 sequences, each consisting of five images. Half of the sequences consisted solely of neutral images. In each of the other 60 sequences, there was a single arousing image, be it positive or negative. After the participants saw each image, they had to press a key on a keypad to report whether they thought it showed something that was positive, negative or neutral; after each sequence they had to press a key to start the next. As the participants watched and responded to the images, the electrodes captured data about the intensity of their brain activity in response to the visual input (more specifically, the amplitudes of their late positive potentials).

The average amplitude of the electrical brain response, across all participants and all images, was 2.9 metres per second for neutral images, 7.4 metres per second for positive images and 10.9 metres per second for negative images. Not only did both positive and negative images cause more intense brain responses than neutral images, negative images caused a more intense brain response than positive images. We are affected much more physiologically by negative information than by positive information. Not only are we loss averse, valuing the loss of something approximately twice as much as we value gaining the very same thing, our brains react more strongly to negative information in general. This means we are more likely to remember negative information and to have our behaviour affected by it. This is our negativity bias.

In their review of the evidence of the negativity bias in both humans and animals, Paul Rozin and Edward Royzman suggest there is more to this cognitive trait than that of negative events simply causing us to have more intense mental responses than positive events (Rozin and Royzman 2001). They refer to that part of this trait as negative potency. In addition, they find that

- Our feelings about a future negative event grow in intensity more quickly as the event approaches than do our feelings about a future positive event. Our pupils naturally become increasingly stressed and anxious about high-stakes assessments as they approach, and feelings they may have about related positive events, such as the ability to relax after the assessments have ended, simply cannot keep pace with the growing negativity.
- Our overall feeling about an event that consisted of both positive and negative parts is more negative than simply adding up the individual parts would suggest. Following the logic of loss aversion again, we overweight our feelings about the negative parts compared to our feelings about the positive parts, meaning we feel worse about the whole event than perhaps we should.
- Negative events tend to be more varied and so cause our brains to work harder to process them than positive events. We mentally tire more quickly when we experience negative events, leading to the earlier onset of decision fatigue. This is what we are feeling when we are particularly drained having gone through a negative event, such as an unsuccessful interview or a disappointing medical appointment.

Key term: negativity bias

We experience negative events more intensely than positive events of equal size, our feelings about future negative events grow more rapidly as the event approaches than do our feelings about future positive events, our overall feeling about an event consisting of both negative and positive parts tends to be more negative than the individual parts would suggest, and negative events cause us greater decision fatigue than positive events.

The work of John Gottman and his colleagues on couples from the 1970s onwards has led to what they call the magic ratio (see Gottman 1993). For a relationship to remain stable, five positive interactions (such as showing interest and expressing affection) are required to offset a single negative interaction (such as a criticism and eye-rolling). Marcial Losada and Emily Heaphy studied the effectiveness of 60 teams at a large information-processing company, where effectiveness was measured by the financial performance of the team, its customer satisfaction ratings and the 360-degree feedback given by members within the team (Losada and Heaphy 2004). The factor that made the greatest difference to team effectiveness was the ratio of positive-to-negative comments that team members made to one another during meetings. The average ratio was 5.6 positive comments to 1 negative comment for the highest-performing teams, 1.9:1 for medium-performing teams and 0.36:1 for the worst-performing teams. They also found that negative feedback was particularly useful for helping the worst-performing leaders address serious weaknesses, but for those leaders who were already performing above average, feedback focusing on the things they were already doing well led to greatest improvements. The closeness of the positive-to-negative interaction ratio found by Gottman for stable relationships and that found by Losada and Heaphy for the most effective teams is remarkable. However, the journal in which their work was published has since questioned the validity of the data Losada and Heaphy used and so caution should be exercised with their result (Editors of American Behavioral Scientist 2014).

The implications of negativity bias for our teaching and feedback are considerable. How many of our pupils receive fewer than five pieces of positive feedback for each piece of negative feedback in lesson after lesson, and reach the end of the school day demoralised about themselves and their academic abilities? Negativity bias does not just affect the academic performance of our pupils, it also affects their mental health; and if we are not careful as teachers, we can trample on that each and every day. We can avoid having this effect by

- Being careful about the amount of negative-to-positive feedback we give to each of our pupils. John Gottman and his colleagues recommend couples keep a record of the number of times they communicate positively and negatively with one another so they can take corrective action if it is falling below the magic ratio. We should look to do similar, particularly for those pupils with whom we tend to be particularly negative. As noted in the study by Losada and Heaphy, negative feedback is essential as it shows our pupils where their serious shortcomings lie and what they need to work hardest to correct, but we should balance such feedback with many more, genuinely positive interactions.
- Focusing our feedback less on the weaknesses of our pupils and their work, and more on their strengths, reinforcing with them the things they should continue to do. We can also look to reframe our feedback. For example, by responding to a piece of work a pupil has just completed with 'You have taken a big step towards improving your use of adjectives - well done' we are communicating the same message as if we responded with 'You still need to work on improving your grammar', but in a way that is more positive and encouraging.
- Avoiding being pedantic. By flagging one minor error, it is likely that we are offsetting the impact of multiple, more significant, praises. By being pedantic, we are making it almost impossible for a pupil to feel a sense of overall positivity about any feedback we give.
- Developing the ability to gauge our audience. The interaction we have with a pupil is only one of many interactions that pupil will have with teachers and fellow pupils during the course of a day. Providing the same feedback, in the same manner, irrespective of the day a pupil is experiencing risks damaging the pupil's mental wellbeing and alienating the pupil. Our pupils need us to be more sophisticated in the way we provide feedback, adjusting it in response to their emotional and psychological state at that moment in time. We can only do this by building effective professional relationships with each of our pupils and investing time and effort into understanding how to interpret the cues they

give. If in doubt, we should adopt the precautionary principle and shift the balance of focus further towards the positive. It is better for a pupil to leave our classroom having not received a more picky piece of negative feedback than to leave it feeling overwhelmed by negativity.

- Taking advantage of every opportunity we can to give encouragement and praise, however insignificant it may seem at the time, and to challenge the negative things pupils say about both themselves and one another. We should celebrate the small wins with our pupils, acknowledging their efforts and successes.

It is also important that we help our pupils to understand their own negativity bias and teach them the steps they can take to overcome it, such as deliberately focusing more on the positives in events than on the negatives; savouring their successes, however small they may be; challenging their own negative self-talk, and, ultimately, being kinder to themselves. A study by Suzanne Segerstrom is a useful starting point for this. In the study, she tested the relationships between the optimism of 61 former law students and their earnings, status at work, social networks and physical and mental health (Segerstrom 2007). The levels of optimism of the participants, both before they started law school and ten years later, were measured using the Life Orientation Test (see Celestine 2019), which asks respondents to score statements using a scale of zero (highly pessimistic) to five (highly optimistic). The findings show that more optimistic participants had a higher average income ten years later. An increase in average score on the Life Orientation Test of one point per statement is associated with an additional $32,667 in annual income, taking into account the number of hours worked. More optimistic participants also had better physical and mental health. An increase in average score on the Life Orientation Test of one point per statement was associated with two fewer days on which they experienced negative physical health symptoms. Interestingly, higher annual income had no discernible effect on participants' optimism levels, but having more people available to talk to was, with each additional person within their social networks being associated with an average increase of 0.022 per statement in their responses to the Life Orientation Test. Our pupils need us to educate them about the need to be optimistic and about the path to that lying with personal relationships rather than money.

Finally, there are equally important implications of the negativity bias for how schools are run and how staff are managed and treated. Senior leaders who want to elicit the very best performance from their staff should adopt a positive, encouraging approach to their interactions with them, focusing on what staff are doing well rather than their weaknesses. That is the way to create a body of mentally healthy staff who are continually working to improve their performance: teachers who will themselves be able to be positive with their pupils and from whom pupils will learn and progress most.

5.4 Practical takeaways

We can enhance the effectiveness of our marking and feedback by

- Continually altering the order in which we mark a class's work.
- Ensuring we know what we are looking for in work before we start to mark it.

- Listening to our gut feelings about our pupils' work.
- Collecting pupils' work in a way that means we cannot tell which pupil has done which piece.
- Regularly checking the marking of one another in the same department.
- Being careful about the balance of our positive and negative feedback to each pupil, aiming for five positives for each negative.
- Focusing our feedback on what pupils are doing well and on how they are improving.
- Allowing the small errors to pass by.
- Altering our feedback in light of the emotional and psychological state of our pupils.
- Challenging the negative self-talk among our pupils.
- Helping our pupils to be optimistic.

Bibliography

Ahmed, A., *et al.*, 2015. The future of assessment 2025 and beyond. Available from: AQA, https://filestore.aqa.org.uk/content/about-us/AQA-THE-FUTURE-OF-ASSESSMENT.PDF

Cardy, R.L., and Dobbins, G.H., 1986. Affect and appraisal accuracy: Liking as an integral dimension in evaluating performance. *Journal of Applied Psychology*, 71 (4), 672-678.

Celestine, N., 2019. What is the life orientation test and how to use it? (LOT-R). *PositivePsychology.com*. Available from: https://positivepsychology.com/life-orientation-test-revised/.

Dayan, E., and Bar-Hillel, M., 2011. Nudge to nobesity II: Menu positions influence food orders. *Judgement and Decision Making*, 6 (4), 333-342.

Editors of American Behavioral Scientist, 2014. Expression of concern. *American Behavioral Scientist*, 58 (8), 1100-1101. Available from: https://journals.sagepub.com/doi/full/10.1177/0002764214537204.

Gottman, J.M., 1993. *What Predicts Divorce? The Relationship Between Marital Processes and Marital Outcomes*. NJ, USA: Lawrence Erlbaum Associates, Inc. Available from: www.gottman.com/blog/category/archives/.

Hattie, J., and Clarke, S., 2018. *Visible Learning: Feedback*. London, UK: Routledge.

Huber, J., Payne, J., and Puto, C., 1982. Adding asymmetrically dominated alternatives: Violations of regularity and the similarity hypothesis. *Journal of Consumer Research*, 9, 90-98.

Ito, T.A., *et al.*, 1998. Negative information weighs more heavily on the brain: The negativity bias in evaluative categorizations. *Journal of Personality and Social Psychology*, 75 (4), 887-900.

Kaplan, R.M., 1978. Is beauty talent? Sex interaction in the attractiveness halo effect. *Sex Roles*, 4 (2), 195-204.

Kenealy, P., Frude, N., and Shaw, W., 1987. Influence of children's physical attractiveness on teacher expectations. *Journal of Social Psychology*, 128 (3), 373-383.

Losada, M., and Heaphy, E., 2004. The role of positivity and connectivity in the performance of business teams: A nonlinear dynamic model. *American Behavioral Scientist*, 47 (6), 740-765.

Malouff, J.M., *et al.*, 2014. Preventing halo bias in grading the work of university students. *Cogent Psychology*, 1 (1).

OECD, 2014. Assessing problem-solving skills in PISA 2012. *In: PISA 2012 Results: Creative Problem Solving (Volume V): Students' Skills in Tackling Real-Life Problems*. Paris: OECD Publishing. Available from: www.oecd-ilibrary.org/education/pisa-2012-results-creative-problem-solving-volume-v/assessing-problem-solving-skills-in-pisa-2012_9789264208070-6-en.

Ross, L., Lepper, M.R., and Hubbard, M., 1975. Perseverance in self-perception and social perception: Biased attributional processes in the debriefing paradigm. *Journal of Personality and Social Psychology*, 32 (5), 880-892.

Rossmo, K., and Pollock, J., 2019. Confirmation bias and other systemic causes of wrongful convictions: A sentinel events perspective. *Northeastern University Law Review*, 11 (2), 790-835.

Rozin, P., and Royzman, E.B., 2001. Negativity bias, negativity dominance, and contagion. *Personality and Social Psychology Review*, 5 (4), 296-320.

Segerstrom, S., 2007. Optimism and resources: Effects on each other and on health over 10 years. *Journal of Research in Personality*, 41 (4).

6 Rewards and sanctions

Schools tend to publish their reward and sanction policies, outlining the consequences for their pupils of a whole range of positive and negative behaviours. That these are publicly available, setting clear expectations for pupils and their parents and guardians, and all staff are expected to adhere to them is important. Indeed, the need for fairness in the way we use rewards and sanctions stands out clearly from the behavioural science literature, as discussed in Section 6.3. However, behavioural science also shows that we can increase the potency of rewards and sanctions by using them in a more sophisticated manner and cautions us about the danger of overusing rewards and sanctions as external sources of motivation. These issues are the focus of this chapter.

6.1 Segregating and combining rewards and sanctions

The findings relating to loss aversion show that the impact we feel from a loss is approximately twice that we feel from an equal-sized gain. They also show two further things about how we value gains and losses, both of which are illustrated in Figure 6.1.

Firstly, we are characterised by the law of diminishing returns. From the hypothetical values in Figure 6.1, the value we feel from being given a single reward is five. Doubling the number of rewards we receive at a particular time does not double the value we feel from them: the total value we feel from two rewards is only seven. In the same way, a single sanction has an impact on us of minus ten, whereas doubling the sanction has a total impact of only minus thirteen.

Secondly, the overall impact we feel from a number of impacts at different times is found by adding up the separate values of the individual impacts. In other words, we return to the neutral position, zero, after each separate reward or sanction. This explains why, when a colleague received a bottle of wine one morning (feeling, in the case of Figure 6.1, a gain of five) and then had it taken away from him later that day (feeling a loss of ten), he felt overall as though he had experienced a loss that day rather than ending the day feeling no better or worse off than he had at its start.

The implications of these further findings can be seen in the following scenarios (in which the values are taken from those in Figure 6.1):

- A pupil submits two pieces of work, each of which are worthy of a single reward. By giving both rewards at the same time, the pupil experiences a gain of seven. By giving the

DOI: 10.4324/9781003198505-7

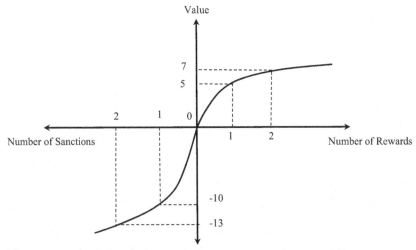

Figure 6.1 Segregating and combining rewards and sanctions
Source: Adapted from Tversky and Kahneman 1981

rewards separately at different times, the pupil experiences two gains of five and so an overall value of ten.

- A pupil does two things wrong, both of which elicit sanctions according to the school's sanctions policy. Issuing a double sanction causes the pupil to feel a loss of 13. Issuing two sanctions on separate occasions causes the pupil to feel two losses of ten and so an overall loss of twenty.
- A pupil submits a good piece of work, worthy of a reward, but in the same lesson also does something that warrants a sanction. Issuing a reward and a sanction separately causes the pupil to feel an overall loss of five (the gain of five from the reward and then the loss of ten from the sanction). This is the negativity bias in operation again. Simply allowing the reward and the sanction to cancel out one another, and so not issuing either, means the pupil feels no impact.

We tend to use our rewards and sanctions as rather blunt instruments. At best we tend to fail in maximising the impacts they have on our pupils, both positive and negative. At worst, our pupils leave our classrooms feeling worse than we had actually intended, with the effects of our sanctions outweighing those of our rewards. By segregating our rewards and sanctions, issuing multiple smaller rewards and sanctions rather than one larger one, we can maximise the impacts of both. By combining them, we can minimise their impacts. We can tailor the impact of our rewards and sanctions to the needs of individual pupils whilst staying in alignment with the policies of our schools.

6.2 The power of ownership

The findings of loss aversion also show how powerful the sense of owning something can be, with us valuing something more when we feel it is ours. The implications of this endowment effect for motivation were tested in an experiment conducted on 150 teachers in nine schools in northeast Illinois by Roland Fryer and colleagues (Fryer *et al*. 2012). The teachers were randomly separated into two groups. Those in Group One were incorporated into a scheme that would see them receive up to an additional $8,000 at the end of the school year conditional on the performance of their pupils in end-of-year assessments. Those in Group Two were instead incorporated into a scheme in which they received an upfront additional payment of $4,000, but at the end of the year would have to return some or all of that money or would receive up to an additional $4,000 based on the same pupil performance conditions as those in Group One.

The two schemes were designed in a way that meant a teacher would receive the same bonus irrespective of which of the two groups they were in and so the performance of the teachers should have been unaffected by the grouping. Their performance should just have been superior to the performance of their colleagues who were not incorporated into either of the incentive schemes. That is not what the researchers found, though. In the end-of-year assessments, the pupils of the teachers in Group Two performed better than those of the teachers in Group One. By controlling for all other possible factors, the researchers concluded that the teachers in Group Two feared losing the $4,000 they had already been given more than those in Group One wanted to gain $4,000, and that motivated the former to work harder than the latter to ensure their pupils performed well.

Key term: endowment effect

We value something more when we feel it is already ours.

Experience shows that we too can take advantage of the endowment effect in our rewards. Rather than simply always giving a reward after a pupil has achieved a target, we can intensify the motivational impact of the reward by giving it at the outset on the understanding that it will be removed if the pupil fails to achieve a target. However, pupils tend not to like such reward schemes, possibly because of its greater potency, and so it is a strategy that should be used judiciously.

6.3 The importance of fairness

Thought experiment: the power-to-take game

This simple game involves only two players. One of the players is the Proposer, and the other is the Responder. Both start the game with £100. In the first stage of the game, the Proposer announces what share of the Responder's money he will seize. In the second stage of the game, the Responder announces what share of their £100 she wants to destroy before the Proposer can get his hands on it. The game ends with the Proposer walking away with his £100 plus the share he announced of what remains of the Responder's money after she has destroyed part of it. The Responder leaves with what remains of her money after she has destroyed some of it and the Proposer has taken his share.

What share of the Responder's money would you seize if you were the Proposer? And what share of your own money would you destroy if you were the Responder?

Thought experiment: the third-party punishment game

This slightly more complicated game involves three players: a Proposer, a Responder and a Judge. The game begins with the Proposer having £100 and the Judge having £50. The Responder starts the game without any money at all. In the first stage of the game, the Proposer distributes the £100 he has been given between himself and the Responder, knowing there is nothing the Responder can do if she does not like the distribution he chooses. In the second stage of the game, the Judge decides whether or not to punish the Proposer for his chosen distribution, which the Judge can do by taking money away from the Proposer. The complication here is that for every three Pounds the Judge takes away from the Proposer, the Judge loses one Pound from his own money. The game ends with the Responder walking away with the amount of money she was given by the Proposer, who in turn leaves with the amount of money he kept for himself minus the money taken by the Judge. The Judge leaves with £50 minus one Pound for every three Pounds he took from the Proposer. Any money taken from the Proposer or lost by the Judge just disappears.

How would you distribute the £100 if you were the Proposer? And how would you respond if you were the Judge?

Our behaviour in the power-to-take and third-party punishment games has been widely studied in behavioural science. When we play the part of the Proposer in the first of these games, we tend to seize approximately 60% of the Responder's money. When we play the part of the Responder, we tend to destroy approximately 8% of our own money if the Proposer has announced to seize less than 60% of it, and we destroy approximately 58% if the Proposer has announced to seize more than 80% (Bosman and van Winden 2002). We cannot alter the Proposer's seizure decision after the Proposer has announced it: all we can do is reduce the amount of money available for the Proposer to seize. By doing so, though, we also reduce the amount of money that is ultimately left for us to keep. If the Proposer declares his intention to seize 80% of our money and we then decide to destroy 60% of it, for example, the Proposer ultimately takes 80% of £40, and we keep 20% of £40: £32 and £8, respectively. It would be better for us not to destroy any of our money, as the Proposer would then take £80, leaving us with £20. But because we so strongly dislike the feeling of being treated unfairly, we willingly harm ourselves just to get back at the Proposer.

When we play the role of the Judge in the second of these games, we rarely take any money from the Proposer if he has shared half or more of the money with the Responder.

In approximately 60% of cases when the Proposer has shared less than half of the money with the Responder, we tend to punish him and increasingly so as the amount shared with the Responder falls (Fehr and Fischbacher 2004).

The results from the power-to-take game show that we are willing to harm someone who we feel has treated us unfairly, even if we hurt ourselves by doing so. The results from the third-party punishment game show that we willingly harm ourselves to punish someone who we feel has treated someone else unfairly. This is how much we dislike unfairness. This is our inequity aversion.

Key term: inequity aversion

We have a natural dislike of unfair behaviour, when it is directed both at ourselves and at others, and are willing to punish such behaviour even if doing so harms us in some way.

Most of the pupils I have punished for misbehaving have not actually minded their sanctions. Pupils tend to understand why they are being punished and accept it. But on one condition: that it is fair. The power-to-take and third-party punishment games highlight the two types of fairness our pupils expect. The first is that the sanction is warranted, that they have misbehaved in a way punishable according to our school's sanctions policy. The important thing here is that our sanctions policies are very clear, made available to pupils in advance and implemented in a consistent manner. The second is that pupils all receive the same sanction for misbehaving in the same way, that the sanctions policy is implemented in a consistent manner irrespective of the pupil's sex, age or history. It is likely that failure to ensure these two forms of fairness will quickly result in protest behaviour by the pupils directly involved and also by their friends, and to an escalation of the problem even though they know it is going to lead to further sanctions. This applies to our rewards as well.

6.4 Unintended consequences

When we design and implement reward and sanction systems, we only consider the behaviour we would like to incentivise or discourage at that moment in time. We largely ignore the wider or longer-term impacts of those rewards and sanctions, apart from assuming that by incentivising desired behaviour now we will be shaping our pupils into good citizens for the rest of their lives. Behavioural science demonstrates that using rewards and sanctions is not as simple as that, though, and that creating the 'right' incentives now certainly does not lead to desired behaviour in the future (Bowles 2008).

A well-known example of the unintended consequences of sanctions is that from the Haifa nurseries experiment, conducted by Uri Gneezy and Aldo Rustichini (2000). Ten nurseries in the Israeli city were involved in the 20-week study during 1998. Each nursery charged 1,400 New Israeli Shekels (NIS) to care for children aged between one and four years from 7.30 am until 4 pm each day. Before the study, there was no sanction for parents and guardians being late to collect their children. The teachers simply took it in turns to stay late to ensure the children were always supervised. On each day in the first four weeks of the study, the observers simply recorded the baseline number of late collections at each of the nurseries. During the next 12 weeks, six of the ten nurseries, chosen at random, fined parents and guardians ten NIS per child if they were ten or more minutes late in collecting their children. They were given advance warning of this small but not insignificant charge (to contextualise it, the fine for illegal parking in the city was 75 NIS at the time but with a less-than-certain probability of being caught). In the final four weeks, the fines were removed without any explanation.

The recordings of the observers are summarised in Figure 6.2. In the first four weeks, there were on average eight late collections each week at each of the six test nurseries and ten each week from each of the four control nurseries. During the 12 weeks in which fines were charged, there were on average 16 late collections each week at each of the test nurseries whilst the weekly average number of late collections at each of the control nurseries fell slightly to nine. And then in the final four weeks of the study, after the fines had been removed, there was an average of almost 19 late collections at each of the test nurseries each week, whilst the weekly average at each of the control nurseries further fell to eight. Not only did the introduction of the fines cause the numbers of late collections to rise at the test nurseries during the period in which they were implemented, it caused a permanent increase in late collections at those nurseries.

In a more recent study by Gerda Kits, Wiktor Adamowicz and Peter Boxall, 160 people from the University of Alberta participated in experiments in which they took on the role of landowners, with groups of ten participating in each experiment (Kits *et al.* 2014). The experiments consisted of 12 rounds, and the participants were each given $2 at the start of each round to represent the earnings from their land for that period of time. The experiments were

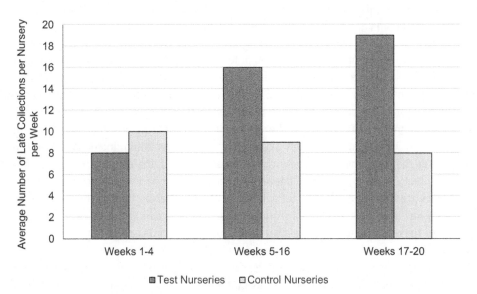

Figure 6.2 Results from the Haifa nurseries study

divided into control and test experiments, with the test experiments in turn being divided into three phases:

- In Phase One, consisting of the first four rounds of the experiment, the participants simply had to choose which of five levels of environmentally friendly practice to implement. For each incremental increase in practice they chose, $0.5 was donated to a Canadian charity. Each participant could cause up to $2 to be donated to charity in each round by being completely environmentally friendly. However, each incremental level of implementation came at a cost to the individual participant, also up to $2 for complete implementation.

It should be noted that each of the participants were to be paid in cash at the end of the experiment an amount equal to the sum of their individual earnings across the rounds minus the sum of their expenditures on being environmentally friendly. They could see a tally of their individual earnings and all of their past decisions throughout the rounds.

- In Phase Two, which consisted of rounds five to eight, each of the participants was able to submit an offer to the experimenters that outlined the level of environmentally friendly practice she was committing to implement in exchange for compensation. (The experiment was designed in this way to resemble the subsidies that farmers can receive in exchange for conservation practices, such as maintaining hedgerows.) They were told the offers reflecting the best deals for charity would be accepted. Successful participants would receive their requested compensations in addition to their $2 for each round of the experiment but then had to select at least the levels of implementation to which they had committed themselves. Unsuccessful participants would continue to receive their $2 for each round.
- In Phase Three, which consisted of the remaining four rounds, the ability of participants to apply for financial compensation for being environmentally friendly was revoked, and the experiment continued in the same way as in Phase One.

In the control experiments, which consisted of 12 rounds, all of which were conducted according to Phase One, the average total expenditure on environmentally friendly practices by the ten participants was approximately $4 per round. In Phase One of the test experiments, the average total expenditure on these practices by the ten participants was also around $4 per round. In Phase Two of the test experiments, this average total expenditure, perhaps unsurprisingly, rose to approximately $6 per round. The interesting finding is that in Phase Three, after the compensatory payments had been removed, the average total expenditure on these practices fell again, but to a level lower than what it had been before the payments were introduced: to approximately $3 per round. The long-term effect of the compensatory payments was to actually reduce environmentally friendly expenditures by 18%.

Both of these experiments reveal that sanctions and rewards can have unintended negative effects on behaviour, either at the time or in the future. They show that the use of external motivators, be they negative or positive, can more than offset our internal motivation to behave in desirable ways. This is known as motivational crowding-out, for which there are three main explanations. The first explanation is that external motivators can create acceptable trade-offs. In the Haifa nursery case, for example, the ten NIS fee was interpreted by parents and guardians as being the price for being able to collect children beyond the advertised end of the day. For many of them, this was a price worth paying, and so they readily took advantage of it. The second explanation is that we are naturally averse to being controlled and that being told we cannot do something often makes us more keen to do that precise thing. The Haifa study is again a possible example of this in action, with parents and guardians rebelling against being told that collecting children late was unacceptable. The third explanation is that external motivators can reduce, and even eliminate, the sense of pleasure we have from doing something that benefits others, from acting in ways that are altruistic, selfless and thoughtful. This is the favoured explanation of the results from the landowner study. In the test experiments, participants were willing to donate money to charity in the first phase because they gained a sense of pleasure from helping others. This is known as the warm-glow effect. The introduction of the compensatory payments diminished this effect as participants felt others would think they were only donating to charity in order to receive a tangible reward from doing so. The positive effect of the reward outweighed the negative effect of motivational crowding-out whilst the payments were available. Once the payments were removed, though, this switched as participants could no longer receive payments and felt others would still think they were only giving to charity because they had become used to doing so in order to benefit financially.

Key term: motivational crowding-out

Rewarding desirable behaviour and punishing behaviour that is undesirable can inadvertently lead to effects opposite to those intended, both at the time of the rewards or sanctions and in the future.

We want our pupils to behave in a manner that we and our schools deem desirable whilst they are with us, but also when they leave and make their own ways in life. Part of our role as teachers is to help our pupils to develop into compassionate and thoughtful citizens who strive to make the societies in which they live better places. If we are to see this, we need to take care with how we wield our rewards and sanctions. We can best achieve our objective by

- Deliberately fostering in our pupils' internal motivation to behave well. Rewarding pupils out of the sight of others, by simply commenting on their positive behaviour or issuing rewards at a later time, can weaken the link between the behaviour and the external reward, and so strengthen the pupil's awareness of the internal reward.
- Creating opportunities for our pupils to help others without us asking them to do so, trusting that they will notice and act on them. How often do we feel a sense of disappointment when we are already doing something nice for someone and then they ask us to do it? Allowing pupils to be altruistic of their own volition eliminates this disappointment for them and avoids triggering their aversion to being controlled. By comment-

ing on whether or not a pupil chose to take advantage of an opportunity, not issuing a reward or sanction in response, we can help them to notice such opportunities in the future and to feel the internal sense of reward for acting upon them.

- Avoiding trade-off situations. We often create an incentive structure along the lines of, 'For each day you are late in submitting a piece of work, you will lose five marks from its score' and 'For each morning you tidy away the equipment, you will receive a star, and five stars means five further minutes of play'. These allow our pupils to mentally calculate whether or not the desired behaviour is worthwhile on each occasion, which is likely to decline over time due to the logic of diminishing returns illustrated in Figure 6.1. Reward and sanction systems that are both more absolute and more general are more effective in fostering the behaviour we want to see our pupils develop.

6.5 Practical takeaways

We can make our use of rewards and sanctions more powerful by

- Segregating the rewards and sanctions we want to have a large impact and combining those from which we want a smaller effect.
- Taking advantage of our pupils' feelings of ownership and inducing a fear of losing a reward they have already received.
- Ensuring our use of rewards and sanctions is warranted.
- Ensuring our use of rewards and sanctions is consistent across pupils.
- Focusing on fostering our pupils' internal motivations to behave in desirable ways.
- Affording our pupils opportunities to behave well of their own volition.
- Avoiding inadvertently creating trade-offs in our pupils' behaviour, in which they settle for a certain amount of desirable behaviour.

Bibliography

Bosman, R., and van Winden, F., 2002. 'Emotional hazard in a power-to-take-experiment. *Economic Journal*, 112, 147-169.

Bowles, S., 2008. Policies designed for self-interested citizens may undermine "the moral sentiments": Evidence from economic experiments. *Science*, 320 (5883), 1605-1609.

Fehr, E., and Fischbacher, U., 2004. Third party punishment and social norms. *Evolution and Human Behavior*, 25, 63-87.

Fryer, R.G. Jr, *et al.*, 2012. Enhancing the efficacy of teacher incentives through loss aversion: A field experiment. *National Bureau of Economic Research Working Paper* 18237.

Gneezy, U., and Rustichini, A., 2000. A fine is a price. *Journal of Legal Studies*, 29 (1), 1-17.

Kits, G.J., Adamowicz, W.L., and Boxall, P.C., 2014. Do conservation auctions crowd out voluntary environmentally friendly activities? *Ecological Economics*, 105, 118-123.

Tversky, A., and Kahneman, D., 1981. The framing of decisions and the psychology of choice. *Science*, 211, 454.

7 The physical environment

A key finding from behavioural science is that our decision-making and ability to function effectively in a situation are affected by a whole range of possible influences. We have already seen that when we face the same options on two separate occasions, it is likely that we make different choices because of the different decisions we have had to make previously, differences in the way the options are presented to us, and differences in the decisions of others and in the ways they have been treated. As teachers, we should take all of these things into consideration when we are encouraging our pupils to make the most of the opportunities in front of them.

To this list needs to be added the physical environment in which our pupils are learning: the distractions they have to resist, the other choices they have to make and the information that is on display. The purpose of this chapter is to consider the impact of these features of our classrooms.

7.1 Managing temptations and distractions

In a study by Roy Baumeister and colleagues, 67 university students were told that they were participating in an experiment that looked at their taste preferences, which meant they could not eat anything in the three hours running up to their individual sessions (Baumeister *et al.* 1998). Upon arriving for the experiment, the participants found that chocolate chip cookies had been recently baked in the laboratory, causing the room to be filled with a mouth-wateringly good smell. They also found two displays, one consisting of the freshly baked cookies and other chocolate sweets, and the other consisting of red and white radishes.

In Stage One of the experiment, each of the participants was randomly assigned one of three tasks: to taste items from the chocolate display, to taste the radishes or to taste neither and so move straight to Stage Two. Those assigned to the chocolate and radish tasks were given five minutes to taste two or three items from their assigned display whilst the experimenter was outside the room. They were strictly instructed not to taste anything from the other display. Unbeknownst to these participants, the experimenter observed their tasting through a one-way window.

In Stage Two of the experiment, the experimenter returned and asked the participants to solve two problems on the pretext of allowing their tastes to fade and to see whether they had different problem-solving abilities to high school pupils. The problems involved the

DOI: 10.4324/9781003198505-8

participants tracing patterns without going over lines they had already drawn and without lifting their pens from the paper. Participants were given patterns on which to practise before being given the two test patterns. They were told that they could take as much time and as many attempts as they needed to solve the problems: they would only be judged on whether or not they managed to do so successfully. The researchers failed to tell the participants that the two problems were impossible to complete according to the instructions.

Every participant followed the instructions in Stage One of the experiment. None of them tasted items from the display not assigned to them, even though many assigned to the radish task subsequently described how difficult it was to resist the chocolate items, and a number of them were even observed picking up and smelling the cookies. And there was no real difference between the levels of perseverance with the line-tracing problems of those assigned to the chocolate task and those who were not required to taste anything in Stage One of the experiment. These groups of participants spent similar amounts of time on the problems and made similar numbers of attempts to complete them. There was a large difference between the perseverance of those assigned to the radish task and the others in the experiment, though. The average time it took for participants assigned to the chocolate and no-tasting tasks to give up was approximately 19.9 minutes, and they made approximately 33.6 attempts at completing the problems successfully. The average time it took for participants assigned to the radish task to give up was 8.35 minutes, and they made only 19.4 attempts.

These findings are explained by decision fatigue. We find resisting temptation cognitively tiring, in the same way that we find making decisions tiring: it depletes our mental energy reserves. And as our mental energy reserves shrink, our ability to perform subsequent such acts of volition falls. In this case, resisting the temptation to sample the chocolate cookies and sweets ultimately reduced the ability of those assigned to the radish group to persevere with the line-tracing problems. Unsurprisingly, being assigned to the chocolate group and having to resist the temptation to taste a radish had no such effect.

It has also been shown that distractions have a performance-reducing effect on us. A school situated by a busy train line in New Haven, Connecticut, had a worrying discrepancy in the performance of its pupils across classes. In response, the headteacher ensured the same curriculum was taught in all classes and to the same standard, and even switched teachers so those who had been teaching the high-performing classes taught those falling behind. The discrepancy stubbornly remained, though, with the under-performing classes working at a standard that was a whole year behind that of the others. And so the headteacher invited a team of researchers into the school to identify the cause. What the team found was surprisingly simple: the under-performing classes were taught on the side of the building that faced the train line, where they had to endure a high level of noise distraction all day, every day. The City of New Haven responded by installing soundproofing in all of the classrooms facing the tracks, and the pupils in those classes quickly caught up with the academic performance of their peers in other parts of the building. The under-performance was entirely caused by the noise from the train line, which reduced the ability of the affected pupils to focus on their lessons and process the content they were trying to learn (Monahan 2018). This effect is known as the bandwidth tax. Distractions reduce our mental bandwidth – the amount of information we can mentally process at any one time.

> **Key term: bandwidth tax**
>
> Distractions that compete for our attention reduce the amount of information we can mentally process, thereby reducing our ability to learn or perform cognitive tasks.

Failing to minimise the temptations that our pupils have to resist and the distractions they experience during our lessons can have a dramatic impact on their ability to learn, offsetting the impact of more effective teaching. And yet we tend to spend little time considering these two elements of our classrooms. We can help our pupils to maximise their learning by

- Removing as much temptation from our classrooms as possible. Having our pupils switch off their phones and put away their laptops is a good starting point if they have such devices in our lessons. Insisting that they clear their desks of everything that is not needed for the task at hand can further help them focus.
- Continually removing as much distraction as possible, from both outside and inside our classroom. Closing windows when the grounds people are using their leaf blowers and lawn mowers, removing wasps when they have flown in, and insisting on the highest levels of pupil behaviour during lessons are all possible examples.
- Avoiding scheduling lessons in which our pupils need to focus more than usual at times when there are likely to be more distractions, such as at the end of the school day when the bus engines are idling in the car park outside or just before lunch when we are all thinking about what to eat. Planning ahead can eliminate possible behavioural issues before they arise.
- Creating seating plans that ensure pupils who are likely to be tempted to distract one another are seated as far from one another as possible. This reduces both the detrimental effects of being tempted to cause a distraction for one and the detrimental effects of being distracted for the other.

7.2 Wall displays

> **Thought experiment: the letter k**
>
> Does the letter k appear most frequently as the first letter of a word or as the third letter of a word?

Responding to an advertisement posted by Amos Tversky and Daniel Kahneman in the student newspaper at the University of Oregon, 152 students were asked a series of questions such as that in the letter k thought experiment, but including the letters l, n, r and v as well as k. Almost 70% of the participants judged that the majority of these letters occurred more frequently as the first letter of a word than as the third, despite that being incorrect (Tversky and Kahneman 1973).

In a separate experiment in the same study, 98 participants (also recruited through the student newspaper at the University of Oregon) listened to a recording in which 20 pairs of words were read aloud at a speed of one every five seconds. Ten of the pairs consisted of words that were strongly related, five being pairs of words naturally related (such as knife and fork, and table and chair) and five being pairs of words that sounded similar (such as gown and clown, and blade and blame). The other ten pairs were constructed by replacing the first word in each of the strongly related pairs with an unrelated word, meaning each of the second words in the pairs appeared twice. During the recording, ten of the pairs were repeated twice, and the remaining ten were repeated three times, in a way that ensured pairs with the same second word (such as knife and fork, and head and fork) were repeated the same number of times.

At the end of the recording, 30 of the participants were given a list of the 20 first words that they had to pair with the corresponding second words. Unsurprisingly, these participants were more successful at recalling pairs that were repeated three times rather than twice. They were also more successful when recalling pairs that were strongly related. The more interesting part of the experiment concerns the remaining 68 participants, who were each given a list of all 20 pairs and had to identify which of them had been repeated twice and which had been repeated three times. On average, these participants judged the strongly related pairs to have been repeated 2.53 times and the unrelated pairs to have been repeated 2.36 times, even though the two types of pairs actually occurred with equal frequency.

These experiments both provide evidence of how we naturally employ the availability heuristic to help us to make choices and judgements as quickly and efficiently as possible, reducing the effect of decision fatigue. Rather than thinking through all of the possible evidence, we gravitate towards the option for which examples spring most readily to mind. In the letter k experiment, we find it is much easier to think of words that start with the letter k (key, knife, king . . .) than words in which k is the third letter (ask, like, cake . . .) and so, on the basis of that, we conclude that the letter k must occur most frequently at the start of words. In the second part of the word-pairs experiment, we find it much easier to recall pairs in which the words are strongly related and so we judge them to have occurred more frequently.

Key term: availability heuristic

A shortcut we employ to help us to make decisions more quickly and efficiently, by which we gravitate towards options for which we can most easily bring to mind supporting examples.

We all subconsciously employ mental shortcuts such as the availability heuristic when making decisions, especially when we are having to make decision after decision and are feeling the effects of decision fatigue. And so they are likely to play a role in how our pupils answer the questions they face in their assessments. Knowing this, we can harness these shortcuts in a way that increases the chances of our pupils answering those questions correctly by

- Using our wall displays to illustrate examples of important concepts in our subjects. In the case of the multiple-choice questions in economics, for example, pupils are regularly asked questions along the lines of 'Which of the following options is an example of X?' And in trigonometry, pupils have to select the correct equations to solve for certain angles and distances. Having concepts such as these illustrated on our walls can help pupils to more readily recall examples of the correct solutions in assessments without them consciously being aware of it.
- Establishing stronger associations between relevant concepts to help our pupils to move from one to another in their written answers. As the first 30 participants in the word-pairs experiment showed, strongly related pairs are more easily recalled. Finding ways of teaching concepts using terms that already have strong associations for our pupils will help our pupils to recall relevant content and so make it easier for them to structure their responses in a logical and comprehensive manner. Illustrating these associations on our walls will make them easier still to recall.
- Spacing the repetitions of the most important content. We judge items to have occurred more frequently when they are repeated at intervals rather than all at the same time. In other words, we are likely to judge that the letter H appears more frequently in this list of ten letters HTPHZRPHDH than in this list TPHHHHZRPD. Repeatedly returning to the most important content within our lessons rather than devoting a single extended block of time to it helps our pupils to more easily recall it (Underwood 1969). And making the intervals between repetitions longer serves to increase their perceived frequency in the minds of our pupils (Hintzman 1969). Changing our wall displays on a regular basis, so the examples of the most important concepts return most frequently but after extended intervals can further help our pupils to recall them.

However, caution should be taken when it comes to wall displays as they can be a source of unnecessary distraction for our pupils that can even lead to reduced academic achievement. In their study into the distracting effects of displays, Anna Fisher, Karrie Godwin and Howard Seltman randomly separated 24 children with an average age of 5.4 years into two even-sized and even-aged groups (Fisher *et al*. 2014). In the preliminary phase of the experiment, both groups had five lessons with a teacher-researcher in a classroom that had a moderate amount of irrelevant material on display. The purpose of these lessons was to allow the children to get to know the teacher, to become familiarised with the assessment procedures and to take baseline assessments consisting of 70 questions that the teacher read aloud, which the children answered by selecting a picture from a set of four for each question. From these questions, a sample of 36 was selected for use during the experiment itself. Six questions were selected for each of six science topics, for which the children had answered on average 22.7% correctly in the preliminary assessments: a success rate no better than random choice. These six sets of questions were divided equally between the two groups of children in a way that ensured the success rates of the two groups in the preliminary assessments were roughly equal. One group was assigned questions about plate tectonics, volcanoes and bugs, from which they had answered 22% correctly in the preliminary assessments. The other group was assigned questions about stone tools, the solar system and flight, from which they had answered 23% correctly in the preliminary assessments.

The experimental phase of the study involved the teacher taking six lessons with each of the two groups over a two-week period, covering each of the six chosen science topics in turn. The teacher and children sat on the floor in each lesson, and the teacher read to the children from a book about the topic of the lesson, showing them the illustrations after each double-page spread. The pupils answered the six relevant questions at the end of each lesson, in the same way as in the preliminary phase. In half of the lessons, the classroom was highly decorated with educational posters, pieces of the children's own work and maps. In the other half, the walls of the classroom were bare apart from the material needed for the lesson at hand.

Four researchers reviewed the lessons and recorded pupils as being on-task if they were looking at the teacher or at the materials the teacher was showing to them and as being off-task if they were focusing on their own body or clothing, focusing on other children in the classroom, focusing on the wall displays or focusing on something else other than the teacher. Across the two groups, more than 85% of the children spent more time off-task when the classroom was highly decorated than when it was bare, leading to a greater average amount of time spent off-task in the affected lessons. The children also spent a greater proportion of the lesson time focusing on the wall displays rather than on the lesson itself when the classroom was highly decorated. And the amount of time spent off-task directly affected the pupils' average scores in the end-of-lesson assessments. The children answered 55% of the questions correctly when the classroom was bare but only 42% when the classroom was highly decorated.

A balance needs to be struck when it comes to our classroom wall displays. On the one hand, they offer us an opportunity to reinforce our pupils' learning, taking advantage of their natural inclination to use mental shortcuts such as the availability heuristic when answering questions by enabling them to more easily bring to mind key concepts and important steps in their responses. On the other hand, they create unnecessary distractions in our classrooms, which can ultimately lead our pupils to perform less well academically. This balance can be struck by having simple and memorable displays, which are routinely changed and in which examples of the most important content and assessment techniques stand out clearly and return most frequently. Simplicity is the key. Displays should be immediately obvious so as to arouse only a fleeting moment of conscious interest and engagement from our pupils and yet subconsciously reinforce the most important messages and associations between concepts. Displays of any greater complexity than this should be removed, despite their attractiveness and cleverness; as should any irrelevant content. The walls of the classroom of a former colleague were filled, from floor to ceiling, with film posters. It was stunningly attractive but also greatly distracting to pupils who almost certainly achieved less in the teacher's subject than they could otherwise have done.

Before moving on from the availability heuristic, there are two further ways in which it can be harnessed for the benefit of our pupils' learning and progress. The first relates to the perceptions of our pupils about the quality of our lessons. In a study conducted by Craig Fox at Duke University, 64 business students were asked to complete a mid-course evaluation questionnaire when they were three weeks into a six-week course (Fox 2006). This was stand-ard practice at the university. Half of the students were given the first questionnaire to answer whilst the other half were given the second questionnaire. Each of the questionnaires con-sisted of 13 questions, 12 of which were identical across the two, including the final question that asked the students to rate the quality of the course from one (lowest possible quality) to seven (highest possible quality). The only difference between the two questionnaires was that the first had a question that asked the students to list two ways in which the course could be improved whilst this question in the second questionnaire asked students to list ten ways in which the course could be improved. Fox found the students who were asked to suggest ten ways in which the course could be improved gave the course a quality rating of 5.5, whilst their counterparts who were only asked to make two suggestions gave it a rating of 4.9. And this more favourable rating arose despite the two groups of students making similar numbers of suggestions (averaging 2.1 and 1.6 per student, respectively) and despite only 31% of those asked to suggest the greater number actually suggesting more than two.

It is the availability heuristic that is again driving results such as this. The students who had been asked to make only two suggestions about how the course could be improved found it relatively easy to do so. They readily thought of their two suggestions, after which they were able to move on with a feeling of it having been easy to think of flaws in the course. Those who had been asked to make ten suggestions found it much more difficult to complete the questionnaire. They eventually gave up on that question and so moved on with a feeling of not having been able to identify flaws in the course. When it came to the final quality rat-ing, those for whom the required number of flaws had come to mind relatively easily natu-rally scored the course more negatively than did their counterparts who had found it much harder to bring the required number of flaws to mind. The two groups came up with roughly the same number of flaws and so actually had similar feelings about its quality, but their use of the availability heuristic skewed their overall judgements.

The second way we can harness our pupils' use of the availability heuristic relates to their perceptions of their own abilities and likely success. In a study conducted at the University of Michigan by Piotr Winkielman, Norbert Schwarz and Robert Belli, 79 undergraduate students were randomly given one of two questionnaires that asked them about their ability to remem-ber childhood events (Winkielman *et al.* 1998). The structures of the two questionnaires were identical in all but one respect. One of the questionnaires (the 'four-events questionnaire') opened by asking respondents to report two events they experienced between the ages of 5 and seven years and two events they experienced between the ages of eight and ten years. The other (the '12-events questionnaire') opened by asking respondents to report six events from each of these age ranges. Both questionnaires then asked respondents whether there were large parts of their childhoods beyond five years of age that they could not remember, which they answered by selecting yes, no or unsure. And they both ended by asking respond-ents to rate the difficulty of the recall task on a scale of one (very easy) to seven (very difficult).

The students were randomly assigned the questionnaires, and so there should be no dif-ference between the ratings of their memories across the two groups. However, just shy of 20% of those who were assigned the four-events questionnaire reported having a poor memory, whereas over 45% of those assigned the 12-events questionnaire fell into that category. They rated their memory, as with so many things about which we have to make judgements, in a relative rather than an absolute manner. The students required to identify only four childhood events found their task to be much easier than those required to identify 12. And so, on the basis of that experience, those asked to identify only four childhood events judged their memories to be better. This is confirmed by the two sets of scores for how difficult the recall task was, averaging three for the four-events cohort and four for the 12-events cohort.

The findings from these two experiments are instructive. We want our pupils to think positively about our lessons, to enter our classrooms with a sense of eager anticipation and a readiness to learn, and to have positive perceptions of their own abilities, increasing the likelihood that they will persevere when they encounter challenges. Using devices such as termly evaluations about our lessons in which we ask our pupils to identify a small number of things they like and a larger number of things they dislike, before asking them to give an overall rating, can help bolster the first of these. And testing their ability to recall content in ways that require only a small number of recollections before asking them to rate their own learning and memory, perhaps in plenary activities, can bolster their self-perceptions (although this needs to be balanced with the dangers arising from the cognitive trait of overconfidence).

Finally, our pupils will inevitably face difficulties with their learning and will encounter challenges in their assessments. When they do so, they have to decide whether or not they try to overcome them: a decision-making process in which the availability heuristic is likely to loom large. It is only worth their while to persevere if they feel that there is a good chance of them succeeding. Without that feeling of hopefulness, they might as well give up and save themselves the mental effort, its resulting decision fatigue and the likely experience of failure. And our pupils will only be hopeful if, at the moment difficulty strikes, they can more easily recall examples of pupils like them succeeding than examples of similar pupils failing. That is down to us and to the way we seek to encourage them. Choosing to take a negative approach in our lessons, saying things such as 'This previous pupil failed because . . .', increases the ease with which our pupils can recall examples of failure and increases the likelihood that they will give up. Choosing to take a positive approach in our lessons, saying things such as 'This previous pupil succeeded even though they found this difficult . . .', tilts their mental decision-making in favour of perseverance. Our wall displays offer a great opportunity for implanting further examples of success into our pupils' minds.

7.3 The cost of change

Thought experiment: electric shocks

Imagine you find yourself in the (perhaps rather unlikely) situation in which you know there is a high probability that you will receive a serious electric shock at some point within the next few minutes and you have the opportunity to simply press a button to reduce the probability of that shock being delivered. Would you press the button?

Gaurav Suri and colleagues have presented some of the most surprising findings from a behavioural experiment, from their investigation into the reasons why we sometimes choose to ignore beneficial courses of action, such as when we choose not to take medicine prescribed by our doctors (Suri *et al.* 2013). Before running an experiment that actually put participants into the situation described in the electric shock thought experiment, they asked 130 people, including 30 psychologists, what they would do in it. Over 95% of the people they surveyed thought it was not a difficult decision to make and could see no reason why someone would choose not to reduce the probability of a shock.

In their subsequent experiment, 40 university students individually faced 14 trials in which it was highly likely that they would be given electric shocks that had been calibrated to the highest intensity they could bear. The participants were told that the purpose of the experiment was to allow the experimenters to compare their personal perceptions of anxiety with their actual physiological responses. They had devices attached to their fingers that continually measured their heart rates, and they were asked to report their feelings of anxiety at the end of each trial, on a scale of one (not at all anxious) to seven (extreme anxiety). Half of the participants, chosen at random, were faced with two buttons during their trials. If they pressed one of the buttons, the probability that they would receive a shock during that trial was reduced by 90%. If they pressed the other button, the probability that they would receive a shock remained unchanged. These participants were compelled to press one of the buttons but were free to press whichever they liked. They were even explicitly told by the experimenter that the focus of the study was entirely on the difference between their perceived and actual anxiety levels, which was unrelated to their choice of button. The other half of the participants were faced with a single button which, if they pressed it, reduced the probability that they would receive a shock during that trial by 90%. These participants did not have to press the button. Before their trials began, the participants were all told that pressing the probability-reducing button would cause there not to be a shock, whereas not pressing it would almost certainly result in a shock being given in the vast majority of trials.

The researchers found that in over 85% of trials in which the participant was compelled to press one of the two buttons, the participant chose to press the button that reduced the probability of a shock. The corresponding figure for trials in which participants did not have to press a button at all was just over 52%. In almost half of the trials in which pressing a button was optional, participants chose to leave the situation as one in which they would almost certainly be given an almost unbearable electric shock. Eight of the participants in the optional choice situation even chose not to reduce the probability of a shock in at least eight of their 14 trials.

Results such as these, albeit not usually as stark, are evidence of our status quo bias; of our natural inclination not to change the situation we are in unless we absolutely have to. When forced to make a decision, a clear majority of the participants chose to make the situation unambiguously better for themselves. When making a decision was optional, almost half of the participants chose not to do so even though that meant remaining in an unambiguously worse situation.

Key term: status quo bias

Our natural inclination to avoid changing the situation in which we find ourselves.

That we behave and make decisions in this way has also been repeatedly reported outside experimental laboratories. In a study by Raymond Hartman, Michael Doane and Chi-Keung Woo, 1,500 customers of the Pacific Gas and Electric (PGandE) Company in California responded to a survey about the service reliability they had experienced and their willingness to pay for, and their willingness to avoid, alternative scenarios (Hartman *et al*. 1991). Based on their responses about service quality, they were separated into two groups. The first group consisted of those who had reported high service reliability, experiencing an average of only three power outages a year, each of an average duration of two hours. The second consisted of those who had reported low service reliability, experiencing an average of 15 power outages a year, each of an average duration of four hours. The two groups of customers were then presented with one of two menus of six options, from which they could choose a level of service reliability that started at that they were currently experiencing and, in gradual increments, moved to the level of service reliability of the other group along with an offsetting change in tariff. The final option for those in the high reliability group, for example, was to have a service characterised by an average of 15, four-hour power outages each year and a 30% reduction in tariff. The final option for those in the low reliability group was to have a service characterised by only three, two-hour outages each year and a 30% increase in tariff. They were informed that PGandE could alter the amount it spent on the service it provided in response to the wishes expressed in the study, ensuring the respondents made their selections with as much seriousness as possible.

The responses to the initial questionnaire showed that there was very little difference between the two groups of customers. There were minor differences in their average income levels and energy usage, and those in the low reliability group tended to be more rural; otherwise they were demographically very similar. Given such a large sample, the researchers expected the customers to split in a roughly even manner across the different options from which they could choose. This was certainly not the outcome, though. Approximately 60% of the customers in each group opted for the level of reliability and tariff they were already experiencing, whilst just under 6% of each group opted to switch to the reliability experienced by the other group and the corresponding change in tariff. Further analysis of the amounts they reported being willing to pay for different scenarios showed customers even expected to be compensated for switching to a better level of service reliability. The power of the status quo effect was such that they expected to be paid for improving their experience.

Three explanations of our status quo bias have been proposed. The first relates to our natural aversion to loss. It asserts that we would rather keep things as they are than take any risk that could result in us feeling a loss. As the saying goes, better the devil you know. This is certainly plausible in the case of the Californian electricity customers, especially those who were already enjoying a high service level and so would be risking ending up in a situation they regretted. However, this does not apply to the students in the electric shock experiment who had the opportunity to make their situation unambiguously better. Indeed, in a separate iteration of the electric shock experiment, the majority of participants explained to the experimenters that they could not lose out from pressing the button. The second and third explanations relate to our desire to avoid decision fatigue. According to the second explanation, we naturally prefer inaction to action. We would rather not make a decision at all, and so preserve our mental resources, even if that means missing out on a better outcome. Known as our omission predisposition, this is a plausible explanation for both. According to the third explanation, we tend to choose the option that is most clearly signposted. This is the explanation preferred by the researchers in the electric shock study, who argue that the benefits of choosing to reduce the probability of a shock were clearer for those in the mandatory choice group because they were compelled to make a choice.

Key term: omission predisposition

Our natural inclination to prefer inaction to action; to prefer not making a decision if at all possible.

Whichever explanation is correct, the status quo bias looms large in the decisions we make on an everyday basis. And our pupils are characterised by it no less. Just like us, our pupils try to avoid changing the situations in which they find themselves, even if they could change them in beneficial ways. Our pupils do not like change as it imposes a mental cost on them: a mental cost that can ultimately reduce their ability to make other decisions, to learn and to control their own behaviour. And so we can help our pupils by minimising the changes they experience within our classrooms, as that will enable them to devote their mental resources to more productive, learning tasks. We can use seating plans for our classes, so that pupils sit in the same places in each lesson. This removes the need for pupils to decide where to sit as they enter our rooms; it eliminates the possibility of pupils entering social situations they had not expected, and it enables us to seat pupils in a way that minimises distractions. We can also help our pupils by having a routine and rhythm to our lessons that they come to expect and by ensuring they know in advance of any unavoidable changes in our lessons, such as planned absences when they will be taught by different teachers and lessons that are going to be dramatically different to what they expect.

Planning lots of variety into our lessons seems an obvious way to ensure our lessons are engaging, fun and enjoyable. However, that comes at a mental cost to our pupils we usually do not consider. It may be that we are inadvertently making it harder for our pupils to learn.

7.4 Practical takeaways

We can help our pupils to concentrate on their learning and to get the most from our lessons by

- Removing as much temptation and as many distractions from our classrooms as possible.
- Scheduling lessons in which they particularly have to focus for periods in which it is likely there will be fewer distractions.

- Employing seating plans in our lessons, separating those pupils who are most likely to distract one another.
- Using simple wall displays that change periodically to reinforce key associations and examples.
- Linking new content to that our pupils have already learned.
- Spacing the repetitions of the most important content as widely as possible.
- Removing any unnecessary interest from our displays.
- Harnessing the availability heuristic of our pupils to increase their perceptions of the quality of our lessons and of their own abilities, and the likelihood of them succeeding if they persevere during difficulties.
- Minimising change in our lessons.

Bibliography

Baumeister, R.E., *et al.*, 1998. Ego depletion: Is the active self a limited resource? *Journal of Personality and Social Psychology*, 74 (5), 1252-1265.

Fisher, A.V., Godwin, K.E., and Seltman, H., 2014. Visual environment, attention allocation, and learning in young children: When too much of a good thing may be bad. *Psychological Science*, 1-9.

Fox, C.R., 2006. The availability heuristic in the classroom: How soliciting more criticism can boost your course ratings. *Judgement and Decision Making*, 1 (1), 86-90.

Hartman, R.S., Doane, M.J., and Woo, C.-K., 1991. Consumer rationality and the status quo. *Quarterly Journal of Economics*, 106 (1), 141-162.

Hintzman, D.L., 1969. Apparent frequency as a function of frequency and the spacing of repetitions. *Journal of Experimental Psychology*, 80 (1), 139-145.

Monahan, K., 2018. *How Behavioral Economics Influences Management Decision-Making: A New Paradigm*. London, UK: Academic Press.

Suri, G., *et al.*, 2013. Patient inertia and the status quo bias: When an inferior option is preferred. *Psychological Science*, 24 (9), 1763-1769.

Tversky, A., and Kahneman, D., 1973. Availability: A heuristic for judging frequency and probability. *Cognitive Psychology*, 5, 207-232.

Underwood, B.J., 1969. Some correlates of item repetition in free-recall learning. *Journal of Verbal Learning and Verbal Behavior*, 8, 83-94.

Winkielman, P., Schwarz, N., and Belli, R.F., 1998. The role of ease of retrieval and attribution in memory judgements: Judging your memory as worse despite recalling more events. *Psychological Science*, 9 (2), 124-126.

SECTION TWO: BEHAVIOUR

8 Our two selves

In his letter to the Church in Rome, thought to be written around the year 57, Paul of the Bible summed up the focus of this chapter rather well by explaining that we often find ourselves doing things we do not actually want to do and not doing things we know we should (see Romans, Chapter 7, verses 15-19). It is as though there are two of us, the person we want to be and the person we become when we somehow lose control. And we lose control on a regular basis. That Robert Louis Stevenson's 'The Strange Case of Dr Jekyll and Mr Hyde' was such a success, selling 40,000 copies within the first six months and being made into a stage production at London's Lyceum within only a couple of years, suggests this is something to which we all relate (Luckhurst 2006). Behavioural scientists studying our willpower and self-control have begun to shed light on why this resonates so well with us, light that also has implications for the behaviour of our pupils.

8.1 Decision fatigue – again

In a series of experiments, Kathleen Vohs and her colleagues investigated the link between our decision-making and our self-control (Vohs *et al*. 2008). In one of the experiments, 30 undergraduate students were randomly assigned to either a choice or no-choice group. The first phase of the experiment for those in the choice group involved them having to make a long series of choices between different products. At first they had to choose their preferred option from five different categories: t-shirts, shampoo brands, socks, candles and sweets. Some of the options were on display in the laboratory whilst others were simply described. Once they had done that, they then had to choose between their different choices. The experimenters motivated them to make honest choices by giving them the prospect of receiving a product at the end of the experiment based on their choices. Finally, these participants had to choose between a range of different occupations, each of which was described for them. By the end of all this, they had each made 292 choices. In contrast, the first phase of the experiment for those in the no-choice group involved them having to rate, but not choose between, the products and occupations from which their counterparts had to choose. They were motivated by the prospect of receiving a product chosen at random for them. In the second phase of the experiment, the participants from both groups moved into a separate room in which there were 20 cups containing a concoction made from orange juice, water, vinegar and sugar: an unpleasant but not

DOI: 10.4324/9781003198505-10

Table 8.1 Results from the unpleasant drink and cold water experiments

Measure	Choice Participants	No-Choice Participants
Average cups drank	2.06	7.67
Average time in cold water	27.7 seconds	67.42 seconds

harmful recipe. They were paid one nickel for each cup they drank. The results are shown in Table 8.1.

In a related study by the same researchers, 25 undergraduates were also randomly assigned to either a choice or no-choice group. The first phase of the experiment for those in the choice group was identical to that presented earlier. The first phase for those in the no-choice group was different, though. In this experiment they had to write in detail about their thoughts and feelings about eight adverts taken from popular magazines. They were motivated by the prospect of being able to choose a product for themselves. In the second phase of this experiment, all of the participants undertook the cold pressor test. The temperature of a container of water was maintained at 1°C whilst that of the room was maintained at 22°C. The participants initially had to submerge their nondominant arms up to their elbows in a container of room-temperature water for one minute. This ensured they were all in the same condition when they then submerged that same arm up to the elbow into the cold water for as long as they could bear. The results are also shown in Table 8.1.

As Table 8.1 shows, the results across the two experiments align. In both cases, having to make decisions in Phase One reduced the ability of the participants to perform subsequent willpower tasks. Having to make choices depletes our mental resources, causing us to suffer from decision fatigue. Not only does this make us less able to make further decisions and to complete other tasks, it also makes us less able to exert self-control, reducing our ability to persevere with drinking an unpleasant drink and to tolerate the effects of cold water. Becoming mentally tired reduces our ability to behave as we would like to. It opens the door to our inner Mr Hyde.

The ability to drink an unpleasant drink or to keep an arm in cold water may seem rather trivial and unrealistic. However, Megan Oaten and Ken Cheng have more recently tested the levels of self-control of university students at different times during a semester, finding the students' performance in their self-control tests declines as the term progresses (Oaten and Cheng 2005). More importantly, they find this reduction in test performance corresponds with negative changes in the students' behaviour outside the study. As the term progresses and their self-control weakens, they exercise less, smoke more, double their caffeine intake, increase their consumption of junk food by half and reduce the time they spend on their personal hygiene. The students also become increasingly irritable. Most interestingly, though, the researchers also see a worsening of the students' study habits as the semester progresses and the exams approach, with them spending more time with friends and more time oversleeping. It is as though the students devote so much of their mental resources to studying hard that they actually study less: an example of the ironic effect.

> **Key term: ironic effect**
>
> A situation in which our efforts to behave in one way actually cause us to increase the behaviour we want to avoid.

As our pupils become mentally tired, both during a given day and throughout a week and term, they become less able to control their own behaviour. They are naturally less able to put up with things they deem unpalatable, as shown by the unpleasant drink and cold water experiments; they are increasingly likely to behave in ways they know they should not, and they are likely to be increasingly prone to lashing out, both at us as their teachers and at their fellow pupils. This does not make these behaviours excusable, but being aware of this correspondence between our pupils' mental tiredness and these behaviours enables us to reduce the likelihood of them happening in the first place. We can set activities for our pupils to complete that involve fewer possible distractions, are less likely to cause pupils to disagree and fall out with one another, and are most obviously sensible and useful at times when they are mentally fatiguing. And we can be judicious about when we challenge our pupils for behaviour that is unusual for them. Tackling it when it arises in the last lesson of the day, for example, may trigger a backlash that causes the situation to escalate. This could be avoided by leaving the conversation until the following morning. Poor behaviour should never be allowed to go unchallenged, but it is important to choose when to challenge it.

That our pupils can naturally lose sight of other important things when they are mentally tired, such as eating, sleeping and exercising properly, is a subconscious cry for help. They often cannot avoid doing this or realise that they are doing it. They need our help to behave as they actually want to. A pupil in a boarding house that I used to supervise would make himself a six-cup cafetière of coffee at 9 pm each evening during the exam term, thinking it would fuel him through his revision until the early hours. Without realising it, he was caught in a vicious cycle in which he simply became increasingly tired and less productive, increasingly anxious and stressed, and yet less able to escape these unhelpful behaviours. Our pupils often need us to intervene, to make them aware of their self-harming behaviour, to compel them to break these cycles and to re-establish positive behaviours, and to hold them to account for doing so.

Our pupils also need us to teach them about their willpower being limited and that it draws on the same mental resources they use to fuel their decision-making, their concentration and their learning. They need to know about the inevitable consequences of exhausting their mental resources, consequences that include their self-control failing; them giving into temptation and behaving in ways they later regret; them becoming more irritable with their friends, family and teachers; and their learning being impaired. And they need to know about the steps they can take to avoid such outcomes, for example,

- Noticing the symptoms caused by decision fatigue: heightened irritability, increased mind-wandering, reduced ability to make choices and increased urge to delay tasks until the next day.

- Choosing the battles they have with themselves. For example, not trying to give up gaming, eating unhealthy food and coffee all at the same time and not trying to change their lifestyles at all in the run-up to important assessments and public exams. Our pupils need to learn how to effectively plan the use of their limited mental resources.
- Engaging in precommitment strategies through which they either prevent themselves from giving into temptation or make commitments to others that they will or will not behave in certain ways, so that when their self-control is at its weakest, they have the additional motivation that comes from knowing they will have to 'fess up' and explain themselves.

We have been using precommitment strategies to tame our own behaviour and cognitive traits since at least our ancient civilisations, and no doubt much longer than that. The example that most readily comes to mind is that of Odysseus in *The Odyssey*, which was written by Homer in the eighth or seventh century BCE (see, for example, Guerber 1993, p. 313). Travelling home from the Trojan War, Odysseus deliberately sailed close to the sirens' island so he could hear their enthralling songs, which famously lured sailors to destruction on the surrounding rocks. Following the advice of Circe, daughter of the Sun God, Odysseus successfully guarded against the same fate by filling the ears of his crew with wax, so they would be immune from the sirens' songs, before instructing them to secure him to the mast and to maintain their course safely past the island irrespective of any change of mind he might have.

The effectiveness of a less extreme form of precommitment is shown in a field study by Xavier Ginè, Dean Karlan and Jonathan Zinman, which assessed the impact of the Committed Action to Reduce and End Smoking (CARES) scheme launched by the Green Bank of Caraga on the island of Mindanao in the Philippines (Ginè *et al.* 2010). The bank sent representatives out onto the streets to enlist volunteers for the scheme, which required a minimum deposit of 50 pesos to open an account. Those who signed-up and opened accounts were then encouraged to use their accounts as a place to save the money they would have spent on cigarettes each week for six months. To make this as easy as possible to do, the bank offered most of the participants a weekly deposit collection service, saving them the time and effort of making trips to the bank. At the end of the six months, the participants were asked to take a urine test. Those who passed the test, thereby demonstrating they had abstained from smoking in the run-up to it, had their savings returned. The savings of those who either failed the test or refused to take it were given to charity.

The researchers recruited 2,000 participants aged 18 years or older, who were randomly assigned to one of three groups. The 781 assigned to the first group were invited to participate in the CARES scheme in the way outlined above. A further 603, assigned to the second group, were given cue cards showing pictures of the damage that can be caused by smoking, such as those of a premature baby and a blackened lung. The final 616 were assigned to the control group and neither participated in the CARES scheme nor received the cards. From those assigned to the first group, only 83 CARES accounts were actually opened, with an average opening balance of 57 pesos. These 83 participants made deposits roughly every fortnight and by the end of the six months had an average balance of 553 pesos, which represented approximately 20% of their monthly incomes.

At the end of the six months, the probability that those who had participated in the CARES scheme passed their urine tests was between 3.3 and 5.8 percentage points higher than that of those in the other two groups. This was also the case 12 months after the start of the experiment. Signing-up to a scheme in which they could lose not insignificant amounts of money if they smoked was effective in helping the participants quit. Thomas Schelling writes about another precommitment strategy, adopted by recovering drug addicts to help stop themselves from relapsing (Schelling 1992). The addicts wrote incriminating letters that were held in trust and, in the event of them relapsing, mailed to the people they least wanted to know about their addiction. We can help our pupils by educating them about the effectiveness of precommitment strategies and by designing, perhaps less extreme, strategies through which we hold them to account.

8.2 Cognitive load – again

In a study related to those in the previous section, Baba Shiv and Alexander Fedorikhin investigated the link between our cognitive load and our self-control (Shiv and Fedorikhin 1999). The studies discussed earlier, by Kathleen Vohs and her colleagues, focused on how mental exertion affects our subsequent ability to regulate our behaviour. The study that follows focused on how the amount of information we need to process affects our willpower at the same moment in time. Shiv and Fedorikhin explained to the 80 or so undergraduate students who participated in their study that the objective of the experiment was to better understand memory, which required the students to remember a number in one room that they would then have to recall in a separate room. In exchange, the students would receive a snack as a reward for participating in the study.

Whilst in the first room, each of the students was given a sheet of paper that explained how they could get to the second room. They were also briefly shown a number by the experimenter, which they had to remember. They were then asked to leave the room one at a time and to go to a trolley from which they could choose their snack before proceeding to the second room. The trolley was visible from the first room, but its contents could only be seen once they were in front of it and so they had no idea about the nature of the snacks before they made their choices. The trolley contained two snacks, each in a container: a chocolate cake with a cherry topping and a fruit salad. A label with 'one dollar' written on it was attached to each of the two containers to ensure the students did not choose the one they thought was more expensive. The students simply had to pick out of the trolley a card that represented their choice. All the while, they had to remember their number.

Having selected their snack, each student then proceeded to the second room. Once there, they were given a booklet in which they had to write the number they had been remembering. They also had to score from one to seven the extent to which they had made their snack decision according to each of five scales shown in Figure 8.1. Each of the students' scores from these five scales were added together and then averaged, creating an overall 'decision score' for which an increase in number represented an increase in the influence of impulse, desire and emotion on the decision.

The pivotal part of the experiment was that when the students were shown the number they had to remember, half of them were shown a two-digit number whilst the other half

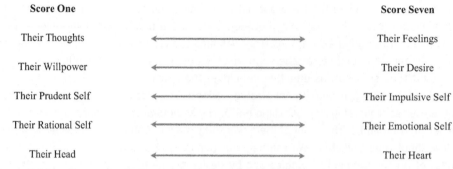

Figure 8.1 The five scales in the snack choice experiment

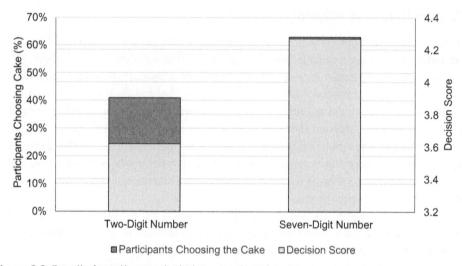

Figure 8.2 Results from the snack choice experiment

were shown one with seven digits. The results from the experiment, illustrated in Figure 8.2, show that a much greater proportion of the students who had to remember the seven-digit number chose the chocolate cake. Not only that, they also reported a much greater average decision score, meaning they made their snack decisions based more on desire and impulse than their counterparts who had to remember the smaller number.

The researchers repeated this study with a further 69 undergraduates. The experimental design was the same apart from the booklet the participants had to complete upon arriving at the second room. In this follow-up study, the booklet included an additional task that asked the students to score how often they could be described by three adjectives (impulsive, careless and easily tempted), each on a scale from one (seldom did it describe them) to seven (usually it described them). Again, these scores were added together and then averaged for each student, creating a single score for self-reported impulsiveness for which an increase in score represented an increase in impulsiveness. The 69 participants were separated into two groups on the basis of this score, with those reporting a score lower than the median

Table 8.2 Results from the supplementary snack choice experiment

Measure	Two-digit Number		Seven-digit Number	
	Impulsive	*Prudent*	*Impulsive*	*Prudent*
Participants				
choosing the cake	40%	37%	84.2%	38%
Decision score	2.93	2.80	4.80	2.85

being assigned to the 'prudent group' and those with a score greater than the median being assigned to the 'impulsive group'.

The results from this supplementary study are summarised in Table 8.2. As in the initial study, those who had to remember the longer number were, on the whole, much more prone to selecting the chocolate cake rather than the fruit salad. They also reported that, on average, they made their snack decisions much more on the basis of desire than their less mentally burdened counterparts. The interesting finding from this supplementary study is that this effect was not common across all the students in the seven-digit group, though. In fact, this overall difference in the behaviour between students given different sized numbers to remember was driven entirely by those who acknowledged that they are impulsive. Those who had to remember the longer number but reported having greater self-control made snack decisions that were almost indistinguishable from those made by students who had to remember the smaller number.

As in the previous section, it could be argued that the snack choices made by undergraduate students in a rather artificial experiment in a laboratory somewhere on a university campus are immaterial to our everyday lives. But Sendhil Mullainathan and Eldar Shafir present a particularly sad example of this effect in real life (Mullainathan and Shafir 2014). On 23 April 2005, Brian Hunton, a firefighter from the Texas city of Amarillo, died whilst responding to an emergency call. He was not killed by the heat nor by the smoke. In fact, he was not killed by the fire at all. He was killed whilst on route to the fire when the door of the truck in which he was riding opened as it went round a corner at speed, causing Brian to fall from the vehicle and to hit his head on the pavement. He died because in the rush to respond to the call, and in his effort to save the lives of those in danger, he did not buckle his seat belt. And this was not an isolated case. The authors note that in the period 1984 to 2000, between 15.8% and 19.8% of firefighter fatalities in the USA were caused by firefighters not fastening their seat belts and then being involved in road accidents. It is not that firefighters do not realise the risk that comes from not fastening a seat belt or that they deliberately choose to take the additional risk. They educate thousands of schoolchildren every year about those dangers. It is simply that in responding as quickly as they can, they overlook the need for them to take care of themselves. They focus their cognitive bandwidth so fully on doing their jobs that they inadvertently cause themselves to suffer from the tunnelling effect.

Key term: tunnelling effect

A situation in which we devote so much of our cognitive bandwidth to a particular task that we overlook other important considerations.

When they are focusing on a particular task, event or situation, our pupils are also prone to suffering from the tunnelling effect and to inadvertently ignoring other things in the situation around them. These things they overlook can include our instructions, the feelings of their peers, and, as in the example of Brian Hunton, their own wellbeing. This effect contributes to the findings of Megan Oaten and Ken Cheng in the previous section about students' increasingly harmful behaviours as exams approach. It also explains why significant events at school, such as an accident on the sports field, or at home, such as an illness in the family, can cause academic performance to decline and can trigger unrelated behavioural issues. When they find themselves in these situations, our pupils need us to help them to remember the other important things they need to do. We can do this by drawing their attention to these other things, making it easier for them to complete these other things by earmarking during school hours the time they need to do so and ensuring they have all the necessary resources and instructions, and actually being with them whilst they complete these other things.

Teaching our pupils about their susceptibility to the tunnelling effect and the steps they can take to avoid it is also important. One such step that has been shown to be effective is the use of checklists. In his study of surgical procedures, Atul Gawande demonstrates how powerful it can be to make a list of the important tasks that need to be fulfilled (Gawande 2010). Eight hospitals from around the world were selected to participate in the study, split between developed and less-developed countries. The number of deaths and major complications during surgery in up to four operating rooms in each of the hospitals were recorded over a three-month period. Around 4,000 adult procedures were observed, from which over 400 involved major complications and 56 resulted in the patient's death. Around half of the complications were due to infections and a further quarter arose from technical problems. After this baseline period, a two-minute and 19-step checklist was introduced and followed in these operating rooms. The results were stark. The rate of major complications fell by 36%, with infections being almost halved and technical failures dropping by a quarter, and the number of deaths fell by 47%. Using the checklist essentially spared over 150 patients from harm and saved the lives of 27 others. Itemising in advance the tasks that need to be fulfilled can help us to avoid the tunnelling effect. It can help us to ensure we attend fully to all the important things we need to do even in the midst of stress and pressure.

8.3 Emotions and self-control

In a study involving 60 undergraduate psychology students at Case Western Reserve University, Mark Muraven, Diane Tice and Roy Baumeister studied the impact on our self-control of us trying to regulate our emotions (Muraven *et al.* 1998). In order to gather baseline data about their physical abilities, the participants were timed holding their breath. After it became apparent that there was at least some surreptitious cheating, with participants making small inhalations whilst performing the task, the experimenters focused on a task that involved the participants squeezing a piece of paper between the handles of a hand grip exerciser for as long as possible. The experimenter stopped the timer as soon as the paper was dropped. Having completed this preliminary exercise, the participants were shown a deliberately upsetting three-minute excerpt from the film *A Dog's Life* (*Mondo Cane*), which presented the impact of nuclear waste on wildlife. The participants were randomly assigned one of three tasks whilst they watched the film. Those in the control group were simply instructed to watch it. Those in the emotional group were instructed to respond as emotionally as possible to what they saw. Those in the restrained group were instructed to minimise their emotional responses as much as possible. Those in the emotional and restrained groups were also told that their facial expressions would be filmed as they watched the clip and that those in the emotional group should make them as expressive as possible whilst those in the restrained group should minimise them. In the second phase of the experiment, the participants were asked to complete an assessment of their mood having watched the film; to complete the handgrip exercise again; to score on a scale from one (not at all) to seven (extremely) their tiredness at the start of the experiment, after watching the film and at the end of the experiment; and to score on a scale from one (very little) to seven (very high) the amount of effort that they had put into their assigned task whilst they watched the film. Each of the participants completed the experiment individually.

The researchers found that the participants in the two 'active' groups, those who had to intensify their emotional responses and those who had to suppress them, reported having exerted greater effort during that part of the experiment than their counterparts who simply watched the film. However, they did not report different levels of effort to one another. Correspondingly, those in the emotional and restrained groups reported being more tired after having watched the film than those who did not have to regulate their emotions. And all of the participants reported similar mood assessment scores, signifying that they all found the film equally troubling. The most interesting finding, though, relates to the participants' individual differences in performance at the handgrip exercise, measured as the time they managed having watched the film minus the time they managed during the baseline test. The average difference amongst those who did not have to regulate their emotional responses during the film was −1.57 seconds. The average differences amongst those in the emotional and restrained groups were −25.10 seconds and −18.49 seconds, respectively.

Whereas this study by Muraven, Tice and Baumeister looked at the impact of us trying to regulate our emotions on our ability to perform a task, Daniel Wegner, Ralph Erber and Sophia Zanakos investigated the impact of us performing a task on our ability to regulate our emotions (Wegner *et al.* 1993). In their study, 289 undergraduate psychology students at the University of Virginia were initially tasked with writing freely about their thoughts for three minutes. After they had done that, half of them were asked to think of a sad event in their past whilst the other half were asked to remember a happy event. A third of those given each task were asked to feel the sadness/happiness again, a third were asked not to feel the sadness/happiness again and the remaining third were given no further instruction. In total, then, the participants were randomly assigned one of six thought tasks. The final complication was that half of those assigned to each of these tasks were also asked to remember the number 741296835 and were told that if they were unable to recall it correctly at the end of the experiment, their data would be rejected. The remaining participants in each of the six groups were given no such cognitive load and so were able to engage in their thought tasks free from any encumbrance. They were all left alone for seven minutes to complete their assigned task and to continue writing freely about their thoughts. In the final phase of the experiment, after the seven minutes were up, the participants had to rate themselves for each of three positive emotions (happy, good and inspired) and for each of three negative emotions (sad, blue and gloomy) on a seven-point scale on each of which higher scores represented more positive feelings. Those given the additional cognitive task also had to write down the number at this point, to test whether or not they had remembered it.

The free writing was analysed by trained researchers and scored on a seven-point scale, on which an increase in number also reflected more positive emotions. The results showed that it was possible for the participants to control their emotions if they were not burdened with the additional memory task. The writing of those instructed to make their emotions as negative as possible received an average score of 3.81; that of those given no further instruction was given an average score of 3.92; and that of those instructed to make their emotions as positive as possible was given an average score of 4.09. This ability to control emotions disappeared for participants who also had to remember the nine-digit number.

When it came to the participants' self-scoring of the six emotions, this effect of cognitive load was even more pronounced. The six scores for each participant, all of which were framed such that an increase in score reflected an increase in positivity, were added together and then averaged to give a single self-reported score for happiness that ranged between one and seven. The results are shown in Figure 8.3. The participants without the cognitive load of having to remember the nine-digit number were again able to control their emotions, with those having been instructed to make them as negative as possible reporting a happiness score of 4.55, whilst their counterparts who were instructed to make their emotions as positive as possible reported a score of 5.04. Not only did having to remember the number eliminate this ability, it actually reversed the effect of the efforts made by the participants to regulate their emotions. Those instructed to make them negative reported a happiness score of 5.19, whilst those instructed to make them positive reported a less-happy score of

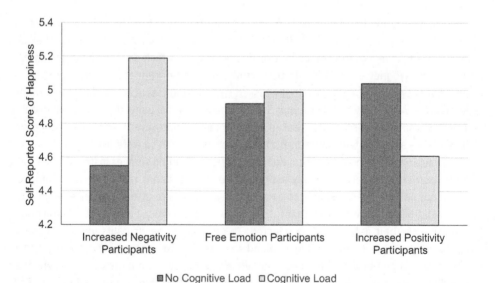

Figure 8.3 Results from the emotion control experiment

4.61. This is another example of the ironic effect, whereby our mental efforts to control our behaviour in some way actually have the opposite impact when we are constrained mentally.

Our pupils are daily beset by emotions. Some are positive, whilst others are negative. Some relate to how they view themselves, whilst others relate to those around them. Some are rational, whilst others are unexplainable, even to themselves. What these studies show is that our pupils' emotions are inextricably linked to their behaviour. If our pupils attempt to either intensify or suppress their feelings, they inadvertently use up more of their limited mental resources, which causes them to feel the effects of decision fatigue and reduces their ability to exert self-control: to concentrate, resist distractions, learn and behave as they know they should. And if their cognitive bandwidths are already taken up with other mental tasks, which is likely in the setting of a classroom and school, they are much less able to control their emotions. In this case, they may even cause the opposite to what they intend when they try to regulate their emotions. It is no wonder that our pupils struggle to learn as we know they could or have outbursts of emotion that seem to come from nowhere.

If our pupils are to maximise their progress in our lessons and schools, and to behave as they know they should, they need the following:

- Safe spaces in which they can release their emotions and teachers who listen to and accept them rather than seem to pass judgement. Only by being able to release their emotions will they be able to focus on their learning and behaviour. By not enabling them to do so, we are backing them into a situation in which they are increasingly unable to control themselves as they know they should.
- Us to recognise when they are struggling emotionally and to remove from them any unnecessary cognitive loads at those times. Piling them with cognitive tasks when they are grappling with emotions is likely to intensify their emotions and to trigger behaviours they regret afterwards, which escalate situations in a way that is completely unnecessary and, ultimately, caused by us.
- Protecting from unnecessary emotional demands at times when they need to particularly focus on their studies. Ashley, a former Sixth Form tutee, is a good example. His parents had gone through a rather unpleasant and hostile separation whilst he was in primary school, which led to the courts prohibiting his father from contacting him. Despite the court injunction, his father periodically attempted to make contact, and every time he did, Ashley's studies suffered. This happened during his SATs and then again during his GCSEs. In the run-up to his final A-level exams, an email appeared in my inbox from his father explaining that he had recently been diagnosed with terminal cancer and was scared he would lose touch with Ashley once the exams were over and Ashley headed off to university. It seemed like a heartfelt plea to be put back in contact with his son. Through discussions between the school's Designated Safeguarding Lead and Ashley's mother, it was decided that I would respond to Ashley's father to explain that I would let Ashley know he had been in touch after Ashley's exams had finished, allowing Ashley to focus on the task ahead. Ashley would also have had his eighteenth birthday by then and so would be able to reciprocate the contact if he chose to do so. I do not know the relational outcome from that situation, but Ashley was grateful for the intervention we took to protect him at such an important and already stressful time.

Our pupils also need to understand this relationship between their emotions and self-control. They need to understand the need for them to release rather than restrain their emotions and to avoid emotional situations when they are cognitively loaded.

8.4 Procrastination – again

Procrastination is a symptom of both decision fatigue and the Rubicon effect, but it is also a behavioural choice, related to our willpower to do what we know we should. And it does not just arise with learning and academic work: we procrastinate in every area of our lives.

Wanting to understand the effects of procrastination on both the standard of what we achieve and our mental wellbeing, Diane Tice and Roy Baumeister invited psychology students to participate in an experiment, 57 of whom volunteered (Tice and Baumeister 1997). At the start of the semester, the students were informed of the submission date for the major piece of coursework for that part of the course. They were also informed that those who were unable to meet the deadline would automatically be granted an extension until a specified later date, and there would also be an exam at the end of the semester. Four weeks into the semester, the students completed Lay's General Procrastination Scale test (Lay 1986), which involved them scoring the extent to which each of 20 statements described them on a scale of one (extremely uncharacteristic) to five (extremely characteristic). Statements included, 'When I am finished with a library book, I return it right away regardless of the date it is due' and 'I always seem to end up shopping for birthday or Christmas gifts at the last minute'. Reversing the scores relating to half of the statements and then adding up the 20 gives the most widely used score of a person's susceptibility to procrastination. The participants also completed checklists about their symptoms of stress and reports about their work requirements and health care appointments throughout the rest of the semester. The participants' coursework was marked by teachers blind to their stress, work and health care reports.

The researchers found that participants who had scored highly for procrastination four weeks into the experiment tended to submit their coursework late, much more so than their counterparts who scored lower for procrastination. Out of the six who missed the first deadline, only one scored below average on Lay's test. Those who scored highly for procrastination also tended to perform less well in both the coursework and the end-of-semester exam. And in terms of health impacts, those who scored highly for procrastination reported fewer symptoms of stress and reported lower workloads and fewer health appointments throughout the majority of the semester than their less procrastinating peers. But these findings were markedly reversed in the final week of the semester when the coursework was due and the exam was looming. As with many of our behaviours, procrastination brings us a short-term gain. It allows us to focus on more enjoyable tasks and reduces our stress levels and feelings of being unwell. However, it comes with two costs. The quality of what we do is ultimately lower when we get around to doing it, and we end up suffering from stress in a more concentrated way. The researchers found that the procrastinators in their study overall experienced more symptoms of stress and attended more stress-related health care appointments than did their less procrastinating peers.

A worrying and surprising trend emerged whilst I coordinated the Extended Project Qualification (EPQ) at a previous boarding school, which involved Sixth Form pupils completing a significant independent research project on a topic of their choice for accreditation equivalent to half of an A level. The pupils knew months in advance the dates for their first draft and final submissions and that, unlike in the Tice and Baumeister study, they were unextendable. However, large numbers of them deliberately chose to leave making their final amendments and additions until the night before the second deadline. They would even prepare for this in advance by moving their desks and chairs from their bedrooms out into the corridors so that they could work together, setting up coffee machines to fuel their all-night efforts and making a trip to the local shop to stock up on sugary provisions. It was as though 'pulling an all-nighter' was something of which to be proud. It was a strange rite of passage. What they did not appreciate was the negative impact of this approach on their final grades for the qualification, their performance in their other subjects and their mental health in the days following their marathon efforts.

On the one hand, it is good for our pupils to experience things such as the EPQ all-nighter. Many of those pupils expressed afterwards their regrets of having taken that approach and explained how they had at least in part succumbed to the planning fallacy and wished they had spread the workload over a longer period of time. Our schools should be places in which our pupils can make mistakes from which they learn and yet are protected by us and the systems we have in place from the full repercussions from doing so. It is better for our pupils to learn the consequences of leaving work until the last minute whilst in a protective Sixth Form than when they are much more on their own at university, for example. However, on the other hand, our pupils need us to teach them the importance of planning their work and doing what they can to overcome their tendencies to procrastinate, such as making a small start on the work to get across their individual Rubicons.

The work of Meng Zhu, Rajesh Bagchi and Stefan Hock casts further light on how we can help our pupils to avoid the consequences of leaving things they need to do until the last minute (Zhu *et al.* 2019). They invited university students to take part in an online study about saving for retirement, from which they received 236 positive responses. The participants had to complete a questionnaire that asked them to describe factors that are important when saving, how they would determine the monthly amount they will need after they have retired and the steps they could take now to increase their savings for the future. They also had to score on a scale of one (not at all) to seven (very) how important it is to save for retirement and how important it was to answer the survey; and to answer a number of questions about things such as their age, sex and marital status. The key to the study was that, in a random fashion, half of the participants were given seven days to complete the questionnaire whilst the other half were given double that time. In order to avoid creating a possible link in the participants' minds between the length of time they had been given to complete the study and the difficulty of completing it, the participants were informed that these deadlines were imposed by the IT server company because it needed to upgrade its systems.

In the end, only 126 of the participants completed the questionnaire before their deadline: 47% of those who had been given the longer deadline and 60% of those who had been given the shorter deadline. The length of the deadline also affected how long it took the participants who managed to complete the questionnaire in time to actually start working on it: 38.75 hours for those given the longer deadline compared to 21.14 hours for those given the shorter deadline. Finally, the length of the deadline also affected the time and effort the participants spent completing the questionnaire. Those who had been given the longer deadline spent an average of 437.3 seconds on completing it and wrote an average of 590.8 characters for the three questions, whereas those with the shorter deadline spent an average of 235.4 seconds on the task and wrote an average of 377.1 characters.

Having a shorter deadline increases the likelihood that we will complete the task set and reduces our susceptibility to procrastination. Knowing time is short, we force ourselves to get the task done much more quickly, whereas we become complacent when we feel time is unconstrained, pushing back making a start on it and ultimately not getting round to it in time. What the study here shows is that a possible reason for this is that we subconsciously think tasks for which we have been given longer deadlines take longer to complete. This intensifies the Rubicon effect, making it more difficult for us to make a start on the task.

Our pupils often ask us for longer deadlines to complete homework, to prepare for applications, to make decisions and to contribute to groups and activities outside the classroom. Sometimes the extra time is genuinely needed, but oftentimes we may actually be doing our pupils a disservice by granting additional time, making it more likely that they fail to complete the tasks on time and that we have to issue sanctions, and increasing the overall stress they feel. Knowing the time pressures borne by pupils, helping them to organise their time and avoid the procrastination trap, and providing advice to their teachers about the individual suitability of different deadlines, are further important roles that should be played by personal tutors. We usually assume our pupils are by nature able to organise their time effectively, but they need our help to do so. They need to be taught about the negative consequences of procrastination, for both their grades and their mental health; the negative effect that asking for longer deadlines and extensions is likely to have on their time management, causing them to procrastinate even more; and the mistake of assuming longer deadlines equate to more time-consuming and resource-costly tasks. They also need to understand the power of tracking their own progress towards their goals, especially longer-term goals. Having a visual representation of their progress can be very motivating, such as a list of the sections in a dissertation they need to write that they put up on a wall and tick when they have completed them. Making this tracker public by showing it to their friends, family or teachers harnesses the power of precommitment strategies and makes this even more effective.

Setting our pupils the Lay's General Procrastination Scale test is a good way to start these conversations. Repeating the test on a routine basis, perhaps annually, also enables us to monitor the progress our pupils make in restraining their tendencies to procrastinate.

It should also be noted that procrastination does not just apply to tasks we dislike or find burdensome. It also applies to enjoyable experiences. In a study by Suzanne Shu and Ayelet Gneezy, 64 undergraduates were each given a voucher for a French pastry restaurant to the value of a slice of cake and a drink (Shu and Gneezy 2010). All they had to do was redeem it. The key to the experiment was that the participants were randomly assigned to two groups, with 32 of them receiving vouchers that had to be redeemed within three weeks and the remaining 32 receiving vouchers that could be redeemed for up to two months. The researchers simply monitored the redemption rates and then sent each of the participants a follow-up survey asking them about their reasons for using or not using the vouchers they had received.

Out of the 32 participants who could use their vouchers for up to two months, only two actually did so: a 6% redemption rate. In comparison, out of the 32 participants who only had three weeks in which to use their vouchers, ten did so: a 31% redemption rate. In the follow-up survey, which was completed by a third of the participants, those who had redeemed their vouchers gave their enjoyment at the restaurant an average score of 5.5 on a scale of one (not at all) to seven (very). In the responses from those who had not used their vouchers, the most commonly selected reasons for not having done so, all scored on seven-point scales from one (do not agree) to seven (strongly agree), were those about them having been too busy (average of 5.76) and them thinking they would do it later (average of 5.0). The researchers point to these patterns in the survey responses as evidence that participants who did not avail themselves of the opportunity to have a free slice of cake and drink did not do so because of procrastination rather than anything else. When we would like our pupils to have an enjoyable experience, such as when we award book vouchers, we should give them short deadlines in which to do so. Setting them longer deadlines is likely to lead to the experiences not being enjoyed and our pupils ultimately feeling a sense of regret, as those who missed their opportunity in the pastry voucher experiment felt.

8.5 Practical takeaways

We can help our pupils to behave well by

- Setting less demanding tasks when they are tiring mentally or face more distractions.
- Challenging unacceptable behaviour at times when our pupils are mentally able to respond well to correction and when we are mentally able to challenge them calmly.
- Helping them to break unhealthy cycles of behaviour, in which they can be trapped.
- Helping to make them accountable for adhering to precommitment strategies.
- Helping them to remember and complete other important things when they are at risk of the tunnelling effect.
- Encouraging them to itemise the important tasks they need to complete in advance.
- Setting them shorter deadlines by which they need to complete work.
- Providing them safe spaces to release their emotions.
- Recognising when they are struggling emotionally and removing unnecessary cognitive demands at those times.
- Protecting them from emotional demands when they need to be especially focused.

Bibliography

Gawande, A., 2010. *The Checklist Manifesto: How to Get Things Right*. London, UK: Profile Books Limited.

Ginè, X., Karlan, D., and Zinman, J., 2010. Put your money where your butt is: A commitment contract for smoking cessation. *American Economics Journal: Applied Economics*, 2 (4), 213-235.

Guerber, H., 1993. *The Myths of Greece and Rome*. New York, USA: Dover.

Lay, C., 1986. At last, my research article on procrastination. *Journal of Research in Personality*, 20, 474-495.

Luckhurst, R., 2006. *A Chronology of Robert Louis Stevenson*. Within R. Luckhurst, ed. Robert *Louis Stevenson: Strange Case of Dr Jekyll and Mr Hyde and Other Tales*. Oxford, UK: Oxford University Press, p. xl.

Mullainathan, S., and Shafir, E., 2014. *Scarcity: The True Cost of Not Having Enough*. London, UK: Penguin.

Muraven, M., Tice, D.M., and Baumeister, R.F., 1998. Self-control as limited resource: Regulatory depletion patterns. *Journal of Personality and Social Psychology*, 74 (3), 774-789.

Oaten, M., and Cheng, K., 2005. Academic exam stress impairs self-control. *Journal of Social and Clinical Psychology*, 24, 254-279.

Schelling, T.C., 1992. Self-command: A new discipline. *In:* J. Elster and G.F. Lowenstein, eds. *Choice Over Time*. New York, USA: Russell Sage Foundation, pp. 167-176.

Shiv, B., and Fedorikhin, A., 1999. Heart and mind in conflict: The interplay of affect and cognition in consumer decision making. *Journal of Consumer Research*, 26 (3), 278-292.

Shu, S.B., and Gneezy, A., 2010. Procrastination of enjoyable experiences. *Journal of Marketing Research*, 47 (5), 933-944.

Tice, D.M., and Baumeister, R.F., 1997. Longitudinal study of procrastination, performance, stress, and health: The costs and benefits of dawdling. *Psychological Science*, 8 (6), 454-458.

Vohs, K.D., *et al.*, 2008. Making choices impairs subsequent self-control: A limited-resource account of decision making, self-regulation, and active initiative. *Journal of Personality and Social Psychology*, 94 (5), 883-898.

Wegner, D.M., Erber, R., and Zanakos, S., 1993. Ironic processes in the mental control of mood and mood-related thought. *Journal of Personality and Social Psychology*, 65 (6), 1093-1104.

Zhu, M., Bagchi, R., and Hock, S.J., 2019. The mere deadline effect: Why more time might sabotage goal pursuit. *Journal of Consumer Research*, 45, 1068-1084.

9 Vicious cycles

Katie was doing absolutely fine as she was approaching the end of her time in the school's Sixth Form. She had worked at a consistently satisfactory level in economics, doing everything I asked of her but not a tremendous amount more than that, and was on course for a B-grade in the subject. But with only a few weeks before she went on study leave, her performance took a downward turn. Having received my feedback about one practice essay, which was considerably below the usual standard of her written work, she submitted a flurry of further essays, giving them to me more quickly than I could turn them around, with the essays becoming progressively worse.

How many times have we seen pupils such as Katie seemingly getting themselves stuck in vicious cycles, either of academic performance or discipline? The causes of these cycles are the focus of this chapter.

9.1 Risk takers and risk lovers

> **Thought experiment: death and salvation**
>
> Imagine you lead the medical authority responsible for a small rural village when you are informed about a disease that is going to strike its population of 600. There are two courses of action available to you: Options A and B. Scientists have precisely estimated that by choosing Option A you will save 200 people, whereas choosing Option B comes with a one-third probability that 600 people will be saved and a two-thirds probability that no-one will be saved. Which option would you choose?
>
> Now reimagine the same scenario but this time with there being a different set of options, C and D. The scientists have precisely estimated that if you choose Option C, 400 people will die, whereas if you choose Option D, there will be a one-third probability that no-one will die and a two-thirds probability that 600 people will die. Which option would you choose in this scenario?

DOI: 10.4324/9781003198505-11

That our minds receive and process information in perhaps unexpected ways, such as through heuristics like the Peak-End Rule, is a key theme running throughout the behavioural sciences. We may intend one thing when we communicate to our pupils, only for them to interpret it in an entirely different manner. And so we should consider carefully how what we say and the actions we take are received and understood. When it comes to effective communication, be it verbal, written or physical, the perceptions of the receiver are more important than the intentions of the originator.

The concept of framing is a central part of this, with there now being a significant body of evidence showing that how we express something dramatically affects the impact of what we are trying to convey. A classic example of this from teaching, often used in teacher training courses, is the impact of perceived gender-specific applications on the outcomes of assessment for learning. Experiments have been conducted in which classes were set one of two mathematical assessments that were identical in all respects apart from the applications used, with the questions in the first being applied to a topic that is traditionally deemed to be female-orientated and those in the second being applied to a topic traditionally thought to be male-orientated. Removing the effects of everything apart from the assessment set, such as the mathematical ability of pupils and their ages, has shown that girls tend to perform better in the first assessment whilst boys tend to perform better in the second. Even though the actual questions are identical, down to the numbers used, pupils tend to perform better in the assessment based on topics in which they are traditionally thought to be more interested and which they can access more readily. How our assessments are framed distorts their results.

The two sets of options in the death and salvation thought experiment box are identical. They are just worded differently, with those in the first scenario expressing the outcomes of the two available medical options in terms of the number of people who will be saved and those in the second scenario expressing the outcomes of the two options in terms of the number of people who will be lost. They are just different ways of describing the same outcomes. And so logically, you should have chosen the same option in each scenario: Option C if you had chosen Option A previously and Option D if you had chosen Option B previously. But that is not how our minds work. Amos Tversky and Daniel Kahneman tested an almost identical set of scenarios and options on students at the University of British Columbia (Tversky and Kahneman 1981). From the 152 students who were asked about the first scenario, 72% chose Option A and 28% Option B. From the 155 students who were asked about the second scenario, 22% chose Option C and 78% chose Option D. There was an almost perfect reversal of responses despite the options being identical.

The reason we make choices in this way lies yet again with us being naturally loss averse, feeling the negative impact of losing something almost twice as acutely as we feel the positive impact of gaining that very same thing. The two-thirds probability that no-one will be saved in the first scenario tends to scare us into choosing Option A because we know that we will feel that loss greatly when we have the sure bet option of saving 200 people. Whereas in the second scenario it is the sure bet option of losing 400 people that tends to scare us into taking the gamble. Our decisions in both scenarios tend to be driven by our eagerness to avoid feeling loss. And these findings do not just arise from university students thinking about a rather unrealistic situation to which they probably struggle to relate. An almost identical task was set for experienced and professional financial advisors by Robert Olsen

(1997). The probabilities used in Olsen's study were the same as those earlier but applied to saving and losing proportions of a client's $60,000 investment. In Scenario One, 65% of these experienced professionals selected Option A and 35% Option B. In Scenario Two, 32% selected Option C and 68% Option D. That our choices reverse due to loss aversion is known as the reflection effect.

Key term: reflection effect

We make an opposite choice between uncertain outcomes when the outcomes are expressed as potential losses than when they are expressed as potential gains, even when the outcomes are identical.

That we all tend to make decisions characterised by the reflection effect is important because it shows how much risk we take when we feel we are already in a situation of either gain or loss. This can be seen in Figure 6.1. Consider a pupil who has achieved something positive and so is already set to receive one reward, whatever that might be. That pupil is already anticipating a gain of five. Taking a risk in order to make it two rewards would, if it works out, lead to an increase in the pupil's anticipated gain of two. If it does not work out, though, and she ends up forfeiting the reward she already has coming to her, her anticipated gain would be eliminated. Faced with a potential loss of five and a possible further gain of two, it makes little sense for her to take the risk, and so she will settle for what she has already achieved. Now consider a different pupil, who has done something wrong and so is already expecting to receive a sanction. That pupil is already feeling a loss of ten. Taking a risk in order to avoid the sanction would, if successful, eliminate her feeling of loss: essentially a gain of ten. If it is not successful, though, and it ends up making the situation worse and eliciting a second sanction, her feeling of loss would be increased by three. Faced with a possible gain of ten and a possible further loss of three, it makes sense for her to take the gamble. We are naturally risk averse when we feel we have already gained something and naturally risk loving when we feel we have already lost something.

This explains the experience of Joe and his friends at a previous school. For whatever reason, and quite unlike them, they decided to superglue a Pound coin to a desk at the school – to a desk that was rather old and of some value. Realising the coin was not going to come off easily and no doubt thinking about the reaction of the teacher in whose classroom the table was kept, they decided to use a compass to lever it up and off. To their horror, this only served to gouge holes into the desk. But they did not stop there. Instead, they attempted to dissolve the glue by pouring hot water over and around the coin. Sadly that failed to work as well, and it even took off a whole patch of the varnish in the centre of the desk. Finding themselves in a situation of loss, Joe and his peers took one risk after another as they attempted to get themselves out of a situation, which they ended up escalating. This also explains why Katie, at the start of this chapter, got herself into such a negative spiral as she tried to eliminate her feeling of having underperformed and why gamblers can quickly lose everything they own.

It is important that we educate our pupils about their natural tendency to take more risks when they are already feeling loss and about the techniques they can adopt to offset the effects from doing so. Only by being aware of this behavioural trait can they avoid the situation in which their academic performance spirals downwards or in which a disciplinary situation escalates. In the academic situation, our pupils should deliberately give themselves time to reflect on the reasons they underperformed on the last task, be it an essay in the case of Katie or an activity within class, before trying again. They should first ask themselves whether or not they truly know the reasons for their low performance. If they do, they should create a plan of how they are going to address them before they start the next piece. If they do not, they should ask a teacher for feedback or clarification before doing anything else. Taking a measured and deliberate approach can turn a situation that has the potential to spiral downwards into a cycle of improvement. In the disciplinary situation, our pupils should ask themselves whether they are considering taking the next step because it will go at least some way to making amends for the damage they have already done, whatever that may be, or they are considering it as a potentially easy way of avoiding blame and sanction. Only if it is truly a step towards making amends should they take it. Helping our pupils to develop such thought processes can be invaluable for them in navigating the situations in which they find themselves.

It is equally important for us to educate our pupils about their natural tendency to avoid taking risks when they are feeling a sense of gain. This explains why some pupils seem to become reluctant to participate in a lesson once they have already made a correct contribution. They feel as though they are already in a positive position with us, which they are reluctant to jeopardise by taking further risks. Being aware of this tendency and then challenging themselves to consider the wider benefits for themselves from continuing to test their understanding can enable them to maximise their learning in these situations.

We can also help our pupils to consciously control their decisions in situations such as these through the feedback we give to them. In terms of academic performance, a loss can quickly lead to a larger loss when pupils focus on the whole task. Narrowing our focus and feedback so that it encapsulates a particular part of the task in which a pupil can more easily succeed can transform a situation in which a pupil experiences another large loss into one in which the pupil experiences a small gain. A small boost can break the vicious cycle, at which point the focus can be gradually widened in a way that enables the pupil to achieve success at the whole task through a sequence of smaller successes. Another element in promoting academic performance involves us creating environments in which a success cannot be cancelled out by a failure and in which failures arising from genuine attempts to learn are themselves rewarded. Switching the focus of praise and reward from the outcomes of what pupils do to the desired actions themselves removes the sense of uncertainty and so nullifies the effect of loss aversion on their behaviour. It also promotes the growth mindset advocated by Carol Dweck (2017).

9.2 The vicious effects of scarcity

Jayden in Section 1.7 suffered the effects of a different vicious cycle: that caused by scarcity, which in Jayden's case arose from the death of his father. During the holidays, he would stand at the gate of his father's house, expecting that at any moment his father would walk through the front door. Understandably, he felt there was something missing from his life, in his case something very significant, and this took up his thoughts and attention. As a result, he was constantly tired, he was usually disengaged in lessons and he rarely completed the homework he was set, all of which led to an escalating disciplinary situation.

The effects of scarcity can be seen in the results of a study conducted by Anandi Mani, Sendhil Mullainathan, Eldar Shafir and Jiaying Zhao on 96 shoppers in a shopping centre in New Jersey (Mani *et al.* 2013). The participants were divided into two groups, rich and poor, based on their annual household incomes, of which the average was $70,000 and the lowest was $20,000. Each of the participants, across both groups, was presented with four scenarios, one of which was as follows:

> Your car is having some trouble and requires $X to be fixed. You can pay in full, take a loan, or take a chance and forego the service at the moment. . . . How would you go about making this decision?

The cost of the work required is left unspecified because half of the participants were randomly assigned a high cost for each scenario, in this case $1,500, and the other half a low cost, in this case $150. Participants responded to each scenario and then completed a set of nonverbal computer-based tasks, requiring them to identify missing shapes in given sequences. The results were clear. Rich and poor participants had similar levels of performance on the follow-up mental tasks when given low-cost scenarios but poor participants performed worse than rich participants when given high-cost scenarios.

The scenarios were deliberately designed to make the participants think about their own, real-life, financial situations. The results suggest they certainly had that effect. Those from poorer households, with incomes between $20,000 and $70,000, were no doubt troubled by the thought of an additional $1,500 bill, which may well have also brought real-life financial concerns and pressures back into their minds. Such a bill would have been much less concerning for their counterparts from households enjoying incomes in excess of $70,000. When it came to completing the shape identification tasks, poor participants finding themselves in the high-cost scenarios fixated much more on their financial problems than rich participants facing the same scenarios. And having their minds fixated on their feelings of financial scarcity occupied their cognitive bandwidths, leaving less room for them to use for the computer-based tasks. Their feeling of scarcity led to poorer performance.

That this is not just a product of the artificial shopping centre setting was shown in a subsequent study by the same researchers, for which 464 sugarcane farmers were randomly selected from across 54 villages in the southern Indian state of Tamil Nadu. Sugarcane farming is a natural field experiment of scarcity because there is only a single harvest, so farmers have a relatively large amount of money after the harvest and a relatively small amount in the run-up to it. Within a matter of weeks, sugarcane farmers go from a situation of financial scarcity to one of relative abundance. Before the harvest in 2010, for example, 99% of the farmers involved in the study had taken out a loan, whereas that figure after the harvest was only 13%. These farmers were asked to complete the same shape identification task as that used in the New Jersey shopping centre, some before the harvest and others after it. The results mirrored those in the previous study, with the farmers answering on average 4.35 questions correctly before the harvest and 5.45 correctly afterwards.

That scarcity does not just affect our behaviour when it relates to our finances was shown in an earlier study by Mullainathan and Shafir, this time with Anuj Shah (Shah *et al.* 2012). In this experiment, 68 people played a game similar to that of Angry Birds, in which they used a slingshot to hit targets. The scarcity the players faced related to the number of shots they were able to make, with 'rich' players having 150 shots (15 per round) and 'poor' players having only 30 (three per round). Some of the players, both rich and poor, were able to borrow shots for the current round, but for every shot they borrowed, their remaining budget was reduced by two. The other players simply had to play within their allotted budgets each round. They all played until they had exhausted their budgets and were incentivised by a possibility of winning a prize that increased with the number of targets they hit.

The researchers were particularly interested in how much care the players took when making their shots, which they measured by the amount of time the players spent lining them up. What the researchers found, perhaps unsurprisingly, was that poor players spent longer lining-up their shots than did their less constrained counterparts. And this extra care paid off for them, with poor players scoring on average 2.31 points per shot compared to the 1.67 average achieved by the 'richer' players. They also found that poor players borrowed significantly more shots than the rich, borrowing on average 24% of their budgets compared to the rich's 2%. But this borrowing was counterproductive: the rich had a similar level of success whether or not they could borrow, whereas the poor actually performed better when they were not able to borrow. The final finding was that the amount of shots borrowed by the poor in a given round of the game was related to the amount of time they spent lining-up their shots in that game. The more they focused on their shots, the more shots they borrowed.

What all of this shows is that a feeling of scarcity can be both a curse and a blessing. When we feel as though we are missing something, we tend to fixate on it just as Jayden did. This can be of benefit to us as it can help us to perform better at the related task. When we feel we have less time than we need to meet a deadline, for example, we can end up scoring better for that piece of work as we deliberately try to make the available time count. This has become known as the focus dividend. However, by fixating on what we feel we are missing, we more quickly deplete our mental resources and so suffer more severely the effects of decision fatigue. Dwelling on something that is worrying us is exhausting and ultimately means we cannot complete as many mental tasks. Fixating on our scarcity also diverts our mental resources away from the other tasks we need to complete, effectively reducing our available cognitive bandwidth and our ability to perform other tasks. In the Angry Birds experiment, for instance, scarcity caused players to make poorer judgements about the amount of shots they borrowed than they otherwise would have made. They prioritised the current round they were playing too much. This is the tunnelling effect at work again. It is no wonder that faced with a loss as great as his, Jayden was simply unable to function at school, was simply unable to complete the tasks he was set and, ultimately, ended up wearing out the patience of his teachers and finding himself in an escalating disciplinary situation. If only we had understood the impossible mental situation in which he found himself.

> ### Key term: focus dividend
>
> We naturally tend to focus more on tasks for which the resources at our disposal are limited, ensuring we extract as much benefit from those resources as possible.

There is little that a pupil in Jayden's situation can do. An adult who understands the psychological reasons why the feeling of scarcity is impacting on his everyday life the way it does would find it difficult to mentally overcome it alone, much less a pupil who is having to grapple with all of the other pressures of growing up. Equally, there is little that classroom teachers can do to help a pupil in this situation, with all the other pupils in their classes, although it is important for teachers to be sensitive to the pressures being felt by their pupils. This is an area in which personal tutors, who meet regularly with small numbers of pupils on a one-to-one basis, and school counsellors are so important. Pupils need to be in the right place mentally if they are to learn in lessons. They need to be able to focus on the content and skills that they are being taught, free from the effects of as many wider pressures as possible. And so it is important that schools provide the support required for each of their pupils to be in such a place. Without that, lessons are likely to be ineffective.

9.3 The Zeigarnik effect

Almost 100 undergraduate students participated in a short experiment for E. Masicampo and Roy Baumeister, in which they completed two experimental tasks either as individuals or in small groups (Masicampo and Baumeister 2011). They were each given five minutes to complete the first task, which simply involved them solving as many of the 25 anagrams they were given as they could. They then moved onto the second task, in which they had five minutes to think of as many items in a category as they could. Before they started the first task, they were randomly assigned to one of three groups. Those selected for the control group were told what the second task was going to involve and were advised to work through the letters of the alphabet logically. They were not told what the category would be. Those selected for the goal group were told what the second task was going to involve, were given the same advice as those in the control group and were told the category would be sea creatures. Those selected for the planning group were told what the task was going to involve and that it would focus on sea creatures and were asked to commit themselves to using the alphabetical approach when they got to it.

The researchers found that adopting the alphabetical approach was not significantly helpful for the participants, but that committing to a plan for solving the second task was. On average, those in the goal group solved 6.55 anagrams successfully, whilst those in the control and planning groups on average got 8.39 and 9.55 correct, respectively. Knowing the focus of the second task but not having to commit to a plan for succeeding at it reduced the participants' ability to concentrate on, and succeed at, the preceding task. As with scarcity, having an unfinished task diverts our mental resources away from other tasks. The only thing that can seemingly offset this is committing to a plan for how we are going to finish the task. Having a meaningless plan, to which we are not fully committed, does not help.

That we tend to focus a greater amount of our mental resources on unfulfilled tasks and goals is known as the Zeigarnik effect after the Lithuanian psychologist Bluma Zeigarnik who first studied it in the 1920s after hearing a professor at the University of Berlin talk about her observation that waiters in a local cafè appeared to remember tabs that were still to be settled more accurately than tabs that had been paid. It also accounts for the brain worm effect, when we play music over and over in our minds having only heard a snippet of it. If we cannot complete something, our brains continue to work on it, often without us being aware of them doing so. That our brains do this can be beneficial as it can lead to a type of focus dividend when the answer to a problem we have been trying to solve seemingly pops randomly into our minds at a later time. This often happens when we are doing something that is mentally untaxing such as showering or driving. It can also help us when we need to remember relevant information, such as in the case of the Berlin waiters. However, it can also have a negative effect if it detracts from more important mental tasks.

Key term: Zeigarnik effect

We naturally tend to devote a greater amount of our mental resources to unfinished tasks.

Every Autumn Term, I see Year 13 pupils struggling to concentrate on their work because they are yet to complete and submit, or hear back about, their university applications and it is playing on their minds. And every Autumn Term, I see pupils in this situation fall behind on their school work, which creates further unfinished tasks that widen and prolong the source of their distraction. Not only are they suffering from the Zeigarnik effect, they quickly find themselves in the situation in which the effect escalates, increasing the stress and anxiety they feel. It was originally thought that their only escape lay in completing the task, ticking it off their mental list of things to do and allowing their minds to let it go. However, the work of Masicampo and Baumeister shows that is not the case and that by making a plan about how and when they are going to complete the task, and then committing to implementing that plan when the time arises, they can also find a sense of release. Such planning does not alter the emotions our pupils feel - they will still feel anxious about the unfilled tasks - but it does allow them to concentrate on other things.

We can help pupils who find themselves in such a situation to avoid becoming trapped in vicious cycles by guiding them through the planning process and then holding them to account for their implementation, forcing them to commit to their plans. We can also empower our pupils to do this for themselves by teaching them how to identify the onset of the Zeigarnik effect in their lives, through signs such as having difficulties when trying to concentrate, a mind that keeps returning to a particular task and interrupted sleep, and how to create a plan to offset it. We can equally benefit from this.

9.4 Practical takeaways

We can help our pupils to get the most out of the learning tasks we set them, and to avoid vicious cycles in which they can potentially become trapped, by

- Encouraging them to reflect on both the causes of any failure before taking steps to overcome it and their motivation for taking those further steps.
- Focusing our feedback for improvement on a narrower part of the task, increasing the chances that pupils will be able to respond to it successfully.
- Not creating an environment in which failures of pupils cancel out their successes.
- Focusing our encouragement, praise and rewards on our pupils' actions rather than on the outcomes of those actions.
- Helping them to come to terms with the feelings of loss and scarcity in their lives.
- Guiding them through the process of creating and committing to a plan of action for completing unfinished tasks.

Bibliography

Dweck, C.S., 2017. *Mindset – Updated Edition: Changing the Way You Think to Fulfil Your Potential*. London, UK: Robinson.

Mani, A., *et al.*, 2013. Poverty impedes cognitive function. *Science*, 341, 976-980.

Masicampo, E.J., and Baumeister, R.F., 2011. Consider it done! Plan making can eliminate the cognitive effects of unfulfilled goals. *Journal of Personality and Social Psychology*, 101 (4), 667-683.

Olsen, R.A., 1997. Prospect theory as an explanation of risky choice by professional investors: Some evidence. *Review of Financial Economics*, 6, 225-232.

Shah, A.K., Mullainathan, S., and Shafir, E., 2012. Some consequences of having too little. *Science*, 338, 682-685.

Tversky, A., and Kahneman, D., 1981. The framing of decisions and the psychology of choice. *Science*, 211 (4481), 453-458.

10 Nudges

Introduced in the now-famous book by legal scholar/economist double-act Cass Sunstein and Richard Thaler in 2009, the idea of using nudges to influence our decisions has become an important part of public policy. Nudging is also widely used in the business world, with popular books on nudge management, inclusive nudging and nudge change management. And it is even being advocated for self-help and self-improvement. As is often the case, schools are lagging behind.

Much misunderstanding surrounds nudging, though. With Sunstein and Thaler also coining the term 'libertarian paternalism' for their proposed policies, a nudge needs to satisfy an important criterion: it needs to leave the choices available to us completely unchanged. It cannot restrict our options, and it cannot make any of them either more or less attractive. A nudge is libertarian. Instead, a nudge works by changing the way the options are presented to us or the way we actually make our choice. In the words of Sunstein and Thaler, it involves changing the 'choice architecture' in a given situation in which we make a decision. Sunstein and Thaler also envisaged a nudge being used to encourage us to make decisions that are better for us, for one another and for the world in which we live. Throughout this book we have explored the ways in which we struggle on a daily basis to make good decisions; the ways our decision-making is characterised by cognitive traits that, in the distant past, used to benefit us in our competition for natural selection; and the ways we suffer from our mental resources being insufficient for the challenge of modern life. Sunstein and Thaler intended governments to integrate nudging into their public policies to help people to overcome these mental difficulties and to live happier lives. A nudge should be paternalistic.

Key term: nudge

A policy used to change our decisions by altering the way, or the order, in which available options are presented to us, leaving the actual options unchanged.

The use of plastic bags in the UK offers a good illustration of the power of nudging. In 2014, over 7.6 billion single-use carrier bags were given to shoppers by major supermarkets despite families typically having around 40 carrier bags lying around in their homes. This

DOI: 10.4324/9781003198505-12

amounted to 140 plastic bags per person and to over 61,000 tonnes of plastic (UK Department for Environment, Food and Rural Affairs 2021). With growing awareness of the environmental damage caused by plastic, driven by the documentaries of David Attenborough and the images of turtles having drowned from becoming entangled in plastic and suffering from plastic straws lodged in their mouths and noses, the UK government introduced a mandatory five pence charge for each carrier bag provided by large retailers. Since the tax was introduced, the number of plastic carrier bags used has declined by 95%, and nearly £180 million has been generated for public spending: an unmitigated policy success. However, the five pence charge is not an example of a nudge as it violates the libertarian criterion by making the option of taking a new carrier bag more expensive. It has changed the nature of the options available to us when we find ourselves at a checkout. It is also highly unlikely that five pence is sufficient to deter people from taking a bag when the average cost of a single shop in UK supermarkets in 2020 ranged from £42.67 at Lidl to £68.69 at Waitrose (Statista 2021). The nudging parts of this policy, which more likely explain its success, were the requirement for customers to ask for carrier bags rather than to simply tear them from the reel in the packing area and the change in societal attitudes engendered by the policy, with it becoming 'the done thing' to take our own bags.

Many examples of nudges, for both our pupils and ourselves, have already been examined in the preceding chapters. For example, the importance of considering the order in which we mark work to ensure pupils receive objective feedback; the motivational power of giving pupils (or teachers) a reward before they have achieved a target on the understanding that it will be removed if the target is not met, thereby taking advantage of the endowment effect; and the impact of changing the way we frame the options from which pupils choose, taking advantage of the reflection effect. Despite nudging being used widely for non-paternalistic purposes, oftentimes profit-making and sometimes nefarious, it is a potentially powerful set of tools for schools and teachers that is currently underutilised, especially in classrooms, corridors, playgrounds and assembly halls. The evidence about using nudges in education is rapidly expanding, but it has tended to focus on strategies for increasing school enrollment and parental take-up of financial aid, and reducing drop-out rates. Relatively little work has so far been done on nudges to improve the academic performance of pupils. The purpose of this chapter is to outline a range of nudge types that could be fruitfully used for this.

10.1 Social nudges

'Oh my God, there's a face watching us' exclaimed Sophie, one of my Year Ten economics pupils, halfway through a lesson in which we were looking at some of the problems with free markets. This was one of the highlights of my teaching career to date.

The 48 members of the Psychology Department at the University of Newcastle were accustomed to paying for their teas and coffees using an honesty box placed in the kitchen, having done so for several years. Whenever they made a drink, all they needed to do was to place some money into the box to cover the cost. During a ten-week-long field experiment, Melissa Bateson, Daniel Nettle and Gilbert Roberts placed images above the drink-making equipment, alternating on a weekly basis between images of eyes that were directly looking towards the drink-maker and images of flowers (Bateson *et al.* 2006). The researchers then simply added up the contributions and compared them to milk usage each week. They found that in weeks in which the images were of eyes, the psychologists contributed almost three times as much (averaging 42 pence per litre of milk used) as in weeks in which the images were of flowers (averaging 15 pence per litre). Through experiments such as these, it has become well-established that we behave more honestly when we feel as though someone is watching us, even if it is only by an image of eyes. This effect has also been recorded on our litter clearing and our sorting of recycling (see Ernest-Jones *et al.* 2011; Francey and Bergmüller 2012, respectively).

The reason Sophie made my day by exclaiming that she was being watched was because, unbeknownst to her and her class, I had propped up a coconut on a bookshelf at the front of the room, and it was simply the downward pointing triangle of three coconut eyes that she noticed out of the corner of her eye. There is clearly something to the study that suggested even such abstract representations of eyes have honesty-enhancing effects.

Not only do we change our behaviour when we feel we are being observed, we also base our decisions at least in part on what others are doing. Leon Festinger, an American social psychologist, first introduced this idea in 1954 when he was working at the University of Minnesota. According to Festinger's social comparison theory, we look at those around us when we want to judge ourselves in some way or when we are lacking the objective information we need to make a decision. In one of the many studies that have looked at this, Rachel Croson and Jen (Yue) Shang conducted a field experiment based on three fund-raising campaigns by an undisclosed radio station on the east coast of America in 2003 (Croson and Shang 2008). In the experiment, 225 existing donors were divided randomly into three groups. Before they made their renewal decisions, those assigned to Group One were each informed that the amount they had donated in the previous year had just been exceeded by another donor. Those assigned to Group Two were informed that their contributions in the previous year were greater than an amount just given by another donor. And those assigned to Group Three were informed that their contributions in the previous year had just been exactly matched by another donor. The researchers found that those in Group One increased their donations compared to the previous year by an average of $12.08, those in Group Two reduced theirs by an average of $24.05 and those in Group Three increased theirs by an average of $5.46

Following studies such as this, Elaine Gallagher, at the time a doctoral student in the Department of Psychology at the University of Bath, recorded the length of time fellow students showered in their university accommodation over a number of weeks. Each of the participants in the study was then randomly told that they were either spending more or less time showering than the average for the group as a whole. As has come to be expected, providing such social information caused those involved to change their behaviour. Those informed that they were taking longer than the average went on to reduce their shower times, whilst those informed that they were taking less time than the average went on to increase theirs (University of Bath 2021). That the use of such social information works both ways is important for nudge design, as is the knowledge that there are two types of social information: descriptive, which provides information about what others are doing, and injunctive, which provides information about what is deemed acceptable or unacceptable.

The Petrified Forest National Park in Arizona covers 346 square miles of fossilised ancient woodland and a colourful barren area known as the Painted Desert. Scattered throughout are logs seamed with quartz of the most astonishing reds, yellows and blues, all of which have been there for 200 million years (National Geographic). It is no wonder the area suffers from the theft of more than a tonne of wood by visitors each month. To test the impact of the two different types of social information, Robert Cialdini and colleagues placed secretly marked pieces of petrified wood alongside visitor trails throughout the national park (Cialdini 2003). On five consecutive weekends, the researchers also placed one of two signs at the entrance to the trails. The descriptive sign read 'Many past visitors have removed petrified wood from the Park, changing the natural state of the Petrified Forest' whilst the injunctive sign read 'Please don't remove the petrified wood from the Park, in order to preserve the natural state of the Petrified Forest.' Over the five-week study, the descriptive sign resulted in the theft of 7.92% of the marked wood, whereas only 1.67% of the wood associated with the injunctive sign was stolen. Comparing these figures to the usual 3% rate of theft demonstrates that descriptive signs that highlight the prevalence of undesirable behaviour actually worsen behaviour.

At the start of each new year, a colleague harnesses the power of both social norms and precommitment strategies to motivate her classes. She does this by asking her classes to formulate and agree on group objectives and to commit to one another to work towards achieving them. This is precisely one of the strategies recommended by the UK's Behavioural Insights Team for increasing environmental sustainability on university campuses (United Nations Environment Programme, GRIDArendal and Behavioural Insights Team 2020).

10.2 Fun nudges

As startling as the eye image experiments are, combining impact with simplicity, the most famous nudge is that introduced at Schiphol Airport in the early 1990s. No doubt frustrated by the amount of cleaning that was needed in the male toilets at the airport, Jos van Bedaf suggested to his colleague, Aad Kieboom, that he should place images of flies in the urinal bowls to create something at which users could aim. Repeated in numerous locations, the introduction of such images has been shown to reduce 'spillage' by 50% to 80% and cleaning costs by 8% to 20%. The only condition for success seems to be that the image is something at which users want to aim. The University of Louisville in Kentucky, for example, has seen great effects by using the emblem of the rival University of Kentucky instead of flies (Evans-Pritchard 2013).

Volkswagen introduced a similarly fun nudge in 2009 when it installed the 'piano staircase' in Odenplan subway station in Stockholm on which each step made a different sound when weight was placed on it in the same way the keys of a piano make a sound when pressed. Although it was primarily intended as a piece of advertising, the staircase had the immediate effect of encouraging commuters to take the stairs rather than the escalator, increasing the use of the healthier option by 66%. Similar staircases have since been installed in cities around the world, including Milan, Melbourne, Istanbul and Auckland, and studies show that they may even induce more long-term, positive behavioural change (Peeters *et al.* 2013).

A third example of a fun nudge is the ballot bin, introduced by the London-based environmental charity Hubbub. Rather than consisting of a single receptacle in which people can place their litter, the ballot bin has numerous transparent receptacles each labelled with the answer to a popular question. And so, by placing litter in the bin, a person can both cast and see their vote in answer to the question posed. The original ballot bin reduced the number of smokers who threw their cigarette butts onto Villiers Street by 20% and subsequent ballot bins around the world have reduced litter by up to 46% (see Hubbub).

10.3 Personalised nudges

A field experiment by the UK's Behavioural Insights Team in collaboration with the UK's Courts Service focused on the collection of fines that had been issued by courts but had not been paid (Haynes *et al.* 2012). All of those included in the study had received distress warrants, meaning they had reached the stage of being notified in writing that either they would be arrested or bailiffs would be appointed to collect the money outstanding through forceful confiscation of personal items. In the initial trial, 1,054 people in this situation were randomly assigned to various groups. Those in the control group were treated as usual by the courts, whilst those in two of the other groups each received either a generic or personalised text message about the need to pay their fine. The researchers found that 5% of those in the usual treatment group responded to the courts, compared to 23% of those who received the generic text message and 33% of those who received the personalised text message. In a follow-up study involving 3,633 people in this situation, the researchers found that not only did receipt of a personalised message increase response rate, it also increased the average amount of money paid to the courts by more than 30%.

The power of personalising nudges is reinforced by another Behavioural Insights Team collaboration, this time with the London Offices of Deutsche Bank (UK Cabinet Office: The Behavioural Insights Team and the Charities Aid Foundation 2013). The aim was to help the bank increase the amount of money its employees gave to the 'Help a Capital Child' campaign and to Meningitis Research UK. The bank's existing scheme asked employees to donate amounts of money equal to their salaries for a day, which the bank would match. On the morning of the charity appeal day, employees randomly received from the company's CEO either a generic email, addressed to 'Dear colleague', or an email addressing them personally by name, encouraging them to donate to the chosen causes. Depending on the office they worked in, some were also exposed to posters advertising the causes, volunteers handing out flyers about the causes or volunteers handing out sweets as a small thank you for their later participation. Amongst those who only received the generic email, 5% donated a day of their salary. Amongst those who received the personalised email, 12% donated a day of their salary. The addition of the small thank you increased these figures to 11% and 17%, respectively. The personalised message coupled with the small thank you gesture more than tripled the donation rate and, had it been used with all employees, would have increased the overall amount raised by Deutsche Bank that day from more than £500,000 to more than £1 million.

Countless studies across a range of different settings and involving a range of different decisions now exist that show the power of targeting nudges at individuals and addressing them by name, particularly when encouraging them to perform administrative tasks. Dominique Morisano and colleagues have also published evidence that personalised goal-setting has positive effects on student academic performance (Morisano *et al.* 2010). In their study, 85 students at McGill University who had reported that they were struggling academically were randomly separated into two groups. Each of those in the first group completed a two-and-a-half-hour online course consisting of eight steps that helped them to set personal goals and detailed strategies for achieving them. Each of those in the second group instead completed three tasks: a series of personality trait questionnaires, a task in which they had to write about a positive experience in their past and a career suitability survey. After the 16-week study period had elapsed, they all completed a concluding questionnaire about their experiences of participating in the study, and their grade transcripts from before and after the study period were compared. The researchers found that the academic performance of those in Group One improved by a grade point average of 0.8: a sizeable effect given the GPA scale goes from one to four. Furthermore, none of those in Group One dropped below full-time study in the following semester, compared to 20% of those in Group Two. And those in Group One reported an improvement in their feelings about their studies.

10.4 Ease nudges

Possibly the most widely used and most studied nudge takes advantage of our omission predisposition, of the finding that we naturally prefer inaction to action in order to reduce the number of decisions we have to make and the decision fatigue we subsequently feel. It is the nudge of changing the default option: the course of action that is taken unless we deliberately choose otherwise.

A problem faced by health services around the world is that of them not having enough organs to use in transplant operations. In the UK in 2012, for example, over 1,300 patients either died or saw their health deteriorate to the point of being unable to receive a transplant whilst waiting for suitable organs to be donated (NHS Blood and Transplant 2013). Statistics such as these have led countries to change their organ donation registers from being opt-in registers, in which citizens are not registered as donors unless they explicitly take action to do so, to being opt-out registers, in which citizens are registered as donors unless they explicitly take action to be withdrawn. In an online experiment, 161 respondents were asked to assume that they had recently moved to a new state and were asked whether or not they were willing to donate their organs if they were to die (Johnson and Goldstein 2003). The participants were asked to further assume one of three things about the nature of the organ donation register in the state to which they had moved, that it was either an opt-in register, an opt-out register or a register in which there was no default. The subsequent donation rate in the opt-out scenario was almost double that in the opt-in scenario: an effect that can be seen in the actual organ donor registration rates across countries with opt-out and opt-in registers.

Peter Bergman and Todd Rogers demonstrate the potential power of switching a system from being one in which those targeted have to opt-in to one in which they have to opt-out in their 2014 field experiment into the impact of parental communication on pupil performance (Bergman and Rogers 2017). Working with 12 middle and high schools in Washington, DC, which together covered almost 7,000 pupils, the researchers studied the impact of a system that alerted parents by weekly text messages from the school if their children had missed any classes, failed to submit assignments on time and/or were scoring less than 70% in one or more of their subjects. Within each of the schools, pupils were randomly assigned to one of four groups. The parents of those in Group One were sent a text message inviting them to use a link on the school's website to enrol in the alert system. The parents of those in Group Two were sent a text message inviting them to enrol in the alert system simply by replying to the text message with 'start'. The parents of those in Group Three were automatically enrolled in the alert system and were informed that they could opt-out of it at any time by replying to an alert with 'stop'. Finally, the parents of those in Group Four, the control group, could view the academic performance of their children on the school's parent portal at any time as usual and could sign up for the alert system on the website, but were not sent messages inviting them to do so.

Following the findings from the organ donation experiment presented earlier, the rates of parental enrollment in the alert system were 1% in Group One, 8% in Group Two and 96% in Group Three. Of greater interest, though, is the impact of the system on pupil performance. For the pupils in Groups One and Two, there were no noticeable effects on their performance compared to those in the control group. This is explained by the low parental enrollment rate for those in Group One and the observation that those parents of pupils in Group Two who enrolled tended to have higher-performing children and were more likely to access the parent portal in the first place (only about 30% of parents had ever logged into the portal prior to the experiment): they were not the parents whom the schools most wanted to participate. For the pupils in Group Three, though, alerting parents to these different concerns led to a reduction in course failure of approximately 10% and to an improvement in pupil performance equal to about a third of a grade in one of their subjects. By employing an opt-out system, the researchers and schools were able to engage the parents they most wanted to participate in the system, who would not have done so otherwise. And this harnessed their influence, possibly without them even realising it was doing so, and led to improved outcomes for their children.

The finding that by harnessing parental engagement, schools can improve the performance and achievements of pupils is not unique to the Bergman and Rogers study. In an earlier experiment, conducted during a 2010 summer programme for incoming Year Seven and Year Ten pupils at a middle and high school in Boston, Massachusetts, Matthew Kraft and Shaun Dougherty found a similar result (Kraft and Dougherty 2013). During the programme, 140 pupils were divided into 14 classes, seven of which were treatment groups and seven were control groups. Each of the parents of those in the treatment groups received a daily phone call for five consecutive days during the second week of the programme, through which they were given an update about the progress and behaviour of their child, a description of the homework tasks and tests that were coming up and a suggestion for something their child should continue to do well or even try to improve on. Each of the pupils in the treatment groups also received a daily text message during this five-day period that reiterated the suggestion given to their parents. For fairness and in order to gain parental permission for the study, pupils in the control groups received such text messages, and their parents such phone calls, in the third week of the programme. To assess the impact of this communication, 16 lesson observers were trained to record for each lesson they observed the number of times the teacher had to redirect pupils' attention and the number of times pupils participated. These observers were randomly assigned to lessons in pairs and were kept blind to whether they were observing treatment or control groups. Pupils' completion of homework tasks was also recorded.

The researchers found that, by harnessing the influence of parents, the probability that pupils submitted completed homework tasks on time was increased by 40%, the number of times pupils had to have their attention redirected was reduced by 25%, and pupil participation in lessons increased by 15%. Parental communication can be a powerful tool for schools to use, but Kraft and Dougherty also show that it should not just focus on problematic behaviour. For such communication to be effective, it needs to be a regular, honest update about pupil performance, both positive and negative.

In a completely different study of a nudge intended to make desired behaviour easier for people, Steffen Kallbekken and Håkon Sêlen ran a field experiment to study the effect of plate size on the amount of food taken from buffets at 45 Norwegian hotels between June and August 2012 (Kallbekken and Sêlen 2013). The control group consisted of 38 hotels that maintained the size of the plates they used whilst the remaining seven hotels reduced the size of their plates. The results show that reducing the average plate size used in hotel buffets from 24 to 21 cm caused a 30% reduction in the food waste generated and, presumably, a reduction in the amount of food consumed. One explanation of this effect is based on social cues: the smaller plate signals to us that taking too much food is unacceptable. Another explanation is based on the difficulty we face when objectively judging the amount of food we take, which means we judge the amount relative to the size of the plate and so the smaller plate size helps us to judge sooner that we have taken enough.

10.5 Designing nudges for schools

The studies in this chapter have all shown that nudges can affect our behaviour; that changing the way options are presented to us can alter the decisions we make. As such, they can be a powerful addition to the policy toolkit of teachers and schools for promoting desired behaviour and attitudes amongst their pupils, and yet they are currently far from being fully utilised in the school setting. Teachers and schools have the opportunity to design, introduce and assess the effectiveness of their own nudges. As with the implications from any of the behavioural experiments discussed in this book, nudges should be tailored to the specific pupils, conditions and issues in a school rather than taken off a shelf. Following the guidance produced by the UK's Behavioural Insights Team, they should also follow its EAST structure (Service *et al.* 2014), being

- Easy for pupils and parents to follow, which can be achieved through the use of opt-out designs, minimisation of any hassle and the simplification of messages;
- Attractive to pupils and parents, catching their attention through harnessing the incentive effects of rewards and sanctions;
- Socially important, by highlighting the behaviour of others and establishing commitments between those involved; and
- Timely, targeting pupils and parents when they are likely to be most receptive and when the desired actions are most important.

Once nudges have been introduced, their effectiveness should be assessed so they can be continually improved and so ineffective and counterproductive nudges can be removed. Behavioural experiments can be used for conducting such assessments (see Chapter 13).

10.6 Practical takeaways

We can help our pupils to improve their behaviour and performance by

- Using injunctive rather than descriptive nudges.
- Asking them to formulate and agree on class objectives and to commit to achieving them.
- Making desired behaviour fun.
- Targeting our interventions at individual pupils and helping them to reflect on their personal behaviour.
- Using the opt-out design for enrollment to maximise the likelihood that those we most want to participate in systems to help pupils do so.
- Harnessing parental influence through regular and honest updates about their children's behaviour and performance, both positive and negative.

Bibliography

Bateson, M., Nettle, D., and Roberts, G., 2006. Cues of being watched enhance cooperation in a real-world setting. *Biology Letters*, 2, 412-414.

Bergman, P., and Rogers, T., 2017. Is this technology useless? How seemingly irrelevant factors affect adoption and efficacy. *HKS Faculty Research Working Paper Series*.

Cialdini, R.B., 2003. Crafting normative messages to protect the environment. *Current Directions in Psychological Science*, 12, 105-109.

Croson, R., and Shang, J., 2008. The impact of downward social information on contribution decisions. *Experimental Economics*, 11, 221-233.

Ernest-Jones, M., Nettle, D., and Bateson, M., 2011. Effects of eye images on everyday cooperative behaviour: A field experiment. *Evolution and Human Behaviour*, 32 (3), 172-178.

Evans-Pritchard, B., 2013. Aiming to reduce cleaning costs. *Works That Work*, 1.

Francey, D. and Bergmüller, R., 2012. Images of eyes enhance investments in a real-life public good. *PLOS One*, 7 (5).

Haynes, L.C., *et al.*, 2012. Collection of delinquent fines: An adaptive randomized trial to assess the effectiveness of alternative text messages. *Journal of Policy Analysis and Management*, 32 (4), 718-730.

Hubbub. Available from: www.hubbub.org.uk/ballot-bin.

Johnson, E.J., and Goldstein, D., 2003. Do defaults save lives? *Science*, 302, 1338-1339.

Kallbekken, S., and Sêlen, H., 2013. 'Nudging' hotel guests to reduce food waste as a win-win environmental measure. *Economics Letters*, 119, 325-327.

Kraft, M.A., and Dougherty, S.M., 2013. The effect of teacher–family communication on student engagement: Evidence from a randomized field experiment. *Journal of Research on Educational Effectiveness*, 6 (3), 199-222.

Morisano, D., *et al.*, 2010. Setting, elaborating, and reflecting on personal goals improves academic performance. *Journal of Applied Psychology*, 95 (2), 255-264.

National Geographic. See the enchanting, ancient forest in the middle of a desert. Available from: www.nationalgeographic.com/travel/national-parks/article/petrified-forest-national-park.

NHS Blood and Transplant, 2013. Taking organ transplantation to 2020: A UK strategy. Available from: www.nhsbt.nhs.uk/to2020/resources/nhsbt_organ_donor_strategy_summary.pdf.

Peeters, M., *et al.*, 2013. Social stairs: Taking the piano staircase towards long-term behavioral change. *In*: S. Berkovsky and J. Freyne, eds. *Persuasive Technology*. Persuasive 2013, Lecture Notes in Computer Science, 7822.

Service, O., *et al.*, 2014. *EAST: Four Simple Ways to Apply Behavioural Insights*. The Behavioural Insights Team. Available from: www.bi.team/publications/east-four-simple-ways-to-apply-behavioural-insights/.

Statista, 2021. Average cost of a shopping basket in the United Kingdom (UK) in 2020, by supermarket. Available from: www.statista.com/statistics/1100981/average-cost-of-a-shopping-basket-in-the-united-kingdom-by-supermarket/.

UK Cabinet Office: The Behavioural Insights Team and the Charities Aid Foundation, 2013. Applying behavioural insights to charitable giving. Available from: www.bi.team/wp-content/uploads/2015/07/BIT_Charitable_Giving_Paper-1.pdf.

UK Department for Environment, Food and Rural Affairs, 2021. Policy paper: Carrier bags: Why there's a charge. Available from: www.gov.uk/government/publications/single-use-plastic-carrier-bags-why-were-introducing-the-charge/carrier-bags-why-theres-a-5p-charge.

United Nations Environment Programme, GRIDArendal and Behavioural Insights Team, 2020. *The Little Book of Green Nudges: 40 Nudges to Spark Sustainable Behaviour on Campus*. Nairobi and Arendal: UNEP and GRID-Arendal.

University of Bath, 2021. Understanding water use in private settings: The case of showers. Available from: www.bath.ac.uk/projects/understanding-water-use-in-private-settings-the-case-of-showers/.

SECTION THREE: WIDER ISSUES

11 Wider issues

The chapters up until this point have been largely concerned with the ways in which the findings of behavioural science can drive improvements in pupil learning and discipline. Schools are much more than collections of classrooms in which we interact with our pupils, though. They are communities of pupils, teachers, leaders and parents that are constrained by structures that are often the way they are simply because that is the way they have always been. And schools only function properly when each of these groups of individuals pull in the same direction and are allowed to play their different parts fully. This is the focus of this chapter.

11.1 Overcoming decision fatigue

An important theme running throughout this book is that both we and our pupils find decision-making mentally tiring, which in turn prevents us all from making the choices that would most benefit us. However, behavioural scientists have also provided us with the way to manage the effects of this decision fatigue, at the heart of which lies glucose: the sugar our bodies create from the food we eat, which powers all aspects of our brain functioning. That glucose is so important in this regard is shown by the fact that our brains consume 20% of the glucose our bodies create despite amounting to only 2% of our bodies' mass (Gailliot and Baumeister 2007).

A study conducted by Matthew Gailliot and colleagues at Florida State University involved 62 undergraduate participants, 49 of whom were female, 12 of whom were male and 1 who did not report their sex (Gailliot *et al*. 2007). Before the experiment began, all of the participants completed 20 Stroop tests, in which they were presented the names of colours in different-coloured fonts and had to identify the name that matched the colour in which it was written. Once their performance in those initial tests had been recorded, they then watched a silent six-minute video of a woman talking. During the film, common one-syllable words appeared at the bottom of the screen, each for ten seconds. They all then consumed a drink of lemonade before the final stage of the experiment, which involved them completing 80 further Stroop tests divided into four blocks of 20. Before all of this, the participants were randomly assigned to one of four groups:

- Those in Group One were instructed to focus solely on the face of the woman in the video and to do their best to ignore the stream of words at the bottom of the screen. Their lemonade was sweetened with sugar and so contained approximately 140 calories.

DOI: 10.4324/9781003198505-14

- Those in Group Two were given the same instructions for the video part of the experiment as their counterparts in Group One but were then given lemonade sweetened with artificial sweetener and so contained zero calories.
- Those in Group Three were instructed to simply watch the video of the woman talking in the way they would watch any other video. Similarly to those in Group One, their lemonade was sweetened with sugar.
- Those in Group Four were also instructed to watch the video in their normal way. Similarly to those in Group Two, though, they were given lemonade sweetened with artificial sweetener.

In this way, each of the participants was randomly assigned one of the possible permutations of video-watching instructions (either to focus solely on the woman's face or to watch as usual) and lemonade types (either sweetened with sugar or artificial sweetener). And this assignment was important for their performance in the final Stroop tests. The task of focusing solely on the woman's face was shown to be mentally draining as those in Group Two went on to make on average twice as many errors in the final Stroop test as did their counterparts in Group Four. Spending six minutes exerting self-control to ignore the words appearing and then disappearing at the bottom of the screen caused decision fatigue that made it harder for the participants to concentrate on the later colour and word matching task. However, there was no difference in performance in the final Stroop tests between those in Groups Three and One, once the differences in their baseline tests had been taken into account. Drinking lemonade sweetened with sugar offset the decision fatigue almost perfectly.

Our brains crave glucose when we are mentally tired and if we fail to supply it, we simply cannot concentrate or make decisions as effectively as we otherwise could do. Similar experiments have shown that when we are mentally fatigued and our brains are starved of glucose, our ability to control ourselves is also impaired. David Benton, Veronica Brett and Paul Brain studied precisely this in the behaviour of 60 primary schoolchildren, equally split male and female and all either six or seven years of age (Benton *et al.* 1987). In their study, the children all ate lunch at school between 12.30 and 1 pm and then had nothing else to eat until 2.30 pm, when they were given a drink of orange squash sweetened with either sugar or artificial sweetener. Between 2.45 and 3.30 pm, the children then played a computer game in which they had to place a bat in such a way that it blocked a ball travelling from left to right on the screen. Each of the children played the game in ten sessions of 15 trials. Unbeknownst to them, the game was set at its most difficult level, which made it almost impossible to complete successfully and inevitable that each of the children would find it frustrating. The behaviour of the children was recorded throughout their sessions. Similarly to the results from the Stroop test experiment presented earlier, those children who had been given the sugary squash were much more likely to exhibit behaviour categorised as 'quiet concentration'. The children who had drunk the artificially sweetened orange were much more likely to fidget, talk and show signs of frustration (described as handling the computer controls roughly, kicking their feet and sighing audibly).

It is no wonder that as a school term goes by, I stop increasingly frequently at the supermarket on my drive home to buy a bag of doughnuts. As we become increasingly tired mentally, our brains crave more and more glucose and our ability to resist sugary foods declines. The catch-22 for dieting is that the only way we can bolster our self-control is by eating the sugary foods we increasingly crave. This is why it is so difficult to maintain a healthy diet when we are mentally busy and why we should be kinder to ourselves when we succumb to temptation. Sadly, it is almost inevitable.

As well as enhancing our levels of concentration and self-control, studies show that glucose has an important effect on the ability of our pupils to recall information. Keith Wesnes and colleagues investigated this in their week-long study of 29 children between nine and 16 years of age, with an average age of 12 years, during a half-term break (Wesnes *et al.* 2003). On the Monday of the study, the children were simply familiarised with the tests they would complete during the rest of the week. On the remaining four days, the children were fed breakfasts consisting of a bowl of cereal (two days), a glucose drink (one day) and nothing at all (one day), with the order in which they had these being randomly assigned. They were not allowed to eat or drink anything other than water after 8 pm throughout the study. The children arrived at the research lab at 8 am on each of the test days in order to take a 25-minute series of baseline tests. They then received their assigned breakfast, before completing similar tests at 9 am, 10 am, 11 am and 12 pm. The results shed further light on the role that glucose plays in our cognitive functioning. The researchers found that the children's performance in the tests declined throughout the morning, but the rate of decline was more than halved if the children had been given cereal for breakfast compared to having nothing for breakfast. There was initially no decline in the children's performance when they had the glucose drink, but then a quicker worsening: the beneficial effect was short-lived.

Two important implications arise from these findings. The first and most obvious is the importance of schools ensuring their pupils and staff are fed throughout each day: breakfast, lunch and a snack at least mid-morning. With the increasing decision fatigue we all inevitably experience during the course of a day, allowing blood glucose levels to drop simply leads to falling levels of concentration, deteriorating academic performance and worsening self-control and discipline. The behavioural findings are very clear that sugary boosts are not the solution, though: their immediate effects may be positive but are quickly cancelled out. What is needed instead are foods that release energy slowly and over a longer period of time. The second is the need for us to teach our pupils to allow themselves to eat more at times when they need to be concentrating most intensely, such as during periods when they are revising, taking exams and writing coursework. The cravings they inevitably feel at these times is simply their brains signalling a need for more fuel. They should be kind to themselves during these times, accepting the increased likelihood of them giving into their cravings, but they should again focus on slow-release foods rather than those that cause a sugar rush. They should certainly not try to diet during these times. By heeding this advice, we can also be happier, more productive and more effective, which can only have positive effects in our classrooms and homes.

11.2 Timetabling

It was a Wednesday afternoon towards the end of term. The pupils had already completed four 50-minute lessons that day, along with enrichment activities after lunch and, in a change to their usual timetable, an extended tutor period during which they watched a 40-minute recording of a PSHE consultant talking about sexual consent. There was one thing left before they could finish for the day: a talk by a guest speaker about environmental conservation. Unfortunately, the venue for the talk was the original school hall in which the acoustics were notoriously bad and in which pillars meant there was almost no visibility of the small screen at the front for some of those in the audience.

Once the pupils had taken their seats, the head of environmental activities at the school introduced the speaker, who then started her presentation. She began strongly, talking about her recent experiences in the Indian Ocean, but gradually her nerves took over, she lost her place and, only halfway through the time she had been given, she ran out of things to say. The pupils, who were usually polite, well-mannered and welcoming, were becoming increasingly restless. And then the speaker made a fatal mistake: she invited audience participation and allowed the spotlight to be taken by a pupil who, unbeknownst to her, was always ready to share his rather controversial opinions in as much detail as he could get away with. He did just that and large numbers of the other pupils were on their feet cheering and applauding before any of the teachers could act. The talk had become an unruly shambles, and the guest was left speechless at the front, not knowing what to do.

Rude and disrespectful behaviour should never be excused, but on that Wednesday afternoon it should have been expected. The pupils were undoubtedly suffering the effects of decision fatigue, brought on by the five hours they had already spent exhausting their mental reserves on concentration and resisting temptation. It had also been almost two hours since they had eaten anything, and they were being asked to further control themselves in a setting in which they could barely hear or see a speaker who was unprepared for the task she faced. The deck was stacked against the speaker and, for that matter, against the pupils themselves. The ring leaders were rightly held accountable for their behaviour – there will be times in life when our pupils have to act appropriately in such situations – but there was an element of them being set up to fail that day.

It is important that we consider the mental situations in which we place our pupils when arranging events. The misbehaviour on that Wednesday could easily have been averted by scheduling it for a different time of the day, perhaps switching the talk and the tutor-led PSHE session so that the pupils went straight from lunch to the talk; by holding it in a venue in which it would have been easier for the pupils to concentrate on the presentation; and by helping the guest speaker prepare for the session. Had all three steps been taken, I have no doubt that the pupils would have been their usual, delightful selves and the speaker would have gone away having had a thoroughly enjoyable and positive experience.

These considerations are also important when schools create the structure of a typical day. At a previous school, for example, it was decided that the lesson immediately before lunch would be extended from 40 minutes to an hour in order to give pupils more contact time with their teachers. This seems to be a positive innovation until the findings relating to both decision fatigue and the role glucose plays in fuelling deliberate thought, concentration and self-control are considered. It is no wonder that my colleagues and I ended up adopting the strategies of slowing the pace of these lessons and spreading the learning activities across the greater available time. Counterproductively, by reducing the sense of urgency and purpose in lessons this may even have reduced the amount learned by pupils: especially in the double lessons with the Year 13s that, with the five-minute break halfway through, became 1 hour 45 minute 'super' lessons.

11.3 Subject choices

Thought experiment: occupational choice

Mark has loved animals since before he can remember. Whilst growing up he would harass his parents into taking him to the local zoo, on what seemed to his parents to be a weekly basis. He was always particularly keen to see the large mammals, which gradually caused him to fall in love with cetaceans, especially the great whales. He is now fascinated by the notion that humans and cetaceans can communicate.

Which is more likely now that Mark is an adult: he is working as a marine biologist or as a primary school teacher?

Girls were responsible for achieving 55% of the A-level qualifications awarded in 2018. However, girls received only 43% of the A-level qualifications in subjects relating to science, technology, engineering and maths (STEM), including 39% of those in maths, 28% of those in further maths and 22% of those in physics. And this is at a time when women with degrees in maths enjoy salaries that are 13.4% higher than that of the average female worker five years after graduation, and women with degrees in engineering and economics earn 9.7% and 19.5% more than that average, respectively (Cassidy *et al.* 2018). Of the possible explanations for this worrying and ultimately damaging pattern, two relate to the behavioural sciences and can be overcome with behavioural solutions: representativeness and teacher bias.

In their now-famous study published in 1973, Daniel Kahneman and Amos Tversky asked participants to judge whether individuals were engineers or lawyers based on two pieces of information: descriptions of the individuals, similar to that of Mark in the thought experiment above, and statistics about the numbers of people in the sample who worked in each of these occupations (Kahneman and Tversky 1973). Kahneman and Tversky found that participants overwhelmingly based their judgements on the descriptions and how closely they aligned with their mental images of people who had those occupations, ignoring the statistical data they were given. Most people judge that it is more likely that Mark is a marine biologist rather than a primary school teacher even if they know the number of primary school teachers in the UK is far greater than the number of marine biologists. That we base such judgements on our mental stereotypes is another example of a heuristic we employ to make decision-making simpler and quicker. This is our representativeness heuristic.

> **Key term: representativeness heuristic**
>
> A decision-making shortcut we use that involves us making judgements based on how closely the options align with our mental stereotypes rather than on objective information.

Given our propensity to make decisions based on our mental stereotypes, the work of researchers such as Barbro Grevholm sheds light on the reason why girls are choosing to be under-represented in STEM subjects (Grevholm 2010). Grevholm studied the way Norwegian school pupils perceive professional mathematicians by asking 12 such pupils, each aged 16 or 17 years and specialising in design and media courses, to draw their mental images of a mathematician. From the images they drew, all showed mathematicians to be males working alone, most of whom were old, five of whom wore glasses, four of whom sat behind a desk and three of whom had beards, one of which was particularly impressive. And all of these pupils were taught maths by a female teacher. It is unsurprising that relatively few girls choose to pursue maths if our pupils, both boys and girls, possess such strong mental images of mathematicians, which a significant body of evidence now suggests they do.

Larry Flick worked with a primary school in Eugene, Oregon, to investigate the effectiveness of one way of potentially overcoming such unhelpful stereotypes: the scientist-in-residence scheme (Flick 2010). Over a six-week period, two academic scientists spent one hour a week for three consecutive weeks with two Year Six classes at the school before the classes made a visit to their lab. The pupils in Class One (11 of whom were boys and 14 were girls) drew their mental images of a scientist before the visits began and then again at the end of the scheme. One of their visitors was female whilst the other was male. Those in Class Two (eight of whom were boys and 14 were girls) only drew their mental images of a scientist at the end of the scheme. Both of their visitors were female. The pupils in two Year Seven classes in a separate school were asked to draw their mental images of a scientist in the same week as those at the test school were drawing their post-scheme images as a control measure. Almost all of the images drawn by pupils in Class One at the outset of the scheme showed a scientist working alone, 91% showed scientists working indoors, 64% showed scientists who were male and 27% showed scientists who were female (the gender of the remaining 9% was unidentifiable). From the drawings of pupils from both classes at the end of scheme, 77% showed scientists working alone, 87% showed scientists working indoors, 36% showed scientists who were male and 34% showed scientists who were female (the gender of the remaining 30% was unidentifiable). The scientist-in-residence scheme had a demonstrable effect on the pupils' perceptions about the sex of a typical scientist, making them almost perfectly balanced.

Delving a little deeper into the results shows that the perceptions of the girls in these classes were affected more than those of the boys by their interactions with the scientists. Of those images whose sex could be identified, 63% of those drawn by the boys before the scheme were of men compared to 42% of those drawn by the boys after the scheme had come to an end. These figures for the girls' drawings were 64% and 32%, respectively.

Our pupils are naturally going to rely on the representativeness heuristic, at least in part, when making their subject choices. And so we can help them to make better decisions by correcting their mental stereotypes of the types of people who study and go on to work in different fields. Failing to do that will simply perpetuate the current situation. Arguably more concerning, though, is the finding of researchers such as Victor Lavy and Edith Sand that our pupils' subject choices are also determined by our own biases (Lavy and Sand 2015). These researchers studied three cohorts of Year Seven pupils between 2002 and 2004 in Tel Aviv, which involved 867 pupils in 33 classes in the 2002 cohort; 1,127 in 41 classes in the 2003 cohort; and 1,017 in 38 classes in the 2004 cohort. Lavy and Sand compared the results of these pupils in their Year Six Growth and Effectiveness Measures for Schools (GEMS) exams, a system of assessments in maths, Hebrew and English operated by Israel's Ministry of Education to help schools to improve the academic attainment of children, with the results of these pupils in their Year Seven internal exams. As the GEMS exams are marked blindly at the national level but the internal exams were marked by the pupils' teachers, differences in these scores can be interpreted as representing teacher bias. In maths, for example, girls outperformed boys in the GEMS exams but were outperformed by boys in the internal exams, which the researchers take as an indicator of bias towards boys. In English, on the other hand, the results of girls and boys were not significantly different in the two types of exams.

On the basis of this measure of teacher bias, Lavy and Sand find that such bias in Years Six and Seven increases the overall academic achievement of boys in Year Nine but reduces that of girls in that year. Furthermore, such teacher bias in Years Six and Seven increases the probability that boys will enrol for and complete A-level equivalent qualifications in maths but reduces that probability for girls. Addressing these subject choice patterns needs to start with our own perceptions and biases, however subconscious and insignificant they may seem.

11.4 Meetings

On a clear Tuesday morning on 28 January 1986, the US Space Shuttle *Challenger* broke apart over the Atlantic Ocean, just 73 seconds after its takeoff from the Kennedy Space Centre in Florida. All seven of its crew were killed. After four months of interviews, a select commission appointed by President Reagan identified the cause of the disaster as a failure in the joint between two sections of the rocket that allowed hot gases to escape, ripping apart the craft. One of the now-infamous rubber O-rings failed to secure the joint.

The day before the launch, five engineers at a contractor warned the National Aeronautics and Space Administration (NASA) that the flight may be dangerous because the effectiveness of the O-rings, which had previously been identified as a possible single point of failure, had never been tested below 11°C, and the actual temperature was below freezing. Having already had the launch postponed on three occasions, NASA staff disregarded the engineers' concerns and urged them to reconsider their 'no-go' position, which they did. NASA launches are given the go ahead by three separate space centres, all of which did so without flagging any concerns about the efficacy and safety of the O-rings (Janis 1991).

In 1972, Irving Janis lay the blame for this disaster, along with other notable events such as the Bay of Pigs Invasion, in what he called groupthink, which he defined as a situation in which the desire of members of a group to agree with one another overrides their inclination to fully appraise alternative options (Janis 1972). Janis outlined a number of conditions that make groupthink possible, including a high level of cohesion in the group, organisational faults (such as the group being insulated from the rest of the organisation, there being a historical lack of impartial leadership and there being a lack of decision-making procedures) and specific situational factors (such as a high level of stress, a feeling of low self-esteem amongst the group because of recent failures and difficulties in decision-making). And he argued that the more of these conditions that are satisfied, the greater the risk of defective group decision-making.

Key term: groupthink

A situation in which the desire of members of a group to reach agreement with one another overwhelms their desire to fully appraise the available options and properly evaluate the risks associated with the group's preferred choice, leading to poor group decision-making.

Although there are weaknesses in Janis' theory, such as the ease with which evidence can be arbitrarily found in support of it from almost any notable failure event and the lack of empirical studies that rigorously test its validity, it does relate to three key findings from behavioural science. The first is the halo effect, which in this situation refers to the tendency of members of a group to trust someone's judgement in a given situation more than they should because of other unrelated positive attributes that person possesses. The second is confirmation bias, which in this situation refers to members of a group retaining and even defending a judgement despite being presented with evidence that demonstrates it was misguided. The third is conformity bias, evidence for which was originally found in the laboratory experiments of Solomon Asch in the 1950s (Asch 1951). In these experiments, male undergraduate students at Swarthmore College were organised into groups of eight and instructed to take it in turns to announce in a number of trials which of three lines of different lengths was a match for a fourth line. Unbeknownst to the 50 focal participants, the other seven in each of their groups had previously been instructed to unanimously announce incorrect judgements in certain trials. The extent to which these erroneous announcements were incorrect was large in each case, ranging from an error of half an inch to an error of one and three-quarter inches.

The results were stark. One-third of all the judgements made by the focal participants were in line with that of the purposefully mistaken majority; 75% of the focal participants conformed with the mistaken majority in at least one trial, and there were almost no errors made in the control trials, in which the majority made the correct announcement. And the stronger the majority, the more likely it was that focal participants conformed. As a notable exception to the problem of replication in the social sciences discussed in Section 2.4, these results have been repeatedly replicated, albeit rather inconsistently at times, and have been shown to emerge when the deception is facilitated through technology rather than through the use of primed participants (see, for example, Hanayama and Mori 2011).

A number of solutions have been proposed to overcome the groupthink problem, which certainly seems to feature in school settings. These include barring more senior members of a group from sharing their thoughts early in meetings, thereby weakening potential halo effects; establishing clear decision-making procedures that force the group to properly consider alternatives and evaluate the risks of a favoured option (another use of the checklist approach); rewarding group members for raising challenges and thinking creatively, thereby incentivising non-conformity; and changing the composition of the group from one meeting to another by bringing in and allowing to speak first other, relevant members of staff for specific discussions. Meetings need to be planned in advance if they are to be effective, and not just their timing and location but their format and the roles of each of the constituent members. And the more important the outcomes of a meeting are likely to be, the greater is the need for careful planning.

11.5 Staff wellbeing

Behavioural science has demonstrated that we each possess a limited cognitive reserve that fuels our decision-making and allows us to resist temptation, and as we deplete that reserve, we end up making increasingly suboptimal decisions. Behavioural science has also demonstrated that we each possess a similar reserve that enables us to be resilient in the face of what we perceive to be a personal attack and when that reserve runs low, our ability to make effective judgements and correct decisions can be overwhelmed by a need to defend and justify ourselves. This second reserve consists of one thing: self-esteem.

Niro Sivanathan and colleagues paid $10 to each of 80 undergraduate students from a university in the American Midwest to take part as individuals in an experiment into the function of our self-esteem (Sivanathan *et al.* 2008). In the first stage of the experiment, the participants were asked to solve a financial problem in which they had to allocate $10 million of research and development funding to one of two departments in a declining company on the basis of the greatest financial return for the company as a whole. As an incentive to engage seriously with the problem, the participants were told that the best performer amongst each 50 of them would receive an additional $50 bonus. Following their decisions, the participants received five years of simulated profit information for the company that showed they had made poor allocation decisions, irrespective of what their decisions had been. In the second stage of the experiment, the participants completed a questionnaire about their levels of self-esteem. Finally, in the third stage of the experiment, the participants were asked to revisit the research and development funding allocation problem and to allocate a further $20 million across the two departments but this time in whatever proportions they chose. A number of participants were randomly assigned to a control group that completed only the first and third stages of the experiment.

In the analysis of the results, the scores from the self-esteem questionnaire were categorised as either low or high based on the median score. The results show that participants with higher-than-average self-esteem chose to invest a further $9.27 million into the department they had originally selected for the funding in the first stage, whereas those with lower-than-average self-esteem chose to invest a further $11.52 million into their previously favoured department: almost a 25% increase in reinvestment.

When our reserves of self-esteem are running low and we feel as though we are not fulfilling a role as well as we should or we are not living up to the expectations of others, our decision-making becomes impaired as we seek to strengthen our position. In the previous experiment, we escalate our commitment to a choice even when we are provided with evidence that doing so is misguided. The way we use our self-esteem reserves follows the logic of loss aversion illustrated in Figure 6.1: when we feel as though we are already experiencing a loss, we are more likely to gamble on entrenching our position because the payoff from it being successful outweighs the further loss from it failing (also see Section 9.1). The researchers of the previous experiment show in two follow-up studies that allowing participants to reflect on and reinforce personal values that are important to them or providing them with feedback that reaffirms their strength in areas unrelated to the financial problem reduced such harmful self-justification. Interestingly, though, the researchers also show that providing participants with feedback that reaffirmed their ability at the financial problem only served to make the participants respond in a more intensely self-justifying manner.

Two messages stand out from these results for staff wellbeing and, ultimately, staff effectiveness at our schools. The first message is that our effectiveness depends on our reserves of self-esteem, also known as our 'affirmational resources' by other researchers (Steele *et al.* 1993). And as these reserves are eroded, which can happen when we feel as though we have failed in some way and when we feel criticised, our performance inevitably deteriorates as we increasingly look to justify and defend ourselves rather than acting objectively and choosing the best way forward. The implication of this for us is that we need to be aware of both our levels of self-esteem and how we are prone to make poor decisions when they are running low. Without this self-awareness, it is all too easy for us to find ourselves trapped in vicious cycles of ever escalating criticism and ever worsening decision-making on our part. The implication of this for line managers is that they need to be aware of the self-esteem levels of those in their teams and to tailor their feedback accordingly. Even seemingly constructive feedback can be damaging to staff effectiveness if delivered on the back of a failure or other such feedback. Line managers need to be judicious with their feedback in order to get the best from their staff. The second message is that line managers can inadvertently intensify a team member's impulse to justify himself by trying to reaffirm his ability at the task in which he has just experienced a failure of some sort. Instead, line managers should try to make the team member reflect on one of his other, unrelated, strengths. Both of these messages also apply to our interactions with our pupils as we seek to elicit the very best from them.

In addition to the implications of this important role played by our reserves of self-esteem, behavioural science is full of findings about how line managers can maximise the wellbeing, productivity and effectiveness of staff. Just from the preceding chapters, we have seen the importance of us

- Knowing the purpose of the tasks we do and feeling recognised for doing them, thereby overcoming the demoralising and wellbeing-reducing Sisyphus effect.
- Being able to complete the tasks we do and feeling proud of ourselves for doing so. The nature of the tasks we are set is important in this, with there being a fine balance to strike between being set tasks that are difficult enough to elicit a feeling of pride in completing them and being set tasks that are easy enough to complete in the time available.
- Having ownership of the tasks we do, thereby increasing the amount we value them.

- Receiving more praise than criticism, especially when we are experiencing negative events in our wider lives, thereby offsetting the effects of our natural negativity bias and harnessing the relational power of the magic ratio.
- Feeling as though we are being treated fairly, be it in terms of the way additional workload is divided; the allocation of opportunities to take on more rewarding tasks; decisions about staff promotions, and, of course, pay.
- Having access to sufficient sources of glucose throughout the day but especially later in the day, which we need in order to offset the effects of decision fatigue on the decisions we make and on our ability to cope with the emotions we feel.

Underpinning all of this is the need for line managers to truly know and understand the members of their teams and to be accordingly flexible with the tasks they assign and the feedback they give. Line managers need to know how their team members are feeling about the different aspects of the work they do, their performance across them and the way they are perceived at school; their career and life aspirations, and the things they are experiencing outside of the school environment. Without such deep understanding it is impossible for line managers to maximise the wellbeing of those in their teams. This inevitably takes time and effort, but that will be amply rewarded in the improvement of staff morale and, ultimately, the experiences of pupils.

11.6 Practical takeaways

We can make our schools more effective and compassionate by

- Providing teachers and pupils with the slow-release glucose they need throughout a day and enabling them to consume more of this at times of greatest stress and effort.
- Planning events in a way that makes it as easy as possible for pupils to participate effectively in them, especially when they are mentally tired.
- Structuring a typical school day according to the findings about decision fatigue and the importance of glucose consumption.
- Correcting our pupils' mental stereotypes of people who study different subjects and have different occupations.
- Correcting our own biases about the performance of boys and girls in different subjects.
- Taking steps to reduce the problem of groupthink in meetings.
- Being judicious about the constructive feedback we give to pupils and colleagues based on their levels of self-esteem.
- Reaffirming the strengths of pupils and colleagues in areas unrelated to their feelings of failure.
- Taking steps to maximise staff wellbeing and effectiveness.

Bibliography

Asch, S.E., 1951. Effects of group pressure upon the modification and distortion of judgements. *In*: H. Guetzknow, ed. *Groups, Leadership and Men*. Pittsburgh, USA: Carnegie Press, pp. 177-190.

Benton, D., Brett, V., and Brain, P.F., 1987. Glucose improves attention and reaction to frustration in children. *Biological Psychology*, 24, 95-100.

Cassidy, R., Cattan, S., and Crawford, C., 2018. *Why Don't More Girls Study Maths and Physics?* Institute of Fiscal Studies. Available from: https://ifs.org.uk/publications/13276.

Flick, L., 2010. Scientist in residence program improving children's image of science and scientists. *School Science and Mathematics*, 90 (3), 204-214.

Gailliot, M.T., and Baumeister, R.F., 2007. The physiology of willpower: Linking blood glucose to self-control. *Personality and Social Psychology Review*, 11, 303-327.

Gailliot, M.T., *et al.*, 2007. Self-control relies on glucose as a limited energy source: Willpower is more than a metaphor. *Journal of Personality and Social Psychology*, 92 (2), 325-336.

Grevholm, B., 2010. Norwegian upper secondary school students' views of mathematics and images of mathematicians. *In*: K. Kislenko, ed. *Current State of Research on Mathematical Beliefs XVI: Proceedings of the MAVI-16 Conference, Tallinn University of Applied Sciences, June 26-29, 2010*, pp. 120-136.

Hanayama, A., and Mori, K., 2011. Conformity of six-year-old children in the Asch experiment without using confederates. *Psychology*, 2 (7), 661-664.

Janis, I., 1972. *Victims of Groupthink*. Boston, USA: Houghton Mifflin.

Janis, I., 1991. Groupthink. *In*: E. Griffin, ed. *A First Look at Communication Theory*. New York, USA: McGraw-Hill, pp. 235-246.

Kahneman, D., and Tversky, A., 1973. On the psychology of prediction. *Psychological Review*, 80, 237-251.

Lavy, V., and Sand, E., 2015. On the origins of gender human capital gaps: Short and long term consequences of teachers' stereotypical biases. *NBER Working Paper No. 20909*.

Sivanathan, N., *et al.*, 2008. The promise and peril of self-affirmation in de-escalation of commitment. *Organizational Behavior and Human Decision Processes*, 107 (1), 1-14.

Steele, C.M., Spencer, S.J., and Lynch, M., 1993. 'Self-image resilience and dissonance: The role of affirmational resources. *Journal of Personality and Social Psychology*, 64 (6), 885-896.

Wesnes, K.A., *et al.*, 2003. Breakfast reduces declines in attention and memory over the morning in schoolchildren. *Appetite*, 41, 329-331.

12 Themes

Our goal as teachers is to see each of our pupils enjoy the very best outcomes, both in terms of personal development and academic progress and attainment. We can only achieve this by heeding and acting upon the findings of behavioural science. Many of these have been examined in the preceding chapters, through which seven strong, clear and inextricably inter-linked themes run. Together these themes characterise the behavioural learning classroom in which our pupils can truly thrive in all aspects of their time with us. They are illustrated in Figure 12.1 and discussed in the sections that follow. The chapter ends with a discussion of two principles underpinning these themes.

12.1 Theme one - wider planning

The first theme that can be discerned running through the preceding pages is the need for us to expand our conception of the planning that should go into the lessons we teach and the activities we run. We are taught during teacher training programmes of the need to set out our objectives, both for ourselves and our pupils; to devise tasks that actively involve our pupils in fulfilling those objectives; to consider how much time we allocate to each task, striking the balance between pupils having enough time to complete the tasks but not so much that they lose focus and become bored; to prepare for how we are going to assess the progress being made by our pupils; and to purposefully differentiate lesson activities for pupils with different learning needs, be they relating to a pupil's Education, Health and Care Plan, a pupil's language needs or a pupil's particularly high academic ability. All of these are important, and three of them are reinforced by behavioural findings: first, the need to set out our objectives, making the purpose of the tasks we set our pupils absolutely clear to them in order to overcome the demotivating and effort-reducing Sisyphus effect; second, the need to consider how we assign the available lesson time to ensure our pupils have sufficient time to complete the tasks and so feel the pride from doing so; and third, the need for us to prepare the assessment for learning we are going to use in order to reduce the number of times we interrupt our pupils as they work and so reduce the unnecessary anxiety and stress we cause our pupils by doing so.

We can help our pupils by encapsulating more than this in our planning, though. Firstly, we can help them by planning how we sequence activities within a lesson and how we sequence lessons in a week according to our pupils' inevitable feelings of decision fatigue as a lesson,

DOI: 10.4324/9781003198505-15

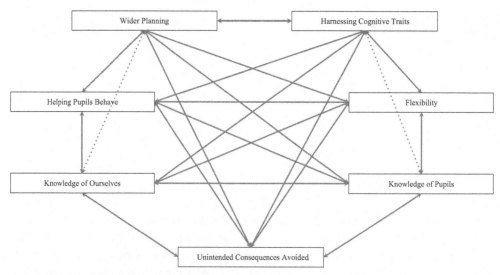

Figure 12.1 The behavioural learning classroom

a day and a week goes on. Maximising pupil engagement and learning is likely to involve scheduling the most important and demanding tasks for lessons that come either at the start of a day and week, in which our pupils' cognitive reserves are most likely to be high, or after a break in which our pupils have had the opportunity to replenish these reserves through eating; and scheduling them for the early parts of these lessons, before we have tired them mentally ourselves. It is also likely to involve us reducing the number of different tasks we set our pupils in a lesson, and reducing the unexpected changes they experience, as switching from one task to another and responding to changes to the norm deplete their cognitive reserves particularly quickly.

When preparing the activities we are going to use in a lesson, we can also help our pupils by considering their difficulty as well as the learning to which they lead. This is partly so they are not too difficult for our pupils to complete, which would deprive them of the motivational and rewarding feelings of pride from seeing them through to their end, but also because with a greater level of difficulty comes deeper learning and a greater sense of pride and achievement. A characteristic of an effective sequence of lessons is that pupils leave each lesson with a sense of accomplishment and with a feeling of motivation to complete any homework tasks we set and to achieve even more in their next lesson with us, that builds over time. This relies on us planning how we want our pupils to feel at the end of each lesson.

Finally, we can help our pupils by planning how we praise and give constructive feedback to them over time. Playing our part in maintaining any healthy relationship, be it personal or professional, requires us to initiate considerably more positive than negative interactions. It requires us to speak positively to someone considerably more regularly than we speak negatively to them. And this is no different as we seek to establish and maintain a positive rapport with each of our pupils. But striking a positively skewed ratio of interactions with each of our pupils requires us to plan how we are going to praise and constructively correct them, being judicious with the feedback we give by overlooking the inconsequential things rather than pedantically correcting everything, and deliberately finding good things to praise. Focusing on actions rather than outcomes can be helpful in this. Without such forethought, it is incredibly easy to revert to a situation in which we inadvertently find ourselves repeatedly praising some pupils and repeatedly criticising others. This is also needed to avoid the damaging wellbeing effects that arise from our pupils' negativity bias.

12.2 Theme two – helping our pupils to behave

When it comes to behaviour, our schools tend to publish clear behavioural policies that link different types of misbehaviour to different sanctions. That such a mapping is made available and we as teachers implement it fully is important for everyone involved: for us, our pupils and our pupils' parents. This is again reinforced by behavioural science as it helps us to treat our pupils fairly, thereby avoiding the self-damaging effects of our pupils' inequity aversion, and it reduces any sense of ambiguity in the minds of our pupils, which would otherwise cause them to disengage with school life. However, simply publishing and implementing such a policy is not enough for it to be effective. We also need to help our pupils abide by it. This is the second theme that runs through the previous chapters.

One thing we can do for our pupils in this regard is to help them meet the deadlines they are set. Perhaps even more so than us, our pupils suffer from the planning fallacy that means they more often than not set aside too little time to complete the tasks they are set, overestimating the speed with which they can achieve them. They are also just as likely as we are, if not more so, to opt for the short-term benefits of procrastination as they find it difficult to make a start on the work we set once they are away from the classroom. Together, these inevitably lead to one of three outcomes: our pupils work late into the night before the deadline to get it done; they take shortcuts to complete the task but to a standard lower than we expect, or they simply miss the deadline. Our pupils end up falling foul of the behaviour policy and end up receiving sanctions in two of these cases; and in the other they cognitively and physically tire themselves more than usual, further exposing themselves to the detrimental effects of decision fatigue on their future learning, behaviour and mental wellbeing. Unless we help our pupils to overcome the planning fallacy and the Rubicon effect, we are simply setting them up to fail. Practically, we can help our pupils to reflect on how long similar tasks actually took them to complete in the past; give them our advice about how long they will need to devote to tasks; and work with them to plan when and where they are going to complete the work they are set. We can also give them opportunities whilst they are in our lessons to plan their responses, write their opening paragraphs and answer the first questions: to make a start. Perhaps counter-intuitively, we can also help our pupils by giving them short but realistic deadlines and by resisting their demands for extensions unless they are truly warranted.

A second thing we can do to help our pupils in this regard is to anticipate and plan for the times when they are most at risk of breaking the rules. This is likely to be at the end of the day when our pupils are mentally tired; at times when they are having to cope with particularly strong emotions, having perhaps received bad news of one kind or another; and at times when they feel as though they are already on the back foot, perhaps having just underperformed in an important assessment. At these times, our pupils simply do not have the mental resources to be able to resist temptation, to persevere as they should with tasks and to control their emotions, all of which is a potent cocktail for misbehaviour. By pressing on with particularly demanding tasks, or placing our pupils in situations in which there are a lot of distractions, or trying to give them constructive feedback at these times is again setting them up to fail. At these times we should instead choose activities that place our pupils under less pressure and involve fewer distractions and temptations, thereby maximising their ability to meet the standards of behaviour we have set and to be in a better frame of mind when they are next able to engage fully in learning.

A third thing we can do is to remove unnecessary distractions in our classrooms, which ultimately cause our pupils to deplete their cognitive reserves by resisting them. Reducing the complexity of our wall displays and the frequency with which we change them is a step in this direction, as is the use of seating plans to separate pupils who particularly distract one another when they sit together, to reduce the urge to catch-up with peers who they have not been with for a while and to remove the need for our pupils to expend mental reserves on adjusting to an unexpected change. However, we should not use well-behaved girls to separate disruptive boys. This is an easy trap we can fall into that simply reinforces damaging stereotypes, particularly in the minds of our female pupils.

12.3 Theme three – being flexible

Whilst it is important that we expand what it means to plan our lessons and we consider within our planning the ways in which we can help our pupils to behave, it is inevitably impossible for us to be able to plan everything in advance. This leads onto the third theme running through the book: the need for us to be flexible. At times we need to be bold enough to discard the plans we have made in light of the situation in which we find ourselves. Three particular situations stand out from the preceding chapters in which we can help our pupils by doing this.

The first is the situation in which either our pupils or ourselves are mentally tired and suffering from the effects of decision fatigue. This may be because it is at the end of a long day or term, or because it is just before lunch on a morning in which our pupils have had to take a stressful exam. It is likely that our pupils will find it difficult to concentrate, resist distractions and control themselves in these situations, and that we will be prone to over-reacting to what they do. The situation is likely to be a tinderbox, with perfect conditions for a disciplinary situation to escalate unnecessarily. And so, instead of pressing on with a particularly challenging task or with a task that involves group work and the pupils to move around in the classroom, we can help our pupils by opting for tasks that involve fewer temptations and at which our pupils can more easily succeed. It is better for our pupils to make less progress with their learning than we had planned, than to find ourselves in a losing battle with them.

The second is the situation in which our pupils are in a negative state of mind, perhaps because they failed at something in their previous lesson, they have already received negative feedback or they are running low on self-esteem. It is likely that our pupils will be unable to objectively process constructive feedback or further failure in such a situation and that such feedback and failure will be received as a further dent in their mental wellbeing, however well-intentioned we are. And so we can help our pupils in these situations by not giving back their marked homework or tests in these lessons as planned, postponing doing that until our next lessons with them, and by swapping the activities we had planned with tasks in which our pupils are more likely to succeed. We can also help them by overlooking more of the minor errors they make in their contributions in class than we would usually.

The third is the situation in which there are more distractions than usual, such as in the week before the Christmas holiday or when a professional sports team is visiting the school, or when a pupil is having to cope with particularly strong emotions. It is likely that trying to press on with mentally demanding tasks in a situation such as these is again going to lead to a feeling of us having to battle with our pupils, especially for the emotional pupil who will have a lower mental reserve on which to draw for positive behaviour. We can help our pupils in such situations by lowering our expectations of what they are able to achieve in these lessons and by taking a longer-term view rather than sticking dogmatically to our plans.

We can help our pupils in every situation by tailoring our interactions with them according to our and their mental states at that moment in time. And as we do so, our teaching and schools will become more effective and more compassionate. But this inevitably means we need to truly know our pupils.

12.4 Theme four – knowing our pupils

We are only ever going to be completely effective at planning, helping our pupils behave and being flexible in the approaches we take if we know each of our pupils and can, as much as possible, treat them as individuals. There are three things we particularly need to know.

The first is the state of mind of each of our pupils as they enter our classrooms, step onto our sports fields and even as they pass us in a corridor. This relates to Figure 3.2, which underpins much of the work in behavioural science. We need to be able to instinctively judge whether our pupils are in a positive mindset, perhaps having achieved something earlier in the day, or whether they are starting their interaction with us feeling a sense of having already lost something. If our pupils have a positive mindset, they are likely to engage in the tasks we set in a thoughtful way, feeling confident in their ability to complete the tasks successfully, and to interact with us in a positive manner. But they are also likely to be less willing to take risks in the contributions they make as they are happy with what they have already achieved that day and do not want to jeopardise that feeling. Pupils in such a positive mindset are likely to need us to give them a greater push than usual to challenge themselves in their learning. If our pupils have a negative mindset, though, it is likely that they will feel a need to either take risks in the way they engage in tasks in order to offset the feeling of loss they already have or to escalate the behaviour that resulted in that loss in an attempt to prove they were right. Pupils in such a negative mindset are likely to engage less effectively with the tasks we set and to interact with us in a defensive manner. It is likely that they need us to minimise the likelihood of them failing again, to reduce the pressure we put on them and to help them to reflect on and reaffirm a personal strength that is unrelated to the source of their loss. Being able to make such an instinctive judgement about the state of mind of our pupils can only come from getting to know them.

The second is the emotions with which our pupils are grappling. When our pupils are controlling emotions, they are doing so using the same mental resource they use when making decisions, switching from one task to another, concentrating on their learning and resisting temptations to misbehave. And so when they are coping with particularly strong emotions, it is inevitable that they become less able to perform these other functions. Likewise, setting our pupils particularly demanding tasks to complete at these times only makes it more difficult for them to cope with their emotions. We need to know when they are experiencing particularly strong emotions so that we can help them to cope by giving them safe spaces in which to release those emotions, helping them to avoid the ironic effect of intensifying their own emotions and by removing any unnecessary school-created pressures from them at these times. We also need to know when they are grappling with the acute emotional demands caused by a feeling of scarcity and when they have a negative experience coming up. Only by knowing the first of these can we help them to avoid the tunnelling effect, in which their focus is so consumed on the cause of the scarcity that they overlook other important things in their lives, both in and out of school. And only by knowing the second can we help them to cope with the stress and anxiety that inevitably intensifies as the event approaches.

The third is the way they feel about their ability to perform in important situations. There is another balance to be finely struck here. On the one hand, we do not want our pupils to be experiencing low self-esteem as that leads to them making poor decisions, which in turn makes the expectation of under-performance self-fulfilling. On the other hand, we do not want our pupils to fall into the overconfidence bias too strongly. We can help by intervening when a pupil is swaying too far one way or the other, in the first case by reaffirming their abilities by helping them reflect on their unrelated strengths and in the second case by targeting our constructive feedback on their actions rather than on their outcomes.

12.5 Theme five – harnessing our pupils' cognitive traits

That our minds, and those of our pupils, work in ways that are predictably surprising at times and predictably illogical at others gives us a wider range of options when trying to help them. This is the underlying premise of the nudge approach. From the works that have been examined in this book, three particularly useful cognitive traits stand out.

The first is the way our pupils naturally value losses and gains, in particular, their aversion to experiencing a loss, caused by them valuing a loss twice as much as they value an equal-sized gain, and their gradually falling sensitivity to either a loss or a gain as it increases in size. These traits are useful in two ways. Firstly, the latter enables us to make much more sophisticated and effective use of our rewards and sanctions policies. By issuing two separate rewards or sanctions, for example, we can increase the impact they have on a pupil compared to issuing them as a single, larger reward or sanction. Similarly, by combining rewards and sanctions we can reduce their impact. Secondly, the former allows us to nudge our pupils to behave in certain ways by reframing the options they face. We can increase the likelihood that our pupils will choose to behave in a certain way, for example, by emphasising how much they would otherwise lose.

The second is the way our pupils often rely on effort-saving heuristics when making decisions, especially when they are mentally tired. We can help our pupils to be more confident and to think more highly of themselves by harnessing their use of the availability heuristic, helping them to more easily recall examples of success. This can strengthen their resilience and their propensity to persevere in difficult situations. We can also help our pupils to make better choices about the subjects they study by harnessing their use of the representative-ness heuristic. By exposing our pupils to the ranges of different people who go on to study and succeed in different subjects, and to work in different occupations, we can correct their unhelpful mental stereotypes about their suitability for the paths on which they would find greatest enjoyment, fulfilment and success.

The third is the way our pupils' thinking is naturally characterised by various types of bias. Two stand out in particular: our pupils' predilection to continue with the status quo and to choose the default option. We can help our pupils by minimising the unexpected changes we deliberately or inadvertently impose on them, which our pupils find particularly mentally draining. Like us all, our pupils like consistency. And like us all, they like to know what to expect in their interactions with us and for their expectations to be realised. We can help our pupils by ensuring there is such consistency as this enables them to focus more on their learning and behaviour. Seating plans can help with this, as can having a usual rhythm to our lessons. We can also harness the power of the default choice bias in our pupils and their parents to increase their enrollment in schemes that will ultimately help our pupils.

12.6 Theme six - knowing ourselves

As we are characterised by the same cognitive traits as our pupils, all of the advice contained in the pages of this book about how pupils can be more efficient, more effective and happier also applies to us. And the more efficient, more effective and happier we are, the better the outcomes and experiences of our pupils will be. Again, three pieces of advice particularly stand out.

The first arises from the evidence that we possess relatively limited mental reserves to fuel our concentration, our ability to behave in the way we feel we should and our ability to cope with emotions and scarcity. We can help ourselves to be efficient by being judicious about how we use our reserves. For example, by prioritising the tasks we need to complete and then tackling those that are most important at the start of a day; by quickly making a start on tasks, however small that start may be; by insulating ourselves from distractions when we need to be productive and to avoid multitasking at all cost; and by reducing the demands we make of ourselves when we are having to cope with difficult situations. We can also ensure we consume sufficient glucose to replenish our mental reserves, especially dur-ing times of particular stress and pressure. And when we have an unfinished task, that we commit to a plan for how we are going to complete it. Through all of these strategies, we can increase the likelihood that we will succeed in situations and meet our objectives by working in ways that align with how our brains naturally function instead of trying to force our brains to do things they simply have not evolved to do.

The second is that we can help ourselves to be effective by taking steps to overcome the ways in which our brains can at times let us down. For example, we all suffer from the plan-ning fallacy; from setting aside too little time for us to complete the tasks at hand. I always seem to fall into this trap when it comes to writing termly reports and university references. We can overcome this by keeping a record of how long it takes us to complete tasks such as these so that we can refer to that when planning our time. Another example is that we naturally find it difficult to mark our pupils' work objectively. Instead, the scores and feedback we provide to our pupils are inevitably influenced by the order in which we marked them, our feelings about our pupils as individuals, and about the expectations we have about the quality of their work. We can overcome the impact of these by first writing model answers against which we can compare the work, changing the order in which we mark it, asking our pupils to anonymise their work and asking colleagues to double-mark it.

The third is that we can be kinder to ourselves in our interactions with our line managers. A former colleague once explained that we should move on from a job in which we feel unvalued and continually criticised as quickly as possible; that remaining in the job for too long would only reduce our ability to make effective career changes. Little did this colleague know that her advice was supported by behavioural science. And little did she know that her advice was even more urgent because remaining in a job too long only leads to us making misjudgements in the workplace, worsening the situation in which we find ourselves and trapping us in a vicious cycle even if the initial treatment by our line managers was unfair. Furthermore, managers who have decided to not value members of their teams are likely to be resistant to changing their opinions because of their confirmation bias and are even more unlikely to change the way they approach and treat those team members because exerting the self-control required to do so is mentally tiring and ultimately is likely to be unsustainable for them. The behavioural science is very clear: anyone who feels unvalued, constantly criticised, undermined and unfairly treated in their school should move to a different school as soon as they can. They should expect their situation to only worsen unless there is a change of management.

12.7 Theme seven – unintended consequences

The final theme that stands out from the preceding chapters is that the perfectly well-intentioned choices we make can often inadvertently lead to negative impacts. These unintended consequences can be separated into two groups.

The first are negative impacts on others. Providing constructive feedback can cause a pupil to simply disengage if she is far from experiencing the magic ratio of positive-to-negative interactions, for example. It can also cause her to react defensively, even to entrench her misguided position, if her self-esteem is particularly low and she receives further negative feedback as personal criticism. And using examples of former pupils who failed to realise their full potential when encouraging current pupils to avoid common pitfalls can simply reduce the likelihood that our pupils will persevere through difficulties by making it easier for them to recall examples of others like them who failed in such situations. We can avoid such consequences by knowing our pupils and how they think.

The second are negative impacts on ourselves. When we are mentally tired and suffering the effects of decision fatigue, striving to behave in a certain way can actually increase the likelihood that we behave differently, and trying to control particularly strong emotions can simply cause us to feel them even more acutely. And when we focus strongly on something, be it a task we need to complete or a feeling of loss in our lives, we can forget to attend to other important things in our lives, such as relationships and our mental and physical health.

We can overcome unintended consequences such as these by being kinder to ourselves, by not depleting our mental reserves to the point at which we lose control of ourselves and our feelings, and by reducing the other demands we place on ourselves when we are trying to cope with difficult tasks and situations.

12.8 Final thoughts

Behavioural scientists have uncovered insights that can undoubtedly help us to make our teaching and schools more effective and more compassionate, which are summarised in the seven themes presented earlier. Before wrapping up, two final thoughts should be raised.

The first is that just as we can help ourselves to be more efficient, more effective and happier by knowing and taking on board all of the preceding findings from behavioural science, so can our pupils. We can help our pupils to help themselves by teaching them about how their minds naturally work and about their cognitive traits. Ten key things that our pupils should know can be found in List One, along with useful tips relating to each.

The second is that it is important that the findings in the preceding chapters are not simply assumed to be universally applicable in our schools and classrooms. Researchers inevitably encounter procedural difficulties when conducting behavioural experiments; they find themselves subject to publication bias that can lead them to distort their findings, even just subconsciously; there are damaging cases of academic fraud in the field, as there are in all fields, and the participants on whom behavioural experiments are run are far from representative of the pupils we teach. The last of these is perhaps the most compelling reason for caution, with only 12.9% of the 70 experiments examined in this book having been run on school pupils, and all of those being in schools in either America or the UK. It is important that these findings are tested in the contexts of our individual schools, especially if they seem surprising and out of alignment with our own experiences. Furthermore, the findings in this book represent just the start of a field of research that has the potential to uncover new ways in which we can give our pupils better educational experiences and see them achieve stronger academic outcomes. Instead of being like the traditional model of research in which university academics tell teachers and schools how to change their practices in the light of findings from narrowly focused projects, though, the behavioural science of education needs our contributions as teachers if its potential is to be realised. It needs to be based as much on the findings from small-scale experiments conducted by teachers in classrooms in different settings as on those from large-scale but narrowly applied experiments conducted by professional academics. Only through collaboration between the two sectors will the questions that remain be answered, the findings that are generated be rigorously tested, and the effects of publication bias be removed. And so the final chapter offers a toolkit for teachers wanting to conduct their own behavioural experiments within their classrooms and schools.

12.9 Summary

Seven key themes from behavioural science that relate to teaching and schools emerge from the pages of this book:

- That we can help our pupils by expanding our conception of planning, including within it how we sequence activities in a lesson and lessons in a week, the difficulty of the tasks we set as well as the learning objectives, and how we praise and provide constructive feedback.
- That we can help our pupils to behave by helping them to meet deadlines, anticipating the times when they are least able to manage their behaviour, and removing unnecessary distractions in lessons.
- That we can help our pupils by adopting a flexible approach to interacting with them, based on their mental tiredness and states of mind, and on the number of distractions they face.
- That we can help our pupils by truly knowing them: their states of mind, the emotions with which they are grappling and their feelings about their own abilities.
- That we can help our pupils by harnessing their cognitive traits: the way they value losses and gains, their use of decision-making heuristics and their susceptibility to the status quo bias and to sticking with default options.
- That we can help our pupils and ourselves by truly knowing how our own brains work: the effects of decision fatigue, the ways we can struggle to be objective and the impact of line managers on us.
- That we can help our pupils by avoiding unintended consequences, both to our pupils and to ourselves.

In addition, we can help our pupils by teaching them about how their minds naturally work and by being researchers ourselves, testing and extending the findings of behavioural science in our own school settings.

13 The teacher-researcher's behavioural science toolkit

13.1 Ethical considerations

Any research should begin with the careful consideration of the relevant ethical issues, especially when children are involved. For behavioural research, the British Psychological Society offers good advice in its Code of Ethics and Conduct, its Practice Guidelines and, most helpful of all, its Code of Human Research Ethics. This third document, which I encourage all researchers thinking about conducting their own behavioural experiments to read, is structured around four principles: (1) respect for the autonomy, privacy and dignity of individuals, groups and communities; (2) scientific integrity; (3) social responsibility; and (4) maximising benefit and minimising harm (Oates *et al.* 2021). The considerations within these that are most pertinent to the school setting are discussed here.

First, it is important that researchers acquire the valid consent of participants before including them in an experiment and that participants are able to retract this consent at any point, upon which they are removed from the experiment. The British Psychological Society suggests young people aged at least 16 years should be able to provide their own consent to participate in a low-risk experiment. In a school setting, though, in which the school needs to build effective relationships and channels of communications with parents, consent should be sought from the parents of all the children involved. For such consent to be valid, it needs to be based on sufficient information for parents to make their decisions but not necessarily on a complete description of the experiment if that would inevitably influence the eventual outcomes of the research. The precise nature of the intervention can be withheld to maintain the integrity of the experiment, but the amount of information withheld should be minimised and the participating children and their parents should know in advance of the experiment when the full details will be revealed to them. And deception should never be used in experiments in the school setting.

Second, it is important that researchers ensure the participants in their behavioural experiments are not individually identifiable whilst also abiding by the principle that participants own the intellectual property rights to the information recorded about them. Participants should be able to request access to, and the deletion of, any information pertaining to them at any time and so records should be kept in a way that facilitates this. These records should be kept completely confidential, with access given only to those who need it for the project to be completed. And any data, analysis and results that are made available to other people must be anonymised to the point that individual participants are not identifiable.

DOI: 10.4324/9781003198505-16

Third, it is important that any risk of harm to participants is avoided. Some psychological research necessarily includes risk, but that should not be the case for experiments conducted by teacher-researchers in a school setting. Researchers must carefully consider experiments from the perspective of the participants involved, and experiments should not be conducted if there is any risk to the participants' physical wellbeing, mental health, personal values, self-esteem, relationships or any other aspect of their lives.

Fourth, it is important that researchers ensure experiments are designed in a way that maximises their likely effectiveness and contribution to knowledge. The aims of any research should be transparent and open to the scrutiny of people not associated with it before it is conducted in order to reduce the risk of groupthink and to expose any problematic outcomes that the researchers have not anticipated. Researchers should also always work within the limits of their experience, training and knowledge, showing humility when presenting their findings rather than making exaggerated claims. And, closely related to that, researchers should always uphold the highest standards of academic honesty, which in this situation particularly means gathering and analysing data truthfully.

Fifth, it is important that the participants in a behavioural experiment are selected in a non-discriminatory manner and are always fully debriefed at its end. Such debriefing needs to reiterate the purpose of the experiment, include a complete description of its design and the role played by the participants, and include an explanation of the findings.

To help with each of these, schools in which teachers conduct research could establish an effective agreement about their research with parents. It quickly becomes burdensome for all those involved when parents are individually contacted each time their children are involved in a research project. Instead, the school could establish a system in which parents give consent at the start of each academic year for their children to be involved in the research projects planned for the year ahead. This would need to be based on an explanation of the purpose of the research, the way pupils will be involved, the way outcomes will be recorded and the data kept confidential, the rights of pupils to the data pertaining to them, the rights of parents to retract their consent at any time, and the way findings are to be communicated.

Schools could also establish an ethics review and research completion process that consists of four elements:

- The need for researchers to outline their research in proposals submitted in time for the school to approve projects prior to the academic year in which the research is to be conducted, enabling it to establish the system of consent outlined earlier. The British Psychological Society provides a suggested template for these in its Code of Human Research Ethics.
- A panel of senior staff that evaluates projects and provides feedback to teachers about them. Such a panel should be independent of the research proposed and should include at least one member trained in research ethics, be they from the school staff or an external advisor. As well as scrutinising each proposal, this panel is able to take a wider perspective to ensure that no single pupil participates in more than one experiment in a given academic year, if that is deemed important, and that the experiments it approves align with the school's values and objectives. The advisory role of this panel is just as

important as its evaluative role, encouraging and helping teachers within the school to realise their research ambitions.

- Transparency and accountability. The decisions made by a review panel should be publicly available, and the panel should be ultimately responsible for the outcomes of the research conducted, giving individual teachers the confidence and security they need to engage in research that is beneficial to the whole school.
- A system by which experiments are monitored and researchers are supported through to the successful completion of their research. Schools could also make sure they benefit fully from their teachers' research by having systems in place for the internal dissemination of the findings, contributing to the sharing of best practice, and the external presentation of those findings in teacher conferences and teaching publications.

13.2 Designing behavioural experiments

After relevant ethical issues have been properly considered, the most important part of behavioural research is the experimental design. If an experiment is designed effectively, statistical tools exist to draw useful findings from it. If an experiment is not designed effectively, though, there are limitations to what data analysis can do.

The most straightforward design, which is also the most widely applicable for us as teachers to use, is that in which each of the pupils involved is assigned to one of just two groups. The two groups of pupils are then exposed to the same conditions apart from a single intervention, to which those in the treatment group are exposed but not those in the control group. Using the same technique to measure the outcomes from both groups then allows the researcher to identify the impact of the intervention. This is the most straightforward design in terms of implementation, thereby maximising the likelihood that the experiment will lead to useful findings, whatever they may be. It is also the most straightforward in terms of data analysis, as standard statistical programmes such as Microsoft Excel and Google Sheets can perform the required calculations with relative ease, as shown in Section 13.3 and Section 13.4. In contrast, analysing the data generated by a three-group experiment requires the use of ANOVA (the analysis of variance) and post hoc tests such as the Tukey procedure. Whilst standard statistical programmes automate the first of these, the second involves considerable manual effort. And even a simple two-group design requires careful thought about the following aspects of its structure:

- The purpose of the intervention and the measurement of its impact. What is the intervention intended to achieve? For example, should it improve pupils' behaviour, engagement or learning? Or something else? And how can that be measured effectively? Through an observer's judgement, through the number of times pupils make contributions in lessons or through pupil performance in tests? It is important that there is a single, clear purpose to the intervention and that it can be measured effectively, minimising any bias and inaccuracy in the process.
- The way in which pupils are assigned to the two groups. Are pupils going to be in their usual classes or is there a way of assigning them to new groups for the purpose of the experiment? Whichever it is, there should not be any discernible differences between the

two groups of pupils in terms of factors that could affect the purpose of the intervention, which could include factors such as their age, sex, academic ability and socioeconomic background. This should be checked before the experiment is conducted as any differences like these will make it difficult, if not impossible, to disentangle the true impact of the intervention.

- The nature of the control group. There are two options for this. Either two different groups of pupils are formed, one of which will be exposed to the intervention (the treatment group) but not the other (the control group), or the same group of pupils is tested both before the intervention (the control data) and after the intervention (the treatment data). The latter is likely to be more palatable to parents as it does not involve purposely depriving one group of children from an intervention that could benefit them. It also brings with it an analytical advantage discussed in Section 13.4. However, the latter option inevitably means the pupils can identify the nature of the intervention, which could cause them to behave differently even if the intervention itself has no effect: akin to the placebo effect, whereby the knowledge of the intervention subconsciously has an impact.

- The way pupils are incentivised to behave seriously. In many of the behavioural experiments examined in the previous chapters, the researchers both paid participants to be involved and included a mechanism that induced participants to make their decisions carefully. For example, the undergraduate students involved in the mug experiment knew they could end up having to pay for a mug out of their own money, which discouraged them from offering sums in excess of what they were actually willing and able to pay. It is unlikely that paying pupils to be involved in experiments will be possible in a school setting, but is there a way of incentivising them to take the experiment seriously? Offering small rewards for good performance in any tests involved, for example?

- The way the data are collected to ensure they are independent. For the eventual analysis of the results to be possible, the data generated from the experiment must be independent. This means the outcome of one pupil must not affect the outcome of another within the same group, and the outcomes of one group must not affect the outcomes of the other. An important part of ensuring this condition is met is that the pupils in the two groups should not be able to identify the intervention, thereby minimising any spillover effect of the intervention on those in the control group. This is why the pre-intervention, post-intervention design may be problematic. Beyond that, this requires the method of measuring the outcome to be applied in isolation to each pupil involved. See Section 13.3 for further discussion of this.

- The way the results are protected from subconscious manipulation. It is important to ensure there are no placebo effects caused by the pupils involved being aware of the nature of the intervention. It is equally important that those collecting and then analysing the data do not influence the outcome of the experiment, even subconsciously, by knowing the structure and purpose of it. Ideally, those collecting the data should be blind to the structure and purpose of the experiment, which is why the researchers in the parental communication experiment trained independent observers to collect the relevant data from lessons and did not inform them whether they were observing control or treatment groups. This is also true of those analysing the data, as that would minimise the impact of the publication bias discussed in Section 2.4, although there are no examples of this happening in the 70 behavioural experiments examined throughout this book. It should be possible to implement these measures in our schools through the creation of communities of mutually supportive teacher-researchers.

13.3 Analysing data and interpreting results: the case of a separate control group

Data analysis is perhaps best demonstrated through an example. In this case, the data come from a hypothetical experiment in which the impact of an intervention on pupils' ability to retain and recall content taught during a two-week period is tested on two classes, each consisting of 15 pupils. Random assignment would probably not be possible in this case as the pupils would be in their usual timetabled classes, but the researcher would select these groups on the basis of there being no notable differences between them in terms of factors such as their sex, academic ability and, in the case of a boarding school, the split between day and boarding pupils. Any notable differences along these lines would make it difficult to disentangle the effects of the intervention from those caused by these differences, and so would potentially invalidate the results. To avoid the ethical problem of denying the control group of the potentially beneficial intervention, an experiment such as this could be conducted during a series of enrichment lessons in the time between the end-of-year assessments and the end of the academic year.

The data generated by this study, in the form of the number of correct answers the pupils give in four different multiple-choice tests, are shown in Table 13.1. The pupils answer a test at the start and the end of each of the two weeks, with each test consisting of 25 questions, each of which is worth one mark. The average score for each pupil from the four tests is also shown and is the basis of the analysis that follows.

The data analysis that follows relates to Excel 2016. Before any analysis can be performed, it is necessary to download the Data Analysis Toolpak, which is free and easy to do.

Table 13.1 Experimental data

Control Group						Treatment Group					
Pupil	Score 1	Score 2	Score 3	Score 4	Average	Pupil	Score 1	Score 2	Score 3	Score 4	Average
1	16	18	15	21	17.5	16	21	23	21	24	22.25
2	11	14	13	14	13	17	18	16	19	20	18.25
3	15	15	11	16	14.25	18	17	16	16	20	17.25
4	19	17	18	22	19	19	19	15	17	22	18.25
5	13	14	13	16	14	20	24	23	24	24	23.75
6	10	11	7	13	10.25	21	15	16	17	18	16.5
7	12	14	12	14	13	22	15	18	16	21	17.5
8	18	16	13	18	16.25	23	20	20	17	20	19.25
9	17	18	17	20	18	24	22	23	18	23	21.5
10	21	23	19	21	21	25	23	22	17	21	20.75
11	9	12	11	13	11.25	26	13	15	11	16	13.75
12	18	20	21	22	20.25	27	12	14	14	18	14.5
13	13	14	15	16	14.5	28	16	16	18	16	16.5
14	19	17	17	18	17.75	29	19	17	16	19	17.75
15	11	15	12	18	14	30	22	23	16	22	20.75

In order to conduct the relevant data analysis, it is important that the generated data have three characteristics. The first important data characteristic is that they are independent, both within each group and between the two groups. The first of these means the outcome for each participant is unaffected by that for any of the other participants in the group. The second means the outcomes for those in the treatment group do not affect those from the control group and vice versa. Whilst we can test the data for the next two data characteristics, there is no test for its independence. It is simply a case of us making sure the outcome for each pupil is gathered in isolation and is immune from any spillover effects. In this particular case, the multiple-choice scores for one pupil must not influence those for the others, and the intervention in the treatment group must not affect the outcomes from the control group. Ideally, the two groups should take each of the tests at the same time so there is no possibility of the pupils in one group telling those in the other about the questions; the pupils within each group should be prevented from any sort of cheating; and the pupils in the two groups should not be able to identify, and those in the control group should not benefit from, the intervention.

The second important data characteristic is that they are normally distributed. This means the outcomes for each group are separately distributed smoothly around their average value in a way that resembles the shape of a bell. This can be tested by plotting a histogram of the outcomes for each group. For the small samples that are likely from experimenting on classes, though, this is likely to be very imprecise, to the point of being unhelpful. A more effective test of the normality of data is to construct its Q-Q Plot. Sadly this is not automated in Excel but can be done quickly through the following steps:

Step One: List the outcomes for the pupils in the group in Column A and then sort them so the smallest value is in the top cell and the largest value is in the bottom cell.

Step Two: Rank these ordered outcomes in Column B. This can be done manually or, for larger samples, using the formula =RANK.AVG(A1,$A$1:$A$15,1) in which the information in parentheses instructs Excel to rank the data starting in cell A1 and ending in cell A15, giving the first value a rank of one. That the ranking ends in cell A15 is simply a function of there being 15 outcomes in the data from the current experiment: this should be changed in accordance with the sample size.

Step Three: Calculate the percentiles of the data in Column C by using the formula =(B1-0.5)/COUNT($A$1:$A$15). The only thing to note in this formula is the use of B1, which instructs Excel to start in cell B1. If you have added column headings in row 1, this would be B2.

Step Four: Calculate the z-values of the outcomes if the data had a perfectly normal distribution in Column D using the formula =NORM.S.INV(C1). Again, this instructs Excel to commence the calculations for the value in cell C1 and so this part of the formula should be altered if a heading row has been inserted.

Step Five: Calculate the actual z-values of the data in Column E using the formula =STANDARDIZE(A1,AVERAGE($A$1:$A$15),STDEV($A$1:$A$15)).

Step Six: Plot the values in columns E and D as a scatter graph and then add a trendline.

Each of these calculated values for the average scores for the pupils in the control group are reported in Table 13.2. The resulting Q-Q Plot for the control group average scores is

Table 13.2 Calculated data for the Q-Q Plot for the control group average scores

Original Data	Rank	Percentiles	Normalised Z-Score	Actual Z-Scores
10.25	1	0.033333	−1.83	−1.65683
11.25	2	0.1	−1.28	−1.34714
13	3	0.166667	−0.97	−0.80519
13	3	0.166667	−0.97	−0.80519
14	5	0.3	−0.52	−0.4955
14	5	0.3	−0.52	−0.4955
14.25	7	0.433333	−0.17	−0.41808
14.5	8	0.5	0	−0.34066
16.25	9	0.566667	0.17	0.201297
17.5	10	0.633333	0.34	0.588408
17.75	11	0.7	0.52	0.66583
18	12	0.766667	0.73	0.743252
19	13	0.833333	0.97	1.05294
20.25	14	0.9	1.28	1.440051
21	15	0.966667	1.83	1.672317

Actual Z-Scores

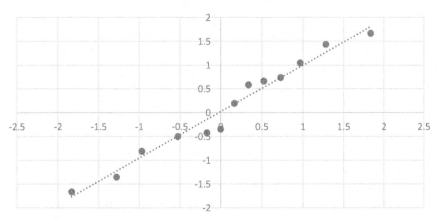

Figure 13.1 Q-Q Plot for control group average

shown in Figure 13.1 and that for the treatment group average is shown in Figure 13.2. The interpretation of these plots is straightforward. The closer the data points are to the 45° trendline, the more normally distributed is the data. In this case, both the average scores for the control and treatment groups are close enough to being normally distributed for the data analysis that follows to be valid.

The third important data characteristic is that the variances of the two sets of data are equal. In other words, their spreads are roughly the same. Again, we can test for this characteristic, this time using an F-test, through the following steps:

Step One: Select 'Data Analysis' and then the 'F-Test Two Samples for Variances' option.
Step Two: Select the relevant columns of data by pressing on the 'Variable 1 Range' box
   and then highlighting the data in the first column and then doing the same for the

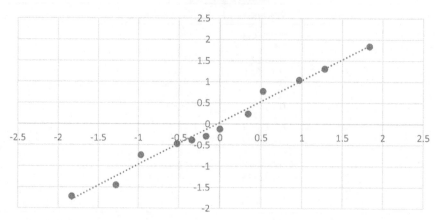

Figure 13.2 Q-Q Plot for treatment group average

'Variable 2 Range' box. Select 'Labels' if you have them in row 1, otherwise the output will simply report Variable 1 and Variable 2. Select an Alpha of 0.05, which is the stand-ard value used in such tests and simply means we are looking for an outcome for which the probability of us rejecting our hypothesis when it is in fact correct is less than 5%. Then select where the output should be produced: I find using a new worksheet for this keeps everything neat.

The resulting output for the averages of the control and treatment groups is reported in Table 13.3. The first thing to ensure is that the variance of the data in the first column of data is larger than that for the second. If this is not the case, swap the columns of data around and run the test again. In this case, this quirky condition in Excel is satisfied, with the variance of the first column of data (the control group average) being 10.43 and that of the second (the treatment group average) being 7.93. The results are then straightforward to interpret again: if the reported F value is greater than the 'F Critical one-tail' value, then the two columns of data have unequal variances. In this case, the F value (1.31) is lower than the 'F Critical one-tail' value (2.48) and so the two columns of data have roughly equal variances.

Once these last two characteristics have been checked and we are confident that the data are independent, we can analyse whether or not the intervention had a significant effect on the outcomes for the pupils in the treatment group compared to those for the pupils in the control group. The characteristics of our data determine which type of test we use for this. If the two columns of data are normally distributed and have roughly equal variances, we want to use a t-test assuming equal variances. If the two columns of data are normally distributed but have unequal variances, we want to use a t-test assuming unequal variances. If the data are not normally distributed, we can continue with a t-test if the sample size is large enough (30 or more). If the sample is smaller than this, we need to use the Mann–Whitney U test. It is unlikely that this will be needed for experiments conducted in classrooms, though, as they

Table 13.3 F-test two sample for variances

Statistic	Control Group Average	Treatment Group Average
Mean	15.6	18.56666667
Variance	10.42678571	7.932738095
Observations	15	15
df	14	14
F	1.31439934	
P(F<=f) one-tail	0.307961158	
F Critical one-tail	2.483725741	

Table 13.4 t-Test assuming equal variances results

Statistic	Control Group Average	Treatment Group Average
Mean	15.6	18.56667
Variance	10.42679	7.932738
Observations	15	15
Pooled variance	9.179762	
Hypothesised mean difference	0	
df	28	
t Stat	−2.68154	
P(T<=t) one-tail	0.006074	
t Critical one-tail	1.701131	
P(T<=t) two-tail	0.012149	
t Critical two-tail	2.048407	

should result in normally distributed data. In the current case, we can use the t-test with equal variances, which we do through the following steps:

Step One: Select 'Data Analysis' and then the 't-Test Assuming Equal Variances' option.

Step Two: Select the relevant columns of data by pressing on the 'Variable 1 Range' box and then highlighting the data in the first column and then doing the same for the 'Variable 2 Range' box. And then insert 0 into the 'Hypothesised Mean Difference' box, which instructs Excel to test whether or not the average of each of the columns of data are different; select 'Labels' if you have them in row 1, an Alpha of 0.05 and where the output should be produced.

The results from this are reported in Table 13.4. The key difference between these results and those for the F-test is that Excel returns two critical values: the first for a one-tail test and the second for a two-tail test. We are interested in knowing whether or not the average outcome from the treatment group is higher or lower than that from the control group and so we should use the two-tail test. (If we were only interested in knowing whether or not it is higher, for example, we would choose the one-tail test.) This time, we interpret these results by comparing the 'P(T<=t) two-tail' figure (the p-value) to our chosen alpha, which is 0.05. If the p-value is higher than the alpha, the averages of each of the columns of data are not different. If the p-value is lower than the alpha, the averages of each of the columns of data are different. In this case, then, with a p-value of 0.012, we can conclude that the two averages are different and so the intervention had a significant impact on the outcomes of the pupils. The intervention was effective.

13.4 Analysing data and interpreting results: the case of the same control group

In the experimental design previously presented, two classes of 15 pupils were used as the separate control and treatment groups for testing an intervention intended to help pupils to retain and recall taught information. A fundamental and ethical problem with such a design is that the pupils in the control group are deprived of an intervention that could strengthen their learning. An alternative experimental design is one in which the intervention is made for all the pupils involved, with their performance before the intervention used as the control. In the particular case of the experiment presented earlier, the pupils could be taught 'normally' for two weeks, during which they are given four multiple-choice tests, one at the start and one at the end of each of the weeks. They could then be taught in conditions that involve the single intervention for two weeks, during which they are again given four multiple-choice tests. The task would then be to establish whether or not there is a significant difference between their scores in the tests before and after the intervention.

To illustrate this process, the data used are the same as in the previous section, but with it relating to a single class of 15 pupils before and after the intervention. This is shown in Table 13.5. Again, it is important that the data generated are characterised by being independent, both within the data either side of the intervention and across them, and normally distributed both before and after the intervention. As the data arise from the same group of participants, it can be assumed that their variances are equal before and after the intervention, but their distributions being normal should be tested using the Q-Q Plot approach as previously presented.

Once it has been established that the two sets of data are both normally distributed, the difference between them can be tested in the following way:

Step One: Select 'Data Analysis' and then the option for 't-Test Paired Two Sample for Means'.

Step Two: Select the relevant columns of data by pressing on the 'Variable 1 Range' box and then highlighting the data in the first column and then doing the same for the 'Variable

Table 13.5 Experimental data

	Before the Intervention					After the Intervention				
Pupil	Score 1	Score 2	Score 3	Score 4	Average	Score 1	Score 2	Score 3	Score 4	Average
1	16	18	15	21	17.5	21	23	21	24	22.25
2	11	14	13	14	13	18	16	19	20	18.25
3	15	15	11	16	14.25	17	16	16	20	17.25
4	19	17	18	22	19	19	15	17	22	18.25
5	13	14	13	16	14	24	23	24	24	23.75
6	10	11	7	13	10.25	15	16	17	18	16.5
7	12	14	12	14	13	15	18	16	21	17.5
8	18	16	13	18	16.25	20	20	17	20	19.25
9	17	18	17	20	18	22	23	18	23	21.5
10	21	23	19	21	21	23	22	17	21	20.75
11	9	12	11	13	11.25	13	15	11	16	13.75
12	18	20	21	22	20.25	12	14	14	18	14.5
13	13	14	15	16	14.5	16	16	18	16	16.5
14	19	17	17	18	17.75	19	17	16	19	17.75
15	11	15	12	18	14	22	23	16	22	20.75

Table 13.6 Paired t-Test results

Statistic	Control Group Average	Treatment Group Average
Mean	15.6	18.56667
Variance	10.42679	7.932738
Observations	15	15
Pearson correlation	0.254466	
Hypothesised mean difference	0	
df	14	
t Stat	−3.10073	
P(T<=t) one-tail	0.003911	
t Critical one-tail	1.76131	
P(T<=t) two-tail	0.007821	
t Critical two-tail	2.144787	

2 Range' box. And then insert 0 into the 'Hypothesised Mean Difference' box, which instructs Excel to test whether or not the averages of each of the columns of data are different; select 'Labels' if you have them in row 1, an Alpha of 0.05 and where the output should be produced.

Interpreting the results of such a paired t-test, which in this case are reported in Table 13.6, is the same as for the t-test assuming equal, or indeed unequal, variances. As we are interested in whether or not the intervention had a significantly positive or negative impact, we want to use the 'P(T<=t) two-tail' value. If this *p*-value is lower than our alpha, set at 0.05, the averages of each of the columns of data are different. In this case, with a *p*-value of 0.008, we can conclude that the two averages are different and so the intervention had a significant impact on the outcomes of the pupils. In other words, the pupils' performance after the intervention is significantly different to, in this case higher than, their performance before the intervention and so the intervention was effective.

13.5 Practical takeaways

To conduct our own behavioural experiment involving pupil participants, we should

- Acquire valid and retractable consent from the parents of the children involved beforehand.
- Ensure pupils are not individually identifiable from the data or results, whilst allowing them to have access to the data that relates to them.
- Avoid any risk of harm to pupils.
- Design the experiment in the way that maximises its likely effectiveness as a study.
- Select pupils to be involved in a non-discriminatory manner.
- Use a two-group design with a single intervention.
- Consider the purpose of the intervention and how its impact can be accurately measured.
- Consider the way we assign pupils to the two groups, ensuring the groups are as similar as possible in terms of all possibly influential characteristics.
- Consider the nature of the control in the experiment, whether it is through a separate group of pupils or through a single group of pupils being measured before and after the intervention.

- Consider how the pupils involved can be incentivised to behave seriously.
- Protect the results from subconscious manipulation by the pupils or those gathering or analysing the data.
- Use either an independent or paired t-test to analyse the data depending on the nature of the control.
- Ensure the data are independent and normally distributed.
- Test the extent to which the variances of the two sets of data are equal and use the appropriate t-test for the analysis.

Bibliography

Oates, J., *et al.*, 2021. *BPS Code of Human Research Ethics*. The British Psychological Society. Available from: www.bps.org.uk/sites/bps.org.uk/files/Policy/Policy%20-%20Files/BPS%20Code%20of%20Human%20Research%20Ethics.pdf.

FURTHER READING

Behavioural Economics by Graham Mallard — A short but wide introduction to the behavioural science on which this book is based. It introduces the findings about our natural biases, but also those about our decision-making processes and social preferences.

Thinking, Fast and Slow by Daniel Kahneman — Written by possibly the leading behavioural scientist and recipient of the Nobel Prize in Economics, this is a detailed overview of the author's own research, much of which is used in the pages of this book.

Predictably Irrational by Dan Ariely — Possibly the most enjoyable introduction to the behavioural science on which much of this book is based. It presents a non-technical, lighthearted and entertaining overview of the key experiments and findings about our natural biases.

Willpower: Rediscovering our Greatest Strength by Roy Baumeister and John Tierney — An exploration of the behavioural findings about our abilities to exert self-control in different situations, based on many of the experiments to which Baumeister has contributed. This book demonstrates the importance of glucose in enabling us to control ourselves.

Nudge: Improving Decisions About Health, Wealth and Happiness by Richard Thaler and Cass Sunstein — Possibly the most famous book on behavioural science, in which the authors introduced the notion of libertarian paternalism or nudge policy. Full of the findings from instructive experiments, this is a must-read for anyone wanting to introduce their own nudges.

Scarcity: The True Cost of Not Having Enough by Sendhil Mullainathan and Eldar Shafir — An exploration of how feelings of being poor or having lost something affects us as severely as they do. The authors cast much-needed light on many situations in which we and our pupils find ourselves.

INDEX